RICH CHURCH,
POOR CHURCH

BOOKS BY MALACHI MARTIN

The Scribal Character of the Dead Sea Scrolls
The Pilgrim (under the pseudonym Michael Serafian)
The Encounter
Three Popes and the Cardinal
Jesus Now
The New Castle
Hostage to the Devil
The Final Conclave
King of Kings
The Decline and Fall of the Roman Church
There Is Still Love

RICH CHURCH, POOR CHURCH

Malachi Martin

G. P. Putnam's Sons / New York

Copyright © 1984 by Malachi Martin Enterprises Ltd.
All rights reserved. This book, or parts thereof, may not be reproduced in any
form without permission in writing from the publisher. Published on the same
day in Canada by General Publishing Co. Limited, Toronto.

Designed by Richard Oriolo

Library of Congress Cataloging in Publication Data

Martin, Malachi.
  Rich church, poor church.

  Includes bibliographical references and index.
    1. Catholic Church—Finance. 2. Catholic Church—
Controversial literature. I. Title.
BX1950.M28   1984   262'.02'0681   84-1939
ISBN 0-399-12906-5

PRINTED IN THE UNITED STATES OF AMERICA

This book is dedicated to
Dolph and Paul Mazur.

CONTENTS

RICH CHURCH,
POOR CHURCH

THE RECENT RECORD

In the last fifteen years, the Vatican has been linked in the public mind with a mind-boggling string of scandals and calamities more often found in sensational novels: big bank failures; gross embezzlements involving up to a billion dollars (and sometimes more); protracted public trials; assassinations and attempted assassinations of police, judiciary and clerical officials; eerily symbolic suicides; defenestrations; counterfeiting of corporate securities; parliamentary investigations without any conclusions; government inquiry boards without any issue; ruination of local economies and of small investors; international money intrigue involving Eurodollars and fiduciary accounts in transcontinental tax havens; the activities of organized crime; and armaments traffic in favor of certain strong-man regimes in the Third World.

Throughout, the name of the Catholic Church has been linked rightly or wrongly with impressive sums of money—impressive even for our modern minds which are so used to hearing of government budgets and corporate assets in the billions. On one occasion in the seventies, when financier Michele Sindona dealt with Vatican money and went bankrupt, there was reliable talk of Vatican involvement to the tune of a billion dollars. On another occasion, counterfeit securities of the same amount were linked with the financial manipulations of certain Vatican employees. When the Banco Ambrosiano of Milan was discovered to be in grave deficit, and the Vatican's involvement was certain (albeit never accurately described), the "hole" in the Ambrosiano's funds was $1.4 billion. More recently, when clearly the Vatican was considering establishing a fund in Poland to aid that country's ailing economy, the monies involved were in the area of $2.5 billion. Where the Vatican is involved, the sums are quite often of this magnitude.

By implication, of course, the three popes who have reigned during those years—Paul VI, John Paul I, and John Paul II (if not their immediate predecessors, John XXIII and Pius XII), together with their Vatican staff and collaborators as well as their colleagues and associates in the Catholic Church throughout the world—have all been linked with these lurid scandals.

Although only the barest details of what happened were gleaned by the press and the media, those details if at all accurate contained implications that should upset many people who have always thought of the Vatican in terms of the Holy Father as the Vicar of Christ and head of the ecclesiastical government of the Catholic Church. Yet the relatively subdued reaction of the general public—Catholic and non-Catholic—means that they either weren't surprised or don't especially care what goes on in the Vatican. Those who have always nourished the prejudice that the Catholic Church, its pope and the entire Vatican, was a hotbed of corruption, merely shake their heads in an "I-told-you-so" attitude.

It is possible that the public has not yet discovered a definite and disturbing pattern in these stories. All it knows for sure is that the Catholic Church is a rich church. Very few have ever thought of it as a poor church. Only once in modern history was it actually a beggarman church on the edge of bankruptcy and reduced to asking for loans it could not itself secure. The revelations of the last ten years would make it out to be a thief—or indicate that at least some of its officials are no better than thieves on a grand scale.

The glare of scandal has been somewhat diffused by the new aura emanating from the very impressive occupant of the Throne of Peter, Pope John Paul II: the dazzling performance of his public—indeed, international—persona, his rare combination of scholarship, integrity, energy, strength of character, and flair for publicity. None but a willful cynic would deny that John Paul II is the right man in the right place at the right time. The world that was mesmerized by the haunting melodic promises of *Close Encounters of the Third Kind*, and enslaved by the childlike, ethereal and nonhuman charm of the helpless but all-wise E.T., is captivated by that robust white-robed figure descending from the sky in his white airplane on all seven continents, speaking in over eleven languages, eloquently proclaiming all mankind's need of justice and peace and love to the millions who flock to hear him and see him.

The full truth behind the Vatican scandals will probably never be accessible to the public. Blame will never be assigned by those uniquely placed to do so.

Besides certain key individuals, some of the participants in the scandals—and the Vatican is certainly to be reckoned among them—are sovereign states and therefore owe no admission of guilt or proof of innocence to the public. It is simply that the finances of a sovereign state are none of the public's business.

Those who *must* know, do generally know. When it is a question of large sums of money, those few who operate at that rarefied level of monetary and fiscal manipulation and who can be construed therefore as having a "professional right to know" are usually quite aware of what is going on. They may not always approve. They may not always be able to stop it. They may not wish to. They may even be beneficiaries, directly or indirectly, of illegal operations. In any case, they are not at liberty to disclose anything vital. The "club" may be quite informal, but its rules are rigidly observed and as rigidly enforced.

Even granting that the Vatican itself was faultless throughout the scandals of the seventies that smelled of malfeasance in high places, how then has its name been indissolubly linked with recent corruption in the world of banking and finance?

The question is urgent since it involves those who rule the Catholic Church. The aim of the Church is to be a publicly recognizable sign of otherworldly salvation for all people, as well as a source of that salvation. But for too long now, those in the higher echelons of the Church have been suspected of quite worldly aims: of secret—almost cabalistic—designs on the rights, liberties, and freedom of ordinary people. Many a sincere modern American Protestant is still convinced that this is true.

There can be no doubt that the higher echelons and inner circles of Catholic hierarchical power bear unmistakable traits of a certain mystery which shrouds those central parts in the awesomeness of high priesthood and privileged admission. Yet those inhabiting this world seem to be gripped and driven by interests as mundane and as diverse as foreign-exchange deals involving rubles, dollars, and yens; the size of Communion wafers to be used in Ruanda; abortion clinics in Cincinnati; apartment complexes in Rio de Janeiro; and the dispute over the Beagle Channel between Chile and Argentina. The ambit of interests seems cosmic. It is.

All the while, however, they are guarded from the prying eyes of outsiders by the most rigid rule of secrecy—a rule bolstered within their ranks by the direst spiritual penalties and outside it with punitive capabilities that no man in his right mind would incur lightly.

Then, quite suddenly, there is an explosion of exposés about
quite mundane wrongdoing, of ordinary, everyday crookedness. A
body of men that gives such paradoxical impressions to outsiders
surely needs a special degree of understanding. Rich church . . . poor
church . . . beggerman . . . thief? What is basic to an understanding of the Catholic Church in these affairs?

Very little attention has been paid to the relationship between
the Catholic Church and its finances. At first, it seems no relationship should exist or, at most, a very minor and tenuous one.
One of the most venerable of religious institutions, the Catholic
Church, with its manifest spiritual mission, should have little to do
with the material-oriented world of power and money. In the past,
the public knew little about general Church finances. But recently
it has become obvious that the relationship is by no means tenuous
and hardly insignificant.

What norms must be used to judge the situation of the Church?

Clearly, the Church must be as pure as Caesar's wife when it
comes to money. The Children of Light—Christ's way of referring
to his followers—must never become identical twins of the money-
worshiping Children of Mammon.

While no one will deny clergymen the economic means of livelihood, neither will any informed person doubt that the Children
of Light are as shrewd as the Children of Mammon. Profits have
been huge. Increasingly, it is difficult to distinguish between Mammon's followers and at least some of the Children of Light—particularly the Church's money managers.

The Vatican emerged from World War II with the functional
structure of its financial departments in good working order and its
realized assets at an appreciable level. From then until the end of
the seventies, its finances flourished, making the Vatican the largest
single stockholder in the world, with about $20 billion traceably
invested (but much more untraceably invested), with gold deposits
exceeding those of most medium-sized countries, and with a worldwide real estate operation that put Vatican lien on territory almost
matching in extent the real estate possessed by popes when they
were sovereign state rulers, and certainly of greater monetary value
than any former papal State.

With prosperity came trouble. Certain officials managing Church monies proceeded unwisely to make serious bids at partnership in a wider management system, to become functionaries in the managerial system of world economics and finance. A strange rot began to surface both within the Church and in its nearest sociopolitical ambient, Italy. Neither the beloved Pope John XXIII nor his successor, Pope Paul VI, was immune from the rot. They unwittingly endangered Catholic unity.

Paul VI in particular seemed at times to act completely outside history. Faced with the financial irregularities of the seventies that revealed moral rot somewhere in the fiscal guts of the Vatican, Paul wanted to resign, but the Roman Curia, his Vatican bureaucracy, would not hear of it. His reasons were that the Catholic Church had lost so much money over his signature, and that such base corruption had been exposed. The Curia's rejoinder was imperative: A pope "resigns" only because he has gone mad (in which case he is ousted) or become a heretic. To make matters worse, Paul abolished a 400-year-old prohibition that threatened papal candidates with excommunication if they tried to buy the votes of the cardinal-electors in a papal conclave, thus almost inviting corruption.

Paul VI lingered on until 1978 to see Mammon's curse descend on the Church and on Italy: High-ranking prelates were members of secret anti-Catholic organizations, and still others belonged to a secret organization trying to destroy the vestiges of democracy in postwar Italy. Money lay at the root of his Church's difficulties.

PART ONE
THE MANAGERS

When one seeks to identify the principal causes for the evident decay and dissolution of the Catholic Church's institutional structure today, two emerge as the most virulently destructive. The first is the patent abuse and prostitution of the unfortunately ambiguous pastoral statements issued by the Second Vatican Council (1962–65). None of the three subsequent popes has been either able or willing to lay himself on the line, scour the abuses out of Church life, and halt that prostitution. Nor is there any indubitable sign on the Catholic horizon as of 1984 that Catholic Church authorities intend to undertake either of those urgently required measures soon.

Pope Paul VI (1963–78), for reasons quite unknown publicly, was neither willing nor able to do so. Pope John Paul I (August–September 1978) simply was not given the time. Pope John Paul II, elected in October 1978, is clearly either not willing or able, chiefly because over the six-year period of his reign, he has not revealed even any recognizably grand papal strategy. Such should have clearly emerged by now, if he were to be ranked with the great popes. For, given our modern telescoping of space and time as well as the astounding instantaneity of global communications, those first six years of his papal reign are the dynamic equivalent of fifteen years in the reign of Pius XII (1939–58). Given his age, John Paul II could yet undertake the necessary measures. But, in Catholic terminology, one could say that, to date, the graces of his office as pope are battling with John Paul's qualities and traits as a man and as a Pole. So, the abuses multiply, and the abasement of Catholic life continues apace and unchecked.

That first cause of Church decline, however, is not as destructive as the second: the emergence of the financial managers at the center of the Church as well as throughout it, and their enormous sphere of influence.

These managers are the latest expression of that play for secular and specifically political power that has been noted as the constant characteristic of the Catholic Church. Unfortunately, the Church's managers share the confusion and aimlessness characteristic of those who engage in power-play in our modern world.

That confusion and aimlessness seems to arise particularly in regard to the demands of political judgment. We are incapable of knowing where our true interests lie, what we should value, what we should discard or avoid. And, further, we seem to be incapable of understanding what effect the sociopolitical and economic-cultural factors in our civilization exercise over our true interests. For we make political judgments, but what these imply as demands is beyond us because we lack any overall vantage-point from which to perceive our true interests.

When the vision, say, of Europeans as a group was that of Catholicism, at least they could see from the outside, as it were, what effects would follow for their lives from political judgments and power-plays. But we moderns have no such vision. In fact, many today would deny that such an overall vision is possible. Hence our thinking is "linear"—from visible causes to their visible effects; we cannot think "vertically," so that the coming inevitable accidents of history are unforeseeable.

The financial managers of the Catholic Church necessarily followed the linear behaviorism of the other secular managers around them. Like their contemporaries, they had the same type of successes and the same kinds of failures, even the same sort of disasters. But their influence, being Church-wide, has been clearly responsible for the growing feeling among many that they could not discern in the institution of the Church any convincing sign of the spiritual salvation the Church claims to have uniquely.

The decline in loyalty to and acceptance of Church dogma and laws was an almost inevitable result. The managers conveyed the impression that Church authorities were no different from their secular counterparts—clever men using modern means to achieve concrete ends. Just like their contemporaries, they suffer from problems, and have only the same linear solutions. The chapter of Church history that concerns the managers is not yet closed because by now not only the economic viability of Vatican and Church is bound up with these men and their managerial system, but also the spiritual ministry and vigor of the churchly institution is dependent on them. And matters must now run their normal course until the bitter end.

THE VACUUM OF POWER

In the year 1870, the papacy was deprived of the papal State. It was an area of about 16,000 square miles with approximately three million inhabitants. With its loss through the Italian wars of national liberation, the pope and his administration were relegated to the few buildings on Vatican Hill in Rome; together with some small land holdings in other parts of Italy, these became the papacy's entire worldly estate. For well over twelve hundred years, the popes had been temporal sovereigns with the power that went along with that absolute sovereignty. They and their followers had always believed that the popes should enjoy independent temporal power in order to be free to fulfill their supernatural mission. Now a vacuum existed in place of that power. The pope was "a prisoner." The "Great Injustice" had been perpetrated. Italy would now be dogged by "the Roman Question" (how to rectify the "Great Injustice") for the next fifty years.

By the turn of the nineteenth century and past the death of Pope Leo XIII in 1903, into the reign of Pope Pius X, the annual budget of the Vatican was a little under $4 million. Annual income kept ahead of that figure by three-quarters of a million on the average. But by the outbreak of World War I, expenses were outrunning income, and the disruption caused by the war threw the Vatican back on its reserves.

Benedict XV succeeded Pius X one month after World War I started. His efforts were more taken up with bringing the warring nations to the peace table than with the Vatican's deteriorating finances. Years before, as a member of the Vatican's Congregation for Extraordinary Affairs, Benedict had negotiated the investment of Vatican funds in the (then) very profitable securities of the Ottoman Empire. His go-between was an Italian, Bernardino Nogara, who headed the Istanbul branch of the Banca Commerciale Italiana. Nogara had served the Holy See well in those times. Now, with the Ottoman Empire about to dissolve forever, Nogara was back in Italy. Vatican investments had been pulled out in time; but that source of revenue was gone. Nogara stayed in touch with Benedict and with Benedict's financial administrators, sometimes advising them, sometimes supervising this or that financial operation. But Nogara's day had not yet come: Perhaps the shrewdest financier Italy had produced since the death of Agostino Chigi in 1520, Nogara would be almost 60 years old before he set about accumulating a huge fortune for the Vatican in 1929.

Bit by bit, the annual budget was cut back, this time to almost one-fourth of the prewar budget. Needed every year now was a sum slightly in excess of $1 million—and this represented a minimum scale of revenue, if the Holy See was to retain some corporate investments in the hope of better times. Money in the form of loans was raised to meet some severe debts after World War I ceased, but the old vigor of contributions never returned; indeed, many of the industries in which Vatican funds were invested had been totally destroyed. Benedict's reign was beset by lack of funds until his death in January 1922.

A new voice was being heard in the confidential councils of the Vatican at this time. It belonged to a young archbishop, Eugenio Pacelli, who had entered the service of the Secretariat of State in 1901 and served under Pius X, Benedict XV, and as of 1922 under Pius XI. In 1917 Pacelli had been posted to Munich, Germany, as papal nuncio to the Bavarian monarchy. The monarchy was swept away, and in 1919 he was sent to Berlin as papal nuncio to the Weimar Republic. From there he monitored the international situation in Germany, Eastern Europe, and Russia. Down in Rome, both Pope Pius XI and Pietro Cardinal Gasparri, Secretary of State since 1914, set great store by the reports and opinions of their nuncio in Germany.

Uppermost in the minds of these three men was the position of the Roman pontiff, his vulnerability to political harassment, his territorial limitations, his economic troubles. All three were convinced that the "Roman Question" had to be solved and "the Great Injustice" repaired not merely for the sake of some abstract principle but because of the political instability and continual economic depression in Italy and the rest of Europe.

When the stocky, square-jawed Cardinal Archbishop of Milan, Achille Ratti, was elected Pope Pius XI on February 6, 1922, he clearly had in mind the solution of the "Roman Question," for he broke with sacred tradition that had kept his predecessor a "prisoner" out of sight in the Vatican. He insisted, one hour after his election, on coming out to be viewed on the central balcony of St. Peter's Basilica, and to give his blessing from there. The last time a pope had done this was in 1846. Romans and Catholics realized that a change was under way.

Immediately after World War I, there were several abortive moves to get communication going between the Vatican and the Italian government about a solution to "the Roman Question." But no government of Italy was sufficiently stable to do anything effective— until Benito Mussolini came to power in 1922.

An old friend of the Vatican showed up about this time. Bernardino Nogara, the man who had helped Pope Benedict XV with the purchase of Turkish securities, had been appointed as an Italian delegate on the economic and finance committee participating in postwar peace negotiations (1921–22) between Austria, Bulgaria, Hungary, and Turkey. Nogara drew one general conclusion from his international experiences since the beginning of the century: The economic face of Europe and the world was changing. Ownership of large territories did not matter so much as participation in international finance. The days of classical capitalism were over.

As if to confirm this, another voice was heard saying much the same thing. From his vantage-point in Munich, Pacelli formed a comprehensive judgment and forecast about the kind of world into which the modern papacy was stepping. In Germany, he had been following the varying fortunes and future promise of a 33-year-old political agitator named Adolf Hitler. Even when Hitler was imprisoned in 1923 for his part in an attempt to seize power, Pacelli told himself that the destiny of Germany rode on Hitler's back.

In his reports to the Vatican, Pacelli analyzed developments in the Soviet Union, Germany, and Italy as part and parcel of a vast and irreversible change in the structure of Europe's economy and therefore of world economic conditions. The Soviet Communist revolution of 1917 had effectively destroyed that fundamental element of capitalism: private property. And it had done this thoroughly by liquidating the old class structure with its division of labor and

rewards and its alliance with Christianity. Hitler and Mussolini—
who was already totalitarian[1] dictator of Italy—were about to abolish
the traditional bases of capitalism, by beating a total retreat from
the free-market philosophy. "Statism," control and direction and
distribution of the nation's resources and production, was going to
be their way.

In the aftermath of World War I, another important change
occurred: Banking leadership passed from Great Britain to the United
States. The gold standard, after a short attempt to reestablish it in
1928, collapsed in Britain and the convertibility of sterling currency
into gold at a fixed price was abandoned. By 1937, all European
nations had abandoned the gold standard.[2] The United States instituted the process of "pegging"—it set a new minimum price for
gold. There was a severe shrinking of international markets, because
the old principles of fourteenth-century laissez-faire economics simply did not work any more.

Between 1924 and 1929, Pacelli was in regular communication
with Bernardino Nogara, who was one of the administrators on the
Inter-Allied Reparations Commission. Nogara's financial skill came
into full play in supervising a reorganization of the Reichsbank in
order to stabilize Germany's postwar internal finances. The loan
of 800,000,000 Deutschmark to the Reichsbank and the payment
of annuities of 2,500,000,000 Deutschmark called for every ounce
of his fiscal ingenuity. Pacelli, at this time, did not really trust
Nogara, principally because Pacelli could not—like many—understand the intricacies of international finance and the manipulation of "paper money." But Nogara's influence on the papal nuncio
was still very great.

As far back as 1925, Pacelli, listening to Nogara, had understood
that all efforts of post–World War I governments to return to prewar
normalcy were in vain. The terrible economic depression of postwar
Germany he witnessed first-hand was, in his opinion, a mere fore-
taste of what was about to assail the whole of Europe and America.

In place of the capitalist system, Nogara predicted the rise of a
managerial system dominated by the masters of industrial technology
and the managers of funds. There was no hope whatever that the
papacy could have its temporal power back in the form of its own
papal State whose revenues would mainly support it in its spiritual
mission. Nor, he recommended, should the papacy aim at such a
futile goal. The revolution that had deprived the papacy of its State
was as yet only halfway on its course. From the French Revolution

of 1789 through the Soviet revolution of 1917, a straight line ran—
and it was still running on. The old privileged classes were on their
way out—at least as the repositories of real power.

How well Pope Pius XI learned his lessons from Nogara and
Pacelli can be judged from a passage he penned in the thirties in
the middle of an encyclical letter directly attacking Mussolini's Fascist regime and its totalitarian vices. Speaking about the modern
economic configuration among nations, he gave the best short summary of what the managerial system portended for the ordinary
masses of people, if it went out of control:

> Immense power and despotic economic domination are con-
> centrated in the hands of a few, who for the most part are not
> the owners, but only the trustees and directors of invested funds,
> which they administer at their own good pleasure. This dom-
> ination is most powerfully exercised by those who, because
> they hold and control money, also govern credit and determine
> its allotment, for that reason supplying, so to speak, the life
> blood to the entire economic body and grasping in their hands,
> as it were, the very soul of production, so that no one dare
> breathe against their will. This accumulation of power is the
> characteristic note of the modern economic order.[3]

Years before he wrote these words, Pius had made up his mind
to try and place the Vatican and therefore his Church beyond the
direct control of the "managers." In order to do that, however, the
great stone had to be removed from the tomb in which popes since
Pius IX had enclosed the papacy. A change of mind was necessary
according to which the papacy would say goodbye to the old, millennial idea of an extensive, temporally powerful papal State. There
must never again be a repetition of that.

The time had come to abandon the juridical fiction that the pope
was a "prisoner" in the Vatican, and to negotiate at least a minimally
satisfactory status for the Vatican in the middle of a world in total
transition and almost certainly facing a repeat performance of World
War I.

Ominously, Pacelli kept warning his Roman superiors that a day
of reckoning was coming. The German high command drawn almost exclusively from the old, established Junker class of Prussia,
had not given up. Faced with economic troubles at home and the
entry of the United States into World War I against them, they had,

in Pacelli's pregnant image, merely folded up their field maps and made peace until *der Tag*, the day of reckoning with Germany's enemies. *Der Tag* would surely come, for the iniquities of the Versailles Treaty had to be avenged, and Germany's humiliation wiped out.

It would not do, Pacelli kept saying, for the papacy to be part of a city and politically unified with any country or polity. The Holy Father had to be juridically independent and acknowledged internationally as a sovereign ruler in his own proper territory. The "Roman Question" had to be solved.

Mussolini was also preoccupied with the "Roman Question." In his earlier days, he had published a pamphlet entitled *God Does Not Exist*. Reading it today, one realizes Mussolini had only economic and political reasons for his doctrinaire atheism and hatred of the *bagarozzi* (monopoly seekers). Perhaps, indeed, that was why, once in power and realizing he could not really control Italians without at least the semblance of reconciliation with the pope and the Church, he decided to perform a volte-face. He had his marriage to Donna Rachele regularized by a priest. He attended mass, not regularly, but he did show up. His children were baptized. He began to treat the Vatican and its pope with greater respect. He forbade Freemasonry, the Church's enemy.[4] He ordered crucifixes to be placed on the walls of classrooms. He granted large subsidies to the Church for repair of the damages wreaked by World War I on Church property. Later, before he became Hitler's lackey, he even went so far as to quote the dictum of Pope Gregory VII that Pius IX (whom Mussolini loathed) had repeated so often sixty years earlier when speaking about another Italian statesman: "Who touches the pope will die," Mussolini said sententiously when Hitler openly threatened the Church in Germany and the pope in Rome.

At the constant urging of Pacelli in Germany, and following his own instincts, Pius XI decided in 1926 to make a first move toward a solution of the "Roman Question." But when Monsignore Luigi Haver was getting his instructions from Secretary of State Gasparri as to his first interview with a member of Mussolini's government, Gasparri predicted the negotiations would last about ten years. The negotiations, which began in earnest in January 1927, could have dragged on without an end, if circumstances had not forced the hand of pope and Dictator. The chief negotiator for the pope was lawyer Francesco Pacelli, brother of Archbishop Eugenio Pacelli.

The negotiations continued for a year and a half until mid–1928 when Pius XI was told that the Vatican's financial situation was extremely endangered. Pius demanded an audit from the Cardinalitial Commission that worked with the Apostolic Camera. It was not the first audit in Church history, but it was the first since the days of Pius IX in the aftermath of the 1870 annexation of the papal State.

When Pius XI got the results, he blanched. Daily running expenses at the Vatican were in excess of $7,000. The leading economists predicted a prolonged economic depression internationally. Italy's economy, and Germany's also, was heading for a chaos of unemployment and staggering inflation. Contributions to the Church were dropping. Legacies were diminishing. Money was immediately needed to pay off loans already spent. But that was only the beginning. What was the source of revenue to be for the next five years? The next ten? Pius called his personal representative in Munich, Archbishop Pacelli.

The Americans, Pacelli advised, were the only ones who could help. And, in particular, one American: George William Cardinal Mundelein, archbishop of Chicago. Born an American, he was nevertheless a true "Roman," Pacelli assured the pope.

Within two weeks, Mundelein had raised a twenty-year loan for $1.5 million, using Church property in Chicago as collateral.

At the same time, Mussolini was considering the near future. A national plebiscite, as he called it, would be taken early in 1929. The Italian people would have to choose "freely" to be governed by the totalitarian dictator and his Fascist Party. For any semblance of a genuine victory at the polling booths, Mussolini would need the support of the Vatican. As of January 1929, he himself undertook to conduct the negotiations to a swift and satisfactory conclusion. By this time, Archbishop Pacelli had been recalled to Rome. Coincidentally, Bernardino Nogara finished his work in Berlin on the Inter-Allied Reparations Committee, and he too returned to Rome. Pacelli was slated to be a cardinal and succeed Cardinal Gasparri as Secretary of State. But first, Gasparri would complete the negotiations with Mussolini. Nogara, in the meantime, went to see his close relative, Giuseppe Nogara, the 58-year-old Archbishop of Udine on the Italo-Yugoslav border, but stayed in touch with Pius XI and Gasparri.

The agreement between the Vatican and the Italian government took place on a rainy day, February 11, 1929, in a ceremony that lasted all of nearly forty-five minutes. Cardinal Gasparri had arranged for it to take place in the Lateran Palace near the room where Pope Leo III had received Charlemagne in 800 A.D. Flanked by his aides, Mussolini signed the agreement on behalf of the government; Gasparri signed for the Vatican.

All Rome was excited once the news broke. Church bells rang. People crowded onto the streets. From abroad congratulatory messages poured in to Pius XI and to Mussolini. The Speaker in the House of Commons declared himself exhilarated at what he called "the decent compromise Signor Mussolini has concluded with the pope."

The anti-clerical Fascists in Mussolini's own party, however, were furious and reproached the dictator with having resurrected the temporal power of the pope that Napoleon and the Piedmontese had so successfully exterminated. Mussolini was immovable. "We have not resurrected the temporal power," he retorted, "we have buried it." To those who reminded him of Cavour's sacred principle ("a free and sovereign Church in a free and sovereign state"), Mussolini had a typically contemptuous answer. "No. What we now have is two sovereign entities, not one within the other, but the two of them separated by a thousand kilometers." Mussolini was right: It took only five minutes to reach the State of Vatican City from his offices in the Palazzo Chigi and, he added, ten minutes to travel the Vatican's entire boundary line. But the physical proximity meant nothing. "Between them and us lies an impassable chasm of time and eternity." Besides, the new State was bound to Italy by Italian law. That was the meaning of the Concordat, he said.

For the moment, there was an uneasy peace between Mussolini and the pope. The only dissenting voice in that year came from some Vatican scholars and archeologists. Mussolini's known plans for Rome's beautification included, they said, the destruction of irreplaceable archeological remains. In time, he would actually tear down whole neighborhoods—churches, residences, monuments— dating from the Middle Ages, in order to make way for his Via Imperiale and two other trans-city highways. *"Fa niente"* ("It doesn't matter"), Pius XI consoled the antiquarians. "We are going to build."

The document they signed had three sections. One, the Concordat, was a list of special powers and privileges accorded to the Vatican so that it would be able to conduct its own affairs independent of the Italian State. A second section, the Lateran Pact, was a legal instrument creating the new State of Vatican City (*Stato della Città del Vaticano*). A third section, the Financial Convention, granted the Vatican certain financial reparations for the losses it had suffered by the merger of the old papal State into Italy in 1870.[5]

The Concordat, among other measures, provided for the full and unimpeded jurisdiction of the Vatican over any and all organizations in Italy, whether clerical or lay or mixed, that professed to work for Catholicism. These organizations, known now as "ecclesiastical corporations," were financially exempt from taxation and state audit. And the Vatican was at liberty to create as many such organizations as it pleased. Clauses 29, 30, and 31 of the Concordat provided for this tax-exempt status, and the word "ecclesiastical" in "ecclesiastical corporations" would be interpreted to mean any corporation founded by Catholics for ostensibly religious purposes whether it worked strictly within the ecclesiastical structure of the Church or outside it. Those clauses would be worth millions to the Vatican in coming years.

The Catholic clergy as well as all citizens of the new papal State were tax-exempt. Religious education was to be provided to all schools, whether run by the Italian government or the Church. Catholicism was declared to be the official religion of Italy, and propaganda in favor of Protestantism was forbidden.

By the Lateran Pact, the new papal State was legally created a sovereign entity. Covering 108.7 acres—mainly the complex of buildings and grounds on Vatican Hill, St. Peter's Basilica, the Apostolic Palace, and other clusters of buildings—the Vatican State had thirty squares and streets, two churches in addition to St. Peter's, four military barracks, and a population of 973 at the signing of the agreement.

The new State also had "extraterritorial" possessions: three basilicas in Rome (St. Mary Major, St. John Lateran, and St. Paul); a certain number of Church-owned offices throughout greater Rome; the papal villa at Castel Gandolfo some 13 miles outside Rome; and several other traditionally papal estates throughout Italy. All these possessions enjoyed the same tax-exempt status as the Vatican State itself.

In return for the creation of the new papal State, the Vatican recognized the Italian State juridically and accepted finally Italy's forcible occupation of the old papal State. The Vatican undertook to exchange accredited representatives with Italy.[6]

The Financial Convention provided that a lump sum of $40 million in cash be paid to the Vatican. Another $50 million in 5 percent government bonds were added to that. The Italian State would pay the salaries of parish priests in Italy. Though this was not part of the official text of the Financial Convention, the Italian State also paid an undisclosed sum into the papal privy purse.

With these documents signed and sealed by parliamentary approval, the Vatican was now ready to attempt its most ambitious nonreligious undertaking: to attain a privileged position at the tables of the international money markets where the future managers of the world system would be sitting.

REENTRY INTO POWER

The creation of the Vatican State and the newly available funds at the disposal of the Holy See prompted a reorganization of the financial agencies of the Vatican.

At the time of signing of the Lateran Pacts, there were four such agencies: the Administration of Holy See Property,[1] responsible for all property on Vatican grounds and all property on extraterritorial grounds throughout the world; the General Administration of Goods of the Holy See, responsible for the normal revenues coming into the Vatican; the Administration of Vatican City, which regulated the payroll, police and armed forces, sanitation, public utilities, Vatican Radio, the Vatican astronomical observatory, and the newspaper, *L'Osservatore Romano*; and the Administration of Religious Agencies,[2] which supervised the investment and distribution of all capital assets.

The pope now proposed establishing a new agency, calling it the Special Administration of the Holy See, and assigning to it the investment and distribution of the monies paid as indemnities by Mussolini. There was no one within the Vatican clergy and certainly no layman judged capable of handling the new funds. The only professional known to Pius XI, Cardinal Gasparri, and the incoming Cardinal Secretary of State, Eugenio Pacelli, was Bernardino Nogara. Between February 11, 1929, the day the Lateran Pact was signed, and June 7 of the same year when Mussolini's rump parliament ratified the Pact into the law of the land, Pius XI had extensive conversations with Nogara, Gasparri, and Pacelli—who had never quite quelled his suspicions about Nogara.

Nogara made his position and outlook quite clear. If he was to shoulder responsibility for the management of the new monies which would accrue to the Holy See on parliamentary ratification of the Lateran Pact, he would have to be given a free hand: to make his own appointees without clearing them with a higher authority; to make his own decisions as to where and how much to invest; to have no other method of control exercised over him except the control of good or bad results.

Moreover, he added, Mussolini was a passing phenomenon in Italian life. As long as he lasted he would need the Church's support. Vatican financial policy should therefore include a positive attitude, an attitude of cooperation insofar as this was possible. Excluded for so long from the innards of Italian industrial and economic life, the Vatican could now reenter that life and secure its stake.

Furthermore, Nogara made it clear that he considered the near-future condition of the world to depend on the monetary policies of the Western democracies, of the United States and Great Britain in particular. The old Catholic heartland in southern Europe would necessarily play second fiddle to them. Therefore, while the funds of the Holy See would be invested heavily in Italy, it was time for the Vatican to look abroad and to widen its horizons: to acquire a solid basis in the gold bullion market; to take full advantage of Swiss banking and currency laws; to invest in foreign money markets, in foreign industrial enterprises, and in real estate holdings on other continents. Catholic countries should not be preferred over Protestant ones. Money was neutral, he declared.

Nogara was perhaps uniquely fitted to meet the needs of the Vatican at this moment. After a childhood and early youth spent in Bellano, some miles from the Swiss border on Lake Como, he had his first training as an architect. Soon after receiving his professional certification, he was offered a position with a mining company, and spent many years supervising first the engineering of mining operations in England, Greece, Bulgaria, and Turkey, then the financing of such operations. Financing became his skill. Subsequently he entered the service of the Banca Commerciale Italiana, becoming vice-president, and heading the Istanbul branch. An expert linguist, he could speak on technical matters in Italian, German, Bulgarian, Greek, Turkish, French, Russian, and English.

Nogara was an aloof and taciturn man. Many who knew him on a day-to-day basis around the Vatican never learned anything about his home life or his tastes, except that he was an avid reader of

Dante. When he died in November 1958, they were still as ignorant about him as they were in 1929.

Nobody, not even Pius XI, seemed to know what Nogara was worth in personal fortune nor even what he earned in his new position or how he earned it—as salary, as honorarium, as commission. Nogara's insistence on confidentiality was not a personal fetish. It was a wise proviso: He was deeply acquainted with the clerical bureaucratic heart and with the powerful temptations that vast sums of money offered laymen and clergy alike. And he was not about to see this already huge Church nest egg channeled into the pockets of personally ambitious men or unworthy causes. When the calamities of the seventies overtook Vatican financiers, many remembered the usually tight-lipped Nogara muttering something about the classic crime, *trahison des clercs*, the treachery clerics were classically reputed to practice on their own caste. At a later stage in his Vatican career, he was the object of the vilest slanders and calumnies, out of which he emerged unscathed.

On June 7, 1929, the day of ratification of the Lateran Pact, Pius XI took two steps: He formally created his new finance agency, the Special Administration of the Holy See; and he appointed Commendatore Bernardino Nogara as its manager and director—his official title was "Delegate"—under all the conditions and rights that Nogara had requested. Nogara picked his own team of aides. Three were laymen, including the distinguished Marquis Enrico de Maillardoz, and there were four accountants. He would personally train them and supervise them. A watchdog ad hoc committee of three cardinals (Pietro Gasparri, Donato Sbarretti, Rafael Merry del Val) was thrown together by Pius. If need be, they could be called on. But any such action would be extraordinary, for ordinarily Nogara would proceed without direct supervision.

This new Special Administration had its headquarters on the same fourth floor of the Apostolic Palace where the pope had his private apartments. (The General Administration of Goods of the Holy See continued on under the secretaryship of Monsignore Domenico Mariani with his eleven accountants.) Nogara now joined the privileged few who had constant and free access to the Holy Father. Under his care were the $90 million of indemnities, the undisclosed sum granted to the pope's privy purse, and—it was said but not confirmed by any documentary evidence—a certain small but still valuable amount of gold deposits. If the sixteenth-century banking genius and art patron Agostino Chigi had started off his professional life with these funds as a basis, he might not have done better than Nogara did between 1929 and 1956, when he retired from active duty as the all-powerful Vatican finance manager and director. But in total contrast to Chigi, Nogara wished for no monument—bronze plaque, marble statue, portrait in oils—erected to his memory, so self-effacing were his methods. He had one consuming purpose: to make the Holy See totally independent financially and thus to give it the power that comes from such independence.

There were few if any in the Vatican offices of 1929–30 whose vision matched Nogara's, who were even capable of assimilating the ideas he had developed, for none had had his experience with currency problems, with international banking and investment. In addition, he was almost unique in his deep knowledge of the Vatican's financial history. He was one of the few men, also, who had studied the history of interest rates as far back as Hammurabi of ancient Babylon and down to the nineteenth-century trade empires.

Mussolini's "donation" to the Church was seen by the general run of Curial officials as a fixed lump sum that, with a little care, would solve immediate problems. Nogara saw those indemnities as a means to a great and long-range goal.

From the beginning, he had his eye on one Vatican financial agency that Pope Leo XIII had established in 1877: the Administration of Religious Agencies.[3] Hitherto, this agency had watched over the administration and distribution of the few capital assets that the Vatican possessed, seeing to the investment of whatever was "marketable." The agency's sphere of power was limited to the few extraterritorial properties throughout the world that the Holy See possessed. It also rendered services to certain ecclesiastical bodies, certain dioceses and landed benefices. But the money at its disposal was sparse, and its operations were as limited by local laws as they were by the "uneducated" hands that managed it all. It was a holdover operation from the days of the papal State, and the revenues it generated were minuscule—never exceeding some few tens of thousands of dollars. As a holdover, it reminded Nogara—and some others—of the time when the papal State garnered funds through a universal collection system from the entire world. Those funds had come into the Camera Apostolica as capital possessions to be spent on the needs and purposes of the papacy.

Nogara's mind, ever attuned to an emerging new order, saw such funds as fodder for investment, as material for money managers, and not so much as revenues to be consumed on immediate needs.

But, in 1929, the Vatican lacked what he knew was essential for such a managerial policy. It lacked the capitalization—self-capitalization—necessary for such a policy, and the indemnities as such were not sufficient for what he had in mind. The Vatican lacked the freedom from local laws of Italy and elsewhere, freedom it needed for such a worldwide operation. Finally, it lacked its own banking facilities; in the long run, no matter what revenues accrued to the Vatican, their management would have to rely on the banking and brokering services of outsiders. This, besides opening the innards of the papacy's economic condition to secular scrutiny, placed the Holy See at the mercy of secular governments, and made it subject to the vagaries of political life and international conflicts.

No one, including Nogara, had any doubt throughout the late twenties that another "Great War" was in the offing. The Versailles Treaty ending the first "Great War" had papered over the lethal cracks, and already the fragile European entente was splitting apart at the seams. In the East, a new colossus had been born, the Soviet Union. In the western hemisphere, a sleeping giant would eventually wake up to "a manifest destiny." One of the few quotations that people remember hearing from Nogara's lips was from that peculiar nineteenth-century genius, Alexis de Tocqueville, who in 1835 declared:

> There are, at the present time, two great nations in the world which seem to tend towards the same end . . . the Russians and the Americans. . . . Their starting-point is different; and their courses are not the same; yet each of them seems to be marked out by the will of Heaven to sway the destinies of half the globe.

Nogara's experiences in the immediate post–World War I period, his cold-blooded appraisal of Germany, Italy, Great Britain, and France and their possible futures—all this told him that an ancient hegemony was passing away from the once-powerful European centers of trade empire and classical capitalism. He knew that de Tocqueville's world—dominated by a sense of grandeur, a profound depth of emotional attachment to land and nation and family, and by the fertile variety and richness of a hierarchical society—would never return. What the world of the 1920s faced was a totally new international arrangement.

"We have time," he remarked. "Just sufficient time." Time to reenter the arena of power. Time to acquire the sinews of power.

To understand the industrial and commercial climate of the Italy in which Nogara launched his first initiatives, one must recall Italian financial traditions. Commodities markets appeared in various Italian cities in the fourteenth century, three centuries before the Doge of Venice established a state-run market with official rules of exchange. But nothing like a market for securities was introduced until the beginning of the nineteenth century, and then it came into being through the occupying French authorities. Milan was the site of the first such exchange. By the beginning of the twentieth century, several other cities—Rome, Genoa, Venice, and Naples among them—had such exchanges.

The prime characteristic of the Italian exchanges was their largely corporate participation. Even today, the bulk of investors are institutional—industries, banks, credit unions. The small private investor was comparatively rare, due in part to the poverty and lack of education among the ordinary people. Nogara's plans included a large-scale entry for Vatican-owned common stocks.

To aid him in his acquisition of equity, he relied heavily on those three clauses in the Concordat by which the Church was allowed to form tax-free ecclesiastical corporations. One reason for Nogara's cultivation of Mussolini and his close advisors was to get the Fascist government to regard any corporation formed by the Church—whether its functions were purely ecclesiastical and religious or whether they were strictly revenue-generating—as a tax-free ecclesiastical corporation in the sense meant by the framers of these three clauses. He succeeded in persuading Mussolini of this, thereby enlarging the tax exemption (or at least the tax abatement) of Church-owned or -controlled companies.

Further tax exemptions and abatements were won from Mussolini through the thirties. In 1936, he granted all Church corporations exemption from the 5 percent corporate tax as well as from a $3\frac{1}{2}$ percent tax on every 1000 lire worth of real estate. (Both taxes were designed to finance the Abyssinian War. Nogara regarded this exemption as due payment for his having devoted one of his Vatican plants to producing munitions for that war.) Other corporate tax exemptions followed: in 1937, from a graduated tax on capital stock; from the sales tax of 1940; from assessments on dividends in 1942.

With these easements to help him, Nogara proceeded with his

investment plans. The general rule was: Enter all phases of Italy's economic and industrial life. Nogara set as his targets mainly banks, credit and insurance organizations, and public utilities. His principal aim was to acquire equity in the major corporations engaged in these branches of business life. It is doubtful if, starting with a capital slightly in excess of $100 million in the autumn of 1929, he could have made as much progress as he did, and as quickly, were it not for still another concession he extracted from the Fascist government.

The Vatican at that time played a major role in the running of the Banco di Roma. Due to the economic depression, the bank had many securities that were drastically reduced in value and with no call-value. Nogara went to Mussolini with his problem.

In 1933 the dictator had established a public law corporation, government run and financed, called the Institute for Industrial Reconstruction. It was Italy's answer to the industrial devastation wrought by the worldwide depression. The IIR's function was to take over or to create industrial firms, to which the government would then assign certain definite business undertakings. It was hoped the central direction provided by the government would help wipe out certain pockets of industrial stagnation or failure. The government, it was argued, would be better equipped to recognize such areas. It was, originally, a typical product of Fascist corporate-state thinking. And in the early thirties it already included about 102 firms.

In principle, none of the firms included under the IIR umbrella could capitalize itself. The state arrangement was that an IIR firm would have to raise 12 lire from investment sources for every lira the government supplied the firm. But then the IIR issued bonds on the open market to be bought by any investor with the funds. The IIR was set up as a temporary measure, but its market success was so great, and its boost to the economy so obvious that it became a fixture in the Italian economy both before and after World War II.

Mussolini was persuaded to allow the IIR to take over the very inactive and practically worthless securities of the Banco di Roma at their original worth, netting the Banco di Roma—and its major shareholder, the Vatican—some $632 million.

This was not Nogara's only or even chief dealing with the IIR. He proceeded to buy up IIR stock on the open market, so that in time the Vatican became IIR's single biggest investor; with that selectively bought stock in hand, the Vatican came to have a major

controlling interest in scores of companies—a move that strengthened Nogara's hand in further corporate investments.

One last major Nogara tactic concerned Vatican accounts in Swiss
and Liechtenstein banks and credit institutions. Under his direction
the Vatican was to acquire a controlling interest in many of these.
But even when the Vatican had only an account—albeit always a
substantial one—in a Swiss bank, Nogara used it to the maximum
in the purchase of Italian and foreign stock, and in buying up Italian
and foreign companies. The system enabled him to bypass currency
regulations, among other things. The advantage of banking procedures conducted in Switzerland and Liechtenstein was the anonymity afforded to the client. Banks and credit institutions could
act as stockbrokers, buying and holding substantial amounts of shares
on behalf of their clients, but not in the client's name. Later on,
in the fifties and sixties, financial circles in Europe and the Americas
would be astounded to find out how far Vatican investments had
penetrated by this anonymous means.

In starting to expand and diversify Vatican participation in the
Italian economy—during the thirties the emphasis was definitely
major, although considerable expansion was recorded in Latin
America—Nogara proceeded in very characteristic ways. For the
first time in Vatican financial history, there appeared on the boards
of companies in Italy and elsewhere the names of various trusted
laymen, some of them recruited from the "Black Nobility," some
of them from less distinguished backgrounds, but all sharing Nogara's extreme devotion to "the material welfare of the Holy See."
As Nogara bought into an Italian company, the name or names of
new board directors, his men, were added to the existing roster,
men like Massimo Spada, Count Enrico Galleazi, Carlo Pesenti,
Antonio Rinaldi, Luigi Mennini, Luigi Gedda, Count Paolo Blu-
menstil, Baron Francesco Maria Oddasso, and the three nephews
of Eugenio Pacelli—Carlo, Giulio, and Marcantonio. These were
the *uomini di fiducia*, the trusted men he himself had picked and
instructed. His own name rarely appeared on a board of directors,
and then only on very important ones. Through his *uomini di
fiducia*, Nogara could reach in at the policy-making level and direct
a company in coordination with the other companies in which he
had secured major or minor representations.

Once control was established over a company, Nogara's policy
followed certain lines he termed "incremental." The idea was always
to increase: the scope, the working plant, the markets, the backroom
research, the output per employee, all were to be continuously on

the move—outward in expansion, forward in initiative, upward in profits.

True to his initial plans, Nogara's first major acquisitions in Italy were in gas, textiles, public and private construction, steel, furnishings, hotels, mining and metallurgical products, farming products, electric power, munitions, pharmaceuticals, cement, paper, timber, ceramics, pasta, engineering, railways, passenger shipping, telephone and telecommunications, and banking. A list of the companies and banks in Italy and abroad in which the Vatican acquired a controlling interest before the outbreak of World War II, when added to a list of those in which it acquired a minor but substantial interest, would fill some sixty or seventy pages of this book.

Nogara's uncanny foresight and business acumen stunned onlookers and associates. He proceeded to deal in the commodities market and, further, to buy up maritime companies busy with the importation of "colonial goods"—bananas, coffee, tea, etc. He bought up real estate within and around Rome in the expectation of future urban expansion. By the late thirties, the number of square feet in Rome possessed by the Vatican was running well beyond 40 million. In time, Nogara would make the Vatican the biggest landowner in Italy after the Italian government. Especially in Rome, the Vatican's holdings were substantial already through bequests, donations, and immemorial possessions. By direct purchase through his companies, or by foreclosures on unpaid mortgages, Nogara kept accumulating land, piece by piece. His agents traveled to other European countries seeking out real estate that would obviously undergo development as urban agglomerates increased. At this time, he was not seeking any real estate in the Americas, although he took several possible purchases under advisement.

In the industrial area, one of his most successful takeovers was of the Società Generale Immobiliare. The oldest of Italy's construction companies, originally based in Turin, SGI presented Nogara with immense possibilities. What had been a construction company more or less limited to Rome was to become a giant conglomerate, the first of the multinationals, active on the national and international scale with political and financial implications that would eventually topple governments, shake the Vatican's inner echelons, be an essential link in the impoverishment of the Long Island, New York economy, and embroiled in international intrigue.

From the beginning, Nogara aimed at a "tripod"—banking facilities in Italy, banking facilities in Switzerland, and a large degree of participation in the industry and economy of Italy. Although the Vatican already owned several medium-sized and many small rural banks in southern Italy, he rightly foresaw that the industrial potential of the north called for the control of banks in that region. They could be used to finance foreign trade transactions, and would afford the Vatican the ability to play a leading part in placing share and bond issues on the stock exchanges. Already before the outbreak of World War II, he had acquired controlling interest in several leading banks—the Banca Commerciale Italiana, Credito Italiano, Banca Provinciale Lombarda, and the Banco Ambrosiano of Milan, to mention a few. From them he started to buy up interests in finance houses, mainly in Europe and a few in Latin America. One of his business ploys was to have one of his wholly owned industrial companies buy controlling interests in financial institutions. It is said that so great were the convolutions of indirect and semi-direct— but always confidential—Vatican control of banks and credit institutions that, even if the fiscal authorities or the Italian Treasury officials wished to trace it all accurately, no one would have the time, the patience, or the filing system adequate to unravel it all. Perhaps, indeed, this was a principle of Nogara's method of money-making—to make identification of sources and relationships difficult, if not impossible. A Treasury official later remarked that one could start such a line of inquiry and follow it laboriously, only to be foiled ultimately by a tax exemption, an untouchable Swiss account, or some similar frustration.

The only hold-up in Nogara's rise to power during those years was momentary and came with the election of Eugenio Pacelli as Pope Pius XII in March 1939. Already before he became pope, Pius had heard rumors about Nogara and the Special Administration— that most of the 1929 indemnities had been frittered away in failed ventures, that Nogara had feathered his own nest, that he was in league with enemies of the Church, with Freemasons, with anti-Catholic circles in France, England, and America. There were even suggestions that he had been coopted by the ultra-secret section of the Masonic Lodge that had been created back in the nineteenth century precisely to make association possible for people like Nogara who could not attain normal Lodge membership.

What fueled the fires of rumor and slander was Pius's own known hesitancy about the taciturn financier. Pius had to know the truth. The world was on the brink of war. Italy would be involved. On what would the Holy See subsist?

As a dedicated and thoroughly trained Roman bureaucrat, Pius set the wheels of inquiry in motion. An ad hoc committee of three Curial cardinals was formed; they were granted carte blanche to rake through the Special Administration files, interrogate the employees, call witnesses, question even Nogara himself.

Characteristically, Nogara submitted quietly to it all. As one cardinal remarked later, the only thing he had to hide was how much he had made for the Holy See since 1929. Independently of the cardinalitial committee, Pius privately set upon investigation into Nogara's personal life, his friends, his haunts, his habits.

The results were astounding. Nogara turned out to be a sober-living, frugal character, with little by way of personal fortune, with hundreds of business colleagues, many acquaintances, and very few friends—all highly placed, all utterly respectable. His daily life read like the schedule of a hard-working monk. More astounding was the report of the three cardinals: The original indemnities of $90 million-plus had been parlayed into a multifaceted business empire that topped $1 billion in value. The Vatican and the papacy were better off, much better off, than ever before in remembered history. Nogara might be a saint or a devil, the remark went, but the major assets of the Holy See were solidly substantial and, into the bargain, quite safe, even if Italy were invaded by the Anglo-Saxons!

"Ma come?" Pius is supposed to have exclaimed on getting the report from the cardinals. How did he do it?

At that, the cardinals shook their heads glumly. "From point A to point B, we have understood all. But, you know, Holiness, this Nogara has gone through the entire alphabet. And we are just ignorant cardinals."

The matter was closed forever after. Never again would Nogara's integrity or his methods be called into question. Nogara had free rein and the full confidence of Pius XII.

It was about this time that Nogara broached with Pius the last tactic in his plans. Since the beginning of his tenure, Nogara had watched over one small working financial agency of the Vatican, the Administration of Holy See Property. From time to time, those in charge of this agency facilitated Italian business friends by transferring funds through the agency to Switzerland or elsewhere. It was always a question of currency exchange and tax exemption, tantamount to a banking service; a small service fee was always tacitly attached to it. Sometimes, the members of the agency came to Nogara for advice on investing of the funds they had for transferral. All of this was done on a very small scale, a service rendered rather than a profitable enterprise. Nogara pointed out the advantages that could accrue to the Holy See if the pope would consider creating another financial agency, an expanded form of the Administration of Holy See Property.

Pius's answer was colored by the pressures weighing on him at that moment from the deteriorating international situation. In principle, he said, he approved of the idea. When Signor Nogara had worked out the details, they would go over it together.

The financier did not return to the subject for another year and ·a half. It was well into 1941 when he submitted a plan to Pius.

The fact was, Nogara said, that the Catholic Church contained over twelve hundred major archdioceses in Europe and the Americas, not to speak of Asia and Oceania (including Australia), besides hundreds of minor ones. There were scores of universities and institutes and societies, besides large-scale monasteries and convents. Involved with this intricate mass of Catholic institutions were sums of money that exceeded by far the liquid assets of most countries. Moreover, the collateral these ecclesiastical bodies possessed was extensive and highly priced. There was also the not inconsiderable sum received each year by these same bodies and by the Holy See in the form of legacies, bequests, and donations. Hitherto, the Congregation for the Clergy managed these funds. But that group, too, suffered from the same limitations as the other financial agencies in the Vatican.

Most assets in Europe and the Americas, besides places like South Africa and Australia, were invested in local or international markets usually by lay brokerage and investment firms. In a few instances, a religious order or a diocese might have one of its own clerics sufficiently "educated" in the management of funds who could therefore do the investing for his superiors. But by and large, this was not the case.

Nogara's proposal: Establish a central ecclesiastical agency for the universal Church which would have the status of a bank within the sovereign State of Vatican City and the advantage of belonging to the papacy and the Vatican, and which would specialize in investing and brokering the funds and assets of ecclesiastical bodies from the entire Church.

Already, the pope's Special Administration could capitalize such an institution with no difficulty. A Vatican agency with the charter and status of a bank would, besides all else, afford the Holy See greater facilities for its own operations, bypassing secular banks and brokerage houses. The whole idea promised the papacy as much economic independence as it ever had enjoyed in its heyday as a temporal power with extensive territories.

Pius liked the idea. In the unsure world of 1941, it seemed a partial answer to the problem of the Holy See's isolation amidst warring nations. In the intervening time since the 1920s, Pius had come to realize where the international monetary system was going and how, with sufficient starting capital and wise management, fortunes could be built on "paper money."

"We should become money managers for the entire Church, Holiness," Nogara advised.

Nogara even had the name of a Vatican employee with whom he himself had worked and whom he had trained in the Special Administration, a man he thought would be an ideal clerical head for the new agency: Monsignore Alberto di Jorio. Nogara would exercise overall supervision of the operation.

Nogara also pointed out, and Pius agreed, that World War II had reached its turning point. The Axis was losing. The postwar world would be dominated by the Anglo-Saxons and the Soviets. The time was opportune for a new initiative, Nogara argued. Pius concurred.

Thus it came about that on June 27, 1942, a new and powerful financial agency was established: the Institute for Religious Agencies.[4] Alone together in the pope's private study, the 66-year-old Pius and the 72-year-old Nogara signed an agreement. Only a few of Pius's cardinals knew of the agreement. Behind the Apostolic Palace, in his office at the bottom of the stairs leading to the famous Tower of the Winds, Vatican librarian and archivist of the Church, choleric Eugène Cardinal Tisserant—one of Nogara's friends—was aware of the secret transaction.

The last time a pope had signed a private agreement with a financier was in 1511: Pope Julius II gave Agostino Chigi total control of the invaluable Tolfa alum mine. There would be one more such fateful meeting between a pope and a financier in this century, in the spring of 1969. But at the moment of the signing of the Pius XII–Nogara agreement, that future pope was merely a 45-year-old archbishop: Giovanni Battista Montini sat at his desk one floor beneath the papal private study in total ignorance of the transaction upstairs. And that other financier, the then 22-year-old Michele Sindona, had only just acquired a degree in tax law from the University of Messina.

The new agency superceded Pope Leo XIII's Administration of

Religious Agencies. The IRA was a separate corporate entity, with a responsibility separate and distinct from all other offices and agencies of the Holy See. From the beginning, it was envisaged as *not* being a unit of the normal Vatican administrative structure. Again and again, both in internal Vatican documents and publicized statements, whenever norms are laid down, there inevitably occurs some phrase that exempts the IRA from any normative charge or ruling— "always leaving intact the special character of the IRA," or "not including the IRA," or "with full respect for the juridical status of the IRA."

The IRA's charter stated that it was established "to take charge of, and to administer, capital assets destined for religious agencies"—agencies being understood in this Roman juridical context to be any legitimate bodies established with the purpose of working within the broad confines of religion and its propagation.

Headed by Monsignore Alberto di Jorio as president and two other clerics as his assistants, it had a staff of qualified laymen. The headquarters of the new agency were assigned to the old tower Pope Nicholas V had built over five hundred years ago as part of his grandiose plans for the defense of the Vatican. To reach the tower today, one enters through the Porta Santa Anna to the right of Bernini's colonnade, past the Church of Santa Anna on the right and the Swiss Guard Barracks on the left. The tower lies straight ahead, beside the walls of the Apostolic Palace and facing the Vatican Polyglot Printing House.

In time, the IRA would come to dominate the Special Administration partly because of its superior supply of liquidity, partly because the Special Administration needed the professional services of the IRA, and partly because the unifying element of both IRA and Special Administration—Bernardino Nogara—was gone by then. Alberto di Jorio became a cardinal, replacing Nogara as "Delegato" at the Special Administration. Monsignore Sergio Guerri took over di Jorio's post at the IRA.

But as of autumn 1942, the financial structure of the Vatican was a smoothly working unit under Nogara's all-encompassing supervision. They would have to sit the war out, operate with immunity between the battling nations, and be ready for the work of reconstruction in Italy and elsewhere once the politicians had signed the armistice. The Vatican now had the sinews of power.

ECONOMIC MIRACLE

Many unjust things have been said about the Vatican's financial secretiveness. Yet Switzerland, Monaco, Saudi Arabia, and Costa Rica all keep their affairs private in this sphere. Why not then accord the same privilege to pope and papacy and Church? Like the affairs of any sovereign State, Vatican affairs are cloaked in confidentiality in the belief that financial matters are best tended when out of reach of those who would use any information to the detriment of the state. Unfortunately, the financial scandals of mid-century only accentuated the call for the Vatican to open its books to public scrutiny, providing fodder for those with lively enough imaginations to attempt a guess at the Vatican's financial resources.

It is possible nevertheless to know with a fair degree of certainty what the worth of the Vatican has been over the last forty years. It is also possible to understand, even if one cannot accept on moral and religious grounds, the outbreak of the calamities that have beset the Church. Finally, it is possible to form a comprehensive view of its finances in that span of time without necessarily losing one's appreciation for the epochal dilemma in which the Vatican finds itself today.

For the purpose of these pages, we need to have some accurate idea of what progress the two chief Vatican financial agencies made in that span of nearly forty years; and we need to know what was the significance of that progress. In order to assess the progress, it should be sufficient to use the period of progress and prosperity between 1945 and 1968 as an example. World War II had to end before real progress could begin; after 1968, an inner change of great significance had been introduced into Vatican financial agencies, and already the calamities were beginning.

Once the sinews of the Vatican were flexed and the officials of the agencies became truly managers of sizable fortunes in marketable assets, certain participants decided to go one step beyond the chartered purpose of the Special Administration and the IRA, and make a bid for partnership in the limited ranks of those who participate in the management of sums of money enormous enough to affect the sociopolitical lives of nations. Much of the stimulus to act came from the political ambient of the Vatican, of Italy, and of Europe in the 1940s, as well as from the background of the people involved. But things went awry. After all, at stake were huge sums of money and a source of immense prestige and leverage—the Vatican and the Catholic Church. "No one can be indifferent to the papacy or its Church," Mussolini remarked once. "They arouse great passions always."

Hence there ensued the calamities of the 1970s, a series of three separate but interconnected scandals involving embezzlement, murder, and illicit financing. As of this writing, the Vatican financial agencies have not yet recovered from those calamities, nor have John Paul II and his administration been able to sift and settle the outstanding questions and puzzles those calamities engender in onlookers, although a start has been made on a restructuring of the Vatican's financial agency.

But in order to be able to appreciate those bids for managerial partnership, and to understand why the calamities ensued, we must first examine how the various financial agencies performed forty years ago.

In the words of one informed and enlightened commentator, Italy at the end of World War II was "one extended poorhouse." Roads, railways, bridges, tunnels, industrial plants, city streets, marketplaces, residential suburbs had been devastated by the rampaging of two vast armies, the pounding by Allied blitzkrieg and German artillery, and the destructive harassment practiced by Italian Partisan forces. In addition, the political fate of Italy—and, with it, of southern Europe and the Mediterranean—hung in the balance. For at the outset of peace, the only organized, well-funded, politically conscious and determined group was the Italian Communist Party, led by Palmiro Togliatti, who had spent most of the war as a house-guest of Joseph Stalin in Moscow.

Not until June 1948 did a settled political configuration embrace

Italy, when a plebiscite eliminated the Piedmontese monarchy in favor of a republic, and a general vote installed the Democristian Party that was to remain in power for some twenty years. There is still an unsolved mystery about the sudden departure of the royal heir, Umberto, from Italy two years earlier. But there is no mystery at all about the Democristian victory: It was to a great extent the doing of Pope Pius XII's Vatican.[1] The pope's national organization, called Catholic Action, brought out the vote. The pope's funding—made possible by Nogara's skillful management—financed the electioneering campaign and oiled the wheels of persuasion. The pope's allies in the caretaker government that supervised the elections made sure that every vote counted. And the leader of the Democristian Party was Alcide de Gasperi, who had been given refuge in the Vatican and who had worked as an assistant in the Vatican Library during the years of Mussolini's vengeful wrath against him.

With such a Church-funded and Church-supported party in power, all the Vatican's privileges conceded by Mussolini were confirmed by the new national government. Financially speaking, the Vatican's Special Administration and its IRA were sitting in the pilot's seat as of that June 1948. Under these circumstances, and given Nogara's mastery, the financial agencies had to flourish. No trouble would arise between Italy and the Vatican until the sixties when the Democristian hold on political power loosened, and a new pope, John XXIII, was elected. Pope John saw no inherent difficulty in an opening up of government to participation by left-wing, i.e. socialist, elements. This was the famous *apertura a sinistra*, a political decision fraught with dire consequences for Italy and the Vatican because it evoked a stiff-backed reaction from traditionalist right-wing elements, and created the circumstances in which Michele Sindona could flourish as "the prime banker of St. Peter," and Roberto Calvi, head of the Banco Ambrosiano, would be lured to a symbolic death in a foreign country.

By about 1968, the impoverished condition of postwar Italy had changed dramatically. Italy had undergone *"il miracolo economico."* Between 1953 and 1968 alone, the country's GNP increased by 150 percent and represented a sum somewhat in excess of $70 billion. At the very center of this "economic miracle" were the Vatican and its financial agencies.

Throughout the description of that "economic miracle," it must be remembered that this is, at best, a partial picture, for certain important elements are necessarily omitted. The Special Administration and the IRA in their heyday beginning about 1948 were operated as one financial agency, although from time to time internal differences and disputes about policy occurred. While the funds originally constituting the Special Administration's resources can be more or less accurately defined, it is impossible to determine how much had accrued in the meantime from those funds and, in particular, from what area of business or where all those increments were banked and invested. This does affect our estimate of Vatican involvement.

For the IRA, the situation is even less exactly definable. We can more or less guess at its initial capitalization as a bank, but indications are this was vastly increased within a relatively short time. The main difficulty in assessing the IRA's performance lies in the functions it performed for ecclesiastical bodies—"the agencies of religion"—scattered mainly throughout Europe and the Americas. For one of the IRA's basic purposes was to provide means whereby these ecclesiastical corporations could invest the monies at their disposal in a manner at once highly confidential and utterly tax-free.

As a concrete illustration of this large and hidden capacity, one can cite the situation of the Church in North America. A conservative estimate of the combined assets of all Catholic ecclesiastical bodies in Canada and the United States around 1968 would settle on a figure somewhere between $85 and $102 billion. Total annual revenues would amount to $11–$14 billion. How much of this revenue was invested through the IRA or its affiliates in Europe and the Americas? What use was made of that total asset value for collateralizing finance procedures—ventures, redemptions, replacements? We cannot omit these factors from a total assessment. Nor can we forget that, all proportions being observed, the same proviso must be made for ecclesiastical bodies in Latin America, Europe, and other parts of the world.

To be added to that estimate of indefinable financial sinews are the monies the IRA undoubtedly managed through its facilities for non-ecclesiastical bodies. This is a very sensitive area: It touches the private fortunes of certain individuals, chosen "friends" of the IRA and the Holy See, who have been granted access to the IRA banking and brokering facilities. It also touches the fiscal and monetary interests—and therefore the vital political interest—of national governments and of nations whether they have an accredited diplomatic representative of their own at the Vatican or whether, like countries such as Israel, they have an unofficial representative in Rome for Vatican connections and enjoy more or less the same access as those in full diplomatic relationship with the Holy See.

The conclusion is that this median span measurement of the success attained by Vatican financial agencies can be taken as one reliable measure. On another page, there is mention of the caution of history as a factor providing Pope John Paul II the main parapets between which any restructuring of Vatican agencies must proceed. The same parapets affect any inquiry, including the present one.

Credit, Banking, and Insuring Institutions

By the midsixties, there were approximately 180 institutions for special credit in Italy. Vatican financial agencies had solidly penetrated roughly half that number. Its mainstay in this vital area of economic and industrial life was La Centrale, which specialized in medium- and long-term credit for projects in agriculture, hydroelectricity, engineering, and mining. La Centrale's stock included 8,235 shares in one power company valued at $24.5 million and 1,417 shares in a second power company valued at $25.2 million. In 1967, La Centrale merged with the Vatican-owned Romana Finanziaria Sifir S.p.A., thus bringing along Sifir's assets of $168 million and capital stock of $72 million. La Centrale's capital was $107 million and its assets $277 million. It had loans of up to $60 million out in industry, over $155 million in long- and medium-range credits. The merger with RFS meant that the La Centrale group were now financing some 90 companies. As of 1967, La Centrale's net profits were in the region of $16 million.

Major or very substantial Vatican equity was to be found in a series of other credit institutions, about a round dozen in all, whose combined capitalization was almost $900 million.[2]

Another Vatican-owned company, Italcementi (which supplied over 30 percent of total cement in Italy and was the fifth largest cement producer in the world),[3] owned a financial house named Italmobiliare which acquired eight banks with cumulative assets of $512 million and a capital resource of $22 million. Italmobiliare had control over the Banca Provinciale Lombarda and the Credito Commerciale di Cremona whose combined deposits exceed $1.2 billion.

Italcementi itself had a capital of $51.2 million, and profits in 1967 topped $5 million.

Another way in which Vatican financial agencies entered the

business of credit institutions was through Vatican participation in the state-run, government-funded Institute for Industrial Reconstruction which at that time accounted for 40 percent of all investments on the Italian market. The Vatican had been and still is one of the single biggest investor participants in the IIR. Nogara himself laid down policy lines in this matter; and, in his day, Vatican funds were used to buy into IIR companies such as Finsider which gave promise of good future expansion and profit.

Finsider, a steel combine, was small in production and output when Nogara invested in it. By the midsixties, not only was Finsider producing over 10 million tons of steel per year, but it had almost 77,000 employees, was making an annual profit of over $24 million, and had diversified into a whole series of wholly owned subsidiaries, with heavy Vatican participation all the way.

Finsider counted among its subsidiaries such giants as the Alfa Romeo automobile company;[4] Finmeccanica,[5] a holding company for thirty-five other companies which operated through them in practically every phase of engineering from electrical engineering to modern armaments; Finmare,[6] specializing in passenger shipping lines; the Dalmine Company (steel ingots and piping); the Terni Company (mostly steel products); and Italsider (steel ingots, pig iron, piping).

In addition to the banks mentioned already as bought up by the Vatican-owned Italcementi through the wholly owned Italmobiliare, Vatican control—total or partial—extended over many other banks.

Three major Italian banks[7]—Banco di Roma,[8] Banca Commerciale Italiana,[9] and Credito Italiano,[10] all affiliated with IIR—were heavily invested in by the Vatican agencies. But Vatican agencies also owned certain banks outright.[11] There were sixteen other banks all around Italy in which Vatican equity was very substantial, and at least another sixty in which Vatican equity was modest but influential on account of the investor's power elsewhere in the economy.[12] The Vatican's most important banks in northern Italy were spread over Lombardy and Emilia. The most prestigious of these was the Banco Ambrosiano of Milan. Founded in 1897 by the "Black" Catholic establishment, the Ambrosiano, with a capital of $6.2 million by the sixties, had bought into Swiss and Luxembourg finance houses. By the midsixties, one of the brightest up-and-coming young men in the Ambrosiano was a 48-year-old ex-cavalry lieutenant turned banker named Roberto Calvi, already director-general of the bank. He had joined the Ambrosiano in 1947 as a simple clerk; by 1971 he had, with the blessing of Vatican financial chiefs, become the Ambrosiano's president. Nogara himself had known Calvi, as he had followed intimately the Ambrosiano's policy of purchasing shares from foreign investment trusts. The Ambrosiano, at this time, was flourishing: It was paying 220 lire per dividend on 3 million shares—topping 1 billion lire in payments.

The Vatican financial agencies through their wholly owned or heavily dominated banking interests had in this period an essential link with two-thirds of all new share and bond issues on the money markets in Italy, and with at least 50 percent of all foreign trade transactions. Through its IIR affiliations and investments, it shared with a few others the management of at least 20 percent of all bank deposits in Italy. The Vatican had acquired two major insurance companies[13] with a combined capital of $30 million, together with nine other insurance companies with a combined capital of $10.7 million. Very large shareholders in all these insurance companies were other industrial and banking corporations—Bastogi, Italcementi, Credito Italiano, La Centrale—that the Vatican owned or in which it had a controlling interest.

As late as February 1982, the Banco di Roma, the Banca Commerciale Italiana, and the Credito Italiano announced that they were going to boost their equity capital. The Banco di Roma, by the issuance of new shares—many at a significant discount to the quoted price on the Milan stock market, is going to double the size of its equity capital from 140 billion lire to 280 billion lire. The Credito Italiano also intends to double its 160 billion lire equity capital to 320 billion lire, by much the same means as the Banco di Roma. The Banca Commerciale had not, as of February, announced how it would proceed.

Industry

There were probably very few areas of industrial manufacture and production in which at least some Vatican money was not invested.[14] Because of the vast need after the destruction of World War II, construction and power were two very profitable business sectors. Nogara launched Vatican money heavily into them.

One of Nogara's first acquisitions was in the textile industry. He bought up four ailing textile companies and merged them into one which he named CISA-Viscosa. After a sufficient period of time had passed to raise CISA-Viscosa's profitability, Nogara financed the takeover of CISA-Viscosa and of another Vatican-owned textile company by the largest textile group in Italy, the SNIA-Viscosa. Over the years, he increased Vatican participation in SNIA-Viscosa until he had the controlling interest in it and its subsidiaries.[15] With its capital of $90 million, its average annual profit around $10 million, and paying 130 lire per dividend to its shareholders, SNIA-Viscosa was a fertile source of income.

In power companies, Nogara enabled the financial agencies under his control to carve out a capital position for Vatican funds. Initially, as he often did, he took over an ailing group of power companies and welded them into one named Italgas.[16] By 1968, Italgas was one of the industrial giants. It was sole supplier for over thirty-five Italian cities. It had a capital of $59 million, producing over 680 million cubic meters of gas annually, and controlled over a dozen other companies engaged in gas-related industries such as tar, coke, distilled water, heating machinery, and stoves. The Vatican's biggest share in telecommunications was through its major participation in the Società Finanziaria Telefonica.[17] Through the SFT, Vatican money has been invested in 10 major subsidiaries[18] and eight minor ones.[19]

In mining and metallurgy, the fate of Vatican funds has largely depended on a company originally named Montecatini which later merged with the Edison Company. Known today as Montedison, it specializes in mining and metallurgical manufacturing, as well as in pharmaceuticals, electric power, and textile fibers. It was one of Nogara's biggest accesses to capital investment, one of which he was most proud—he consented to sit on its board of directors for years, something he rarely did.

By the late sixties, the Vatican had a major share in Montedison. The company's sales ran to $854 million with a net profit of $67 million. Montedison had invested almost $1 billion in other companies, at least nineteen—mainly IIR affiliates. It had foreign subsidiaries in the United States, Holland, Spain, India, Brazil, and Argentina. The company's real estate holdings were valued at $23 million; all its industrial complexes were valued at over $1.5 billion.[20]

Vatican money was also invested in other mining companies.[21] But these were only small parts in a vastly diversified empire of wholly owned or controlled companies dealing in silk, yarn, publishing, furs, buttons, spaghetti, tourism, salt, munitions, pharmaceuticals, paper, electronics, department stores, ready-to-wear clothing, cotton, and children's toys. [22]

If Vatican involvement in the construction industry has been reserved for the last place in this discussion, it is not because its participation was light. It was precisely its dominant successes in this field that provided a beginning of the bids for partnership mentioned previously, and from them the calamities that overtook Nogara's empire.

The Società Generale Immobiliare was founded in 1870. Up to the cessation of hostilities, SGI was mainly confined to Rome and its environs. When Nogara took it over wholly on behalf of the Special Administration, its capital was depleted, its plants largely incapacitated, its reserves low, its technical standards behind the times. But it was one of those business situations in which Nogara's eye detected a potential gold mine.

Ten years after Nogara's death in 1958, SGI had become another giant due to his foresight and management. SGI engaged in construction of residential areas, luxury apartments, department stores and shopping malls, business centers, agricultural projects, and public works. It became a major interest in 62 other Italian companies dealing in real estate, urban and rural development industrial plants, and vast engineering projects. It developed into the bargain a whole series of holding companies: Italo-Americana Nuovi Alberghi and the Compagnia Italiana degli Alberghi Cavalieri (hotels); the Società Italiana Arredamenti Metallici;[23] Bellrock Italiana (construction materials); and Manifattura Ceramica Pazzi—specializing in bathroom fixtures and petrochemical products.

SGI also held a series of private holding companies in Italy and abroad. In Italy, its biggest was the Società Generale per Lavori e Pubbliche Utilità, which engaged in mammoth construction works such as dams, containment embankments for reservoirs, tunnels,[24] highways, hydroelectric plants, subway stations, bridges, viaducts, aqueducts, steel plants, thermoelectric plants—the list was enormous. It also held Ediltechno S.p.A. which did consulting work in Paris, Washington, and New York City. [25]

Abroad it had other holding companies: Ediltechno, Redbrook Estates, Immobiliare Canada,[26] Soyesan Construction Company, Lomas Verdes, Immobiliare Corinto (these last three in Mexico); the Société Immobilière Champs-Elysées in France.

By 1958, the year of Nogara's death, SGI had acquired over 100 million square feet of property within the city limits of Rome itself. Later on, when the Olympic Games were assigned to Rome, SGI would not only sell the land for fifteen sports stadiums and the Olympic Highway, it would also build them; and when they needed repair, it would repair them. The stadiums alone cost the Italian taxpayers $29 million.

The gross assets of SGI itself reached $170 million in 1967; its earnings were $7 million.

It can safely be said that the preceding account offers merely a cross section of what the Vatican finance agencies created between 1945 and 1968. Like all cross sections, it provides a general idea as to how richness and variety were built up over time; but no cross section will convey the full picture, and to take it as such is to invite dangerous assumptions.

In the case of the two Vatican financial agencies, if one were to confine calculations to what is known or knowable, it is possible to conclude that Vatican securities amounted approximately to $5–7 billion dollars spread over 40–50 percent of all shares quoted on the Italian exchange. But that is only part of the picture. Already, and from the earliest years, Vatican monies were invested abroad, principally in Europe, some in the Americas, a little in Africa, the Near East and Far East.

No doubt about it, however, Nogara's goal originally was Pius XII's: to make the Vatican *temporally* an integral and essential part of the European economy. Instead of territorial power, the aim was managerial power. And, between 1948 and 1954, certainly the budding idea of Europe as one political and economic unit was nourished.

The idea was faulty from the beginning, of course, because it really meant only western Europe, and did not include the politically important countries of eastern Europe and the Soviet Union. The Soviets held the key, and they were not prepared to unlock the door. Still the idea persisted in Utopian minds. Only that visionary giant, Charles de Gaulle, kept speaking of Europe "from Calais to the Urals" as the real Europe that had once flourished beneath the aegis of the Catholic Church and that made everything in our fading civilization possible—hope, art, literature, democracy, love of neighbors.

From the midfifties onward, Nogara and his associates began to look further abroad. The "European idea" as a practical aim was as dead as German reunification—and for the same reason: the Soviet colossus. What amount of Vatican monies flourished abroad is at present a matter of speculation. That it matched the Italian investment had been one guess; that it was substantial is as certain as that it existed. In any case, in terms of 1960 dollars, what was now within the hands of the Vatican represented, in terms of liquidity, more than it had ever possessed even in its heyday of universal acceptance among the nations and its universal levy of papal revenues.

The Universal Ministry

All calculations concerning Vatican wealth must include the managerial functions of the Vatican Institute for Religious Agencies. Someday, a later historian will have access to the detailed documents that will tell the complete story of the IRA's universal ministry. For during the first twenty years after World War II, there was a rising graph of religious practice, ecclesiastical control, and financial prosperity that deceived many into thinking that Catholicism was heading into a new Renaissance of flourishing religiosity and churchly organization. In reality, it was a pseudo-Renaissance, merely a last gasp in the gallant attempts made earlier in the century to start a Catholic literature, a Catholic economic system, a Catholic political system, a Catholic persona for man, for woman, for child, for society, for the State. And it was all pointless. But as long as it lasted, the financial gains were considerable.

Acting as advisors, investors, and brokers for hundreds of ecclesiastical bodies throughout the Catholic world—and that was most of the world—the managers of Vatican financial agencies disposed of vast sums for investment. As a by-product of good stewardship and management, from time to time they would act as conduits for funds not of ecclesiastical provenance. The whole mass of funds at their disposal therefore made the Vatican a much sought after co-investor and business partner. It is somewhat surprising to discover that, by and large, the Vatican was not the conduit for tainted funds or for the financial sinews of political oppressors—surprising because it would have been so easy for such corrupt involvement to have gone unnoticed. It was only in the 1960s that actual corruption overtook it on a large scale. By that time, several personalities had emerged within the Vatican financial agencies that were to be central figures in these scandals.

The Rise of Personalities

One of the key personalities was a future pope: Giovanni Battista Montini, elected Pope Paul VI in 1963. Montini's career was spent in the shadow of Pius XII. The contrast between the two men was that of hierarch and clerk, of aristocrat and pleb, of old Italianate tradition and new Italian bravura. Pacelli was quintessentially Italian, hard-headed, devoid of Romantic sentiment, a man of the mystical Roman line—Nicholas V, Dante, Innocent XI, Petrarch, or Savonarola would have recognized his lineaments. Montini was French-educated, a brooding existentialist, dedicated to the Romantic Utopia.

The key difference between the two men was the fire that consumed them: Montini had fire on his brain, but his heart belonged to no throne; Pacelli had fire in his heart, but his brain had a deadly, ice-cold accuracy. Pacelli's rationality saved him from the push of feeling. Montini's brain exploded with passion leading his heart where it should not have gone.

Beginning in the year 1929 and for the next fifteen years, the relationship was close. But after the Democristian victory of 1948, and when Nogara's empire started to emerge, a great rift took place. As Archbishop Pro-Secretary of Internal Affairs at the Secretariat of State, Montini watched carefully and recorded whatever excesses he saw arising from the new postwar regime. In particular, he followed the rising fortunes of Pius's three nephews, Giulio, Marcantonio, and Carlo Pacelli, all princes by title and all highly placed in the Vatican government. All three were numbered among the *uomini di fiducia*, the men of trust, that Nogara placed in key positions on company boards.

Besides many other injustices, Montini claimed to have found irregularities, even illegalities, in the performance of the papal nephews. Montini, who hated injustice as some men hate dirt, catalogued and documented his findings, and one day had them conveyed to Pius XII. It was the right move at the wrong time by the wrong person. There *were* irregularities. There *were* illegalities. But the early fifties were a trying time for Pacelli personally and papally. His health began to deteriorate rapidly, and he became aware of a rising tide of opposition to his strongly authoritarian rule and to certain long-standing Catholic beliefs—notably those concerning priestly celibacy, contraception, and the doctrines of Original Sin and the divinity of Jesus. Internal revolt was the last cross he could bear. Moreover, Montini's name was linked correctly, if discreetly, with people Pius could not abide—Protestant ecumenicists, French ultra-progressive theologians, Italian left-leaning liberal politicians, Latin-American revolutionary thinkers.

The upshot: Giovanni Battista Montini boarded a train for Milan and for exile in 1954. He would never be a cardinal, as far as Pius XII was concerned, and therefore never a *papabile*, a papal contender. But up north, Montini drew closer to two people—one a future pope, the other a financier.

Angelo Giuseppe Roncalli, aged 73, after nearly thirty years of diplomatic service, had recently become Cardinal Patriarch of Venice. Roncalli shared two political views with Montini: the Democristians' reign should end; the hierarchic attitude of Pius XII no longer suited the modern mind. He and Montini had lived in apprehension of Pius for a good deal of their lives, and now they drew together. Four years later, in 1958, one of the first things Roncalli did when he became Pope John XXIII was to make Montini a cardinal.

The way was now open for Montini to inherit the throne of Peter. But, in the meantime, still in Milan, Montini became acquainted with his future *éminence grise*. Michele Sindona was as different from Montini in moral character, method of reasoning, and ambition as Savonarola's Prince is from Dante's Monarch, as King Croesus was from St. Francis of Assisi. Where Montini saw color, heard music, aspired to a transcendent world view, Sindona saw only a black bottom line, heard only the clicking of ticker-tape market reports, aspired only to a geofinancial empire. Since his days as an indigent law student, he had established himself wisely in Milan, the industrial center of Italy. With the *"miracolo economico"* now on the horizon, Sindona aimed to be its master of ceremonies—and much more.

In one sense, he had come a long way from his Sicilian home town of Patti. In another, he had never left it. After obtaining a degree in tax law from the University of Messina, he had begun to work for his living in a local bank, dreaming of becoming an American tycoon one day. Within a year, Messina and all of Sicily would fall to Allied troops. Michele Sindona would take his first steps toward realizing his dream: Purchasing an army truck from the invading Americans, he delivered Patti lemons to the center of Sicily, bringing back wheat and food supplies to his beloved home town. It was an act characteristic of Sindona. To effect this trade, he had to make an arrangement through the Bishop of Patti with the top Mafia leader, Vito Genovese. All his life, Sindona would work with Mafiosi.

He arrived in Milan in 1948, setting up shop as an expert in corporate and tax law. Immediately, he attracted many clients. But his eyes were fixed on one goal: entry into the closed, secret world of Vatican finance. He acquired a reputation for cleverness and resourcefulness in dealing with Italian tax and currency laws, acquired stock in some dozen companies, and was a regular churchgoer and contributor to Church causes.

When Montini arrived in Milan, Sindona secured an introduction to the new archbishop through Massimo Spada, a very important *uomo di fiducia* of the Vatican financial agencies. In time, Sindona would help Montini with his pastoral problems. When, for instance, Montini needed $2 million in order to finance a home for the aged, the Casa Madonnina, Sindona rustled up the money from his business acquaintances in a single day. By 1959, Sindona had the largest practice of all Italian offices specializing in tax and corporate law.

In that same year, he took his first concrete step to his goal: In partnership with the Institute for Religious Agencies, he bought the Banca Finanziaria Privata, 60 percent on behalf of the IRA, 40 percent for himself. The following year, Sindona took complete control of the Banca Finanziaria Privata. From now on, he pursued his goal by devising ways of bypassing tax and currency restrictions. He acquired stock in Swiss companies and banks and started his own Liechtenstein holding companies so that his lines of credit would expand, secrecy would be guaranteed, and currency could be moved in and out of Italy by fiduciary contracts.[27]

From now on, Sindona built up his empire, acquiring companies in Italy, elsewhere in Europe and the United States; buying real estate in Canada and the U.S. for the Vatican's IRA and for himself, always channeling the funds through his Liechtenstein holding companies. He was prestigious enough to sign a contract with the mighty Banque de Paris et des Pays-Bas (Paribas, as it was called), and he was financial representative for many large American corporations such as General Foods, the Ford Motor Company, General Motors, and Crucible Steel of America. By the time Sindona's big moment came in 1969, he owned half a dozen banks in Italy, Switzerland, Germany, and the U.S., and controlled more than 400 corporations. His Euromarket Money Brokers S.p.A., an international brokerage firm, would grow to have 850 client banks and do a gross annual volume of $200 billion. He bought a newspaper and owned real estate on three continents. Sindona's morality was quite flexible: It not only permitted him to bypass state laws; it allowed him to become, in the words of one 1967 Interpol memorandum, a leading member of a group "involved in the illicit movement" of drugs "between Italy and the United States and possibly other European countries." Sindona had explicitly taken as his model the Superman of Friedrich Nietzsche, for whom "there is a higher morality, void of any responsibility to the masses." He aimed at being what Nietzsche described as "the greatest, who can be the most deviating, the human being beyond good and evil."

Michele Sindona shouldered one other vast undertaking in those early years. On All Souls' Day, November 2, 1957, he participated in an international meeting of the Mafia in an upper-floor suite of the Hotel des Palmes in Palermo, Sicily. With him were Lucky Luciano, Joseph ("Joe Bananas") Bonanno, Carmine Galante, Tommaso Buscetta, and Frank Coppola representing the Gambino "family," and others representing the Lucchese and Genovese "families." The subject: investment of profits from the illicit drug trade. The "families" wanted to invest legitimately.

For Sindona, it was a prime chance: Into his hands would fall literally billions of dollars for investment. His companies and banks in Switzerland, Luxembourg, and Liechtenstein provided excellent conduits, for all real ownership of the invested money would be concealed forever. The "families" could go "legit," could buy into respectable businesses, might even pay some taxes. Michele Sindona would have total control over the profits of the heroin trade for investment in Europe and the Americas.

By 1969, he had taken another step: He joined the ultra-secret organization known to the world as Propaganda Due or P–2, a band of men organized on the lines of Freemasonry by a certain Licio Gelli. In joining it, Sindona was doing what the brilliant director-general of the Banco Ambrosiano, Roberto Calvi, had already done and what hundreds of the most prominent professionals in the armed forces, the intelligence community, the judiciary, the bar, the Mafia, the police, what even some highly placed clerics had done: take membership in a powerful organization that promised to uproot Communism.

Sindona's enemies, generally speaking, were on the left: socialists and Communists. But his motives for joining P–2 were undoubtedly financial. Gelli and his associates formed "a state within the state."

In Sindona's business, his safety from the law might well depend on having "friends who had friends." It was why he had cultivated the Mafia since his early days and never lost his association with it. It is speculation to think so, but the rise and power of P–2 may well have been made possible by the original "black Trinity" in Sicily, that strange fellowship of police, mafiosi, and bandits who banded together in 1947 to rid the island of Communists. P–2 was a higher Mafia. Sindona had to belong. It was a stepping-stone.

Another personality among the international money managers had also taken a step forward. Son of a Lithuanian window-washer, Illinois-born Paul Casimir Marčinkus was a priest at age 25 and had been sent to Rome by his patron, Cardinal Archbishop Stritch of Chicago, to study at the Gregorian University. From there, he proceeded to join the Vatican Secretariat of State. From being an *Uditore di Nunziatura Prima Classe* he advanced to being a *Consigliere di Nunziatura Prima Classe*.[28] On August 14, 1964, he became a bishop, a *prelato d'onore*.[29] Soon the burly giant would become known to Paul VI in a vivid way: During Paul VI's visit to the Philippines, Marčinkus saved the pope from an attempted assassination. His acquaintance with Michele Sindona was as yet slight.

In August of 1967, Pope Paul VI restructured the Vatican's financial agencies. Ever since Nogara's death, authoritative direction in the agencies had become a problem. Paul would leave the General Administration of Goods of the Holy See, the Special Administration, and the Institute for Religious Agencies intact as far as working machinery; but he unified command. He appointed a new commission of three cardinals,[30] calling it the Prefecture of Economic Affairs. Under the PECA, there was to be a new financial agency called the Administration of the Patrimony of the Holy See. The APHS would combine in it the old General Administration of Goods of the Holy See and the Special Administration (which dealt with Mussolini's indemnities). But the IRA continued on as before, as did the other financial agencies. The only difference was that authority was more centralized and nearer to the pope, at least in structural appearances. Possibly, Paul VI had already made up his mind on what to do about Vatican investments. They were in grave danger.

By 1969, Pope Paul VI was faced with a staggering problem. After seven years' contention with successive Italian governments, the Vatican was threatened with a loss of tax exemption for dividends and profits. Paul VI knew only one financial genius: Sindona.

If we pay these taxes, we stand to lose hundreds of millions in the long run, Paul complained to Sindona. And this is only the beginning. What can we do?

Very simple and very clear, Your Holiness, Sindona answered: Move the bulk of Vatican resources out of Italy into the tax-free Eurodollar market, using offshore tax corporations.

Paul VI and Sindona met alone in Paul's private study on the fourth floor of the Apostolic Palace. Before Sindona arrived, Paul had drawn up and signed a document giving Sindona total control over all Vatican investments outside of Italy. It was tantamount to control over all Vatican investments. This meant that the funds of the Special Administration as well as those of the IRA were at Sindona's fingertips. Sindona affixed his signature to the document, prayed a little with Pope Paul, and departed. To control the invested assets of the single biggest stockholder in the world, the Vatican! He had attained his goal at last.

Later in the same year, 1969, Bishop Paul Marčinkus replaced Sergio Guerri as Secretary of the IRA after Guerri had been made a cardinal. Roberto Calvi, also in the same year, became director-general of the Banco Ambrosiano of Milan.

As of 1969, it is clear that all the principal actors in the soon-to-erupt scandals—Marčinkus, Calvi, and Sindona—knew each other; it is also clear that they were all acquainted with that distinguished gray-haired Tuscan businessman-turned-cosmopolitan-prince-of-affairs Licio Gelli.[31] There is very little doubt that Michele Sindona was the link between them.

The only other personality missing from this gallery of managers lived in New York at the time and belonged to a world that seems at complete variance with that of pope, Vatican, public and private banks, stock markets, and blue-chip portfolios. Yet few private investors had such a rich, diversified, and well-stocked portfolio—variously estimated at about $1 billion—as Matteo De Lorenzo, a native of Cerignola, a poor town in the Italian province of Foggia. By the late 1960s, Uncle Marty, as he was familiarly called by his associates, had clawed his way to a top position as *capo regime* in the crime "family" originally governed by Sindona's patron in Sicily, Vito Genovese. De Lorenzo's stocks and bonds were accumulated by theft from the storerooms of Wall Street corporations as well as from counterfeit engraving establishments. But they were all working for him, managed with an iron hand by one Vincent Rizzo. Between the two of them, De Lorenzo and Rizzo controlled, in the words of one expert, the distribution of stolen and counterfeit securities throughout the world.

Significantly, any real connection between the managers of Vatican monies and those two New York-based managers came, in the opinion of those specializing in the field, through the all-reaching hands of Michele Sindona. For De Lorenzo and Rizzo knew an American, reputedly the best counterfeiter of securities; and, in 1969, shortly after Sindona initiated (at Paul VI's request) the big changeover in the direction of Vatican investments away from Italy toward the rest of Europe and the United States, some person or persons, clerical or lay or both, working within the financial agencies of the Vatican, requested the services of the two New York managers and their prince-counterfeiter.

PARTNERSHIPS AND
DISASTERS

The complicating factor in any account of the bids for partnership and the subsequent calamities is that all of them are interconnected, the beginning of one arising out of one already begun, the crashing dénouement of another heralding—often necessitating—the similarly noisy dénouement of another, so that at times the two crashes sound like echoes of the same disaster. It is an inescapable conclusion that the interconnecting link between all the elements is provided by the scintillating if erratic genius of Michele Sindona.

One thought runs through the normal person's mind as he or she reads how the bids for partnership led to the calamities: Men of the caliber of Pope Paul VI, Archbishop Marčinkus, Cardinal di Jorio—all were in positions where the prime success of their work depended on accurate evaluation of other human beings; why did none of them, before it was too late, realize Sindona's fatal flaws? The fact is none of them did. Once he arrived on the scene, in one way or another they all became marionettes on strings, with Sindona as the master puppeteer.

So the bids for real partnership began in the fall of 1969. Pope Paul: for a place for his papacy's financial sinews within the markets of Europe and North America. Archbishop Marčinkus: for an equal seat as the pope's banker among the world's most prestigious bankers and brokers. Roberto Calvi of the Banco Ambrosiano: for domination of a multinational financial conglomerate. Licio Gelli, head of P–2: for the post of all-powerful Grand Master of the great Right-Wing World Council that would destroy Communism, wipe out democratic liberalism, and restore a rightful human order. Finally,

Michele Eugenio Sindona: for the unrivaled and unheard of position as sole creator of a new monetary order for all the nations of the world.[1] The cataclysmic events tumbled forth before an astonished world like a line of dominoes toppling in an inevitable chain reaction.

With his power-of-papal-attorney Sindona was free to act. Quickly over the months, relying on his own empire of banks, holding companies, and contacts, he transferred Vatican-owned stocks through a series of companies in Liechtenstein and Luxembourg, then sold the shares on the Italian exchange and reinvested the profits tax-free in American and European stocks. The Vatican portfolio now included stocks in such companies as General Foods, Chase Manhattan, Colgate, Standard Oil, Westinghouse, Procter & Gamble, and Dan River. Sindona sold off the enormous conglomerate of SGI. By the autumn of 1969, he had sold the Vatican's shares in the Lancia Automobile Company to Fiat. Vatican shares in Montedison were disposed of, with the IIR and ENI, two Italian state holding companies, picking them up. Through 1969, 1970, and into 1971, the process went on at a steady, always secret pace, the coordination being perfect between the Vatican's PECA and IRA— with Cardinal Vagnozzi and Archbishop Marčinkus in charge.

Early in 1971, a man who knew Vincent Rizzo and Matteo De Lorenzo came to them and asked for help. A European contact of his had been asked by two members of the Vatican financial agency for $950 million in counterfeit securities. Could they arrange it?[2] After some haggling over details and proof that Vatican personnel were, indeed, involved, Rizzo and De Lorenzo agreed. Back home in the U.S., they assigned the counterfeiting job to two counterfeiters known personally to them: one in New York, the other in Los Angeles. By July, Rizzo and De Lorenzo had an initial sample of $14.5 million in false securities ready. Rizzo's master forger, William Benjamin of Philadelphia, took over from there and put the final finishing touches to the counterfeits. In July, according to the sources, the $14.5 million in counterfeit stocks were shown to the interested Vatican personnel. They were pronounced acceptable, and the remainder were ordered to be ready by October 1971.

But at this stage, something went wrong in the elaborate security arrangements of all the conspirators. The counterfeit nature of some bonds from the batch making up the $14.5 million sample was uncovered by bank authorities. The remainder of the sample bonds disappeared. By 1972, the American police probe into the whole affair was called off by order of President Nixon's Justice Department. Nobody has ever uncovered evidence that the balance of the counterfeit bonds was manufactured or delivered, although for quite a while in Europe rumors flew that certain Vatican officials were using counterfeit bonds. No concrete evidence of such misdoing ever surfaced. The then head of the police strike force's New York office, William I. Aronwald, who directed the extensive surveillance operation in 1971–72, stated in 1983 that the inquiry "had not determined whether the Vatican was involved, as a victim or otherwise."

Meanwhile, in 1972, Michele Sindona tried to buy a $200 million Italian holding company called the Società Italiana Strade Ferrate Meridionali. Control of this company would have made his Sindona Group the most powerful financial combine in Europe. But he was defeated in this attempt by some devoted enemies of his in Italian state-run corporations and finance institutions.

He turned instead to a new proposition: the acquisition of an American bank. By September 1972, Sindona had purchased a controlling interest in the Franklin National Bank of New York. Before that, he sold one of his Luxembourg banks, Compendium, to Roberto Calvi, now the director-general of the Banco Ambrosiano.

Through Compendium, Calvi controlled a number of offshore finance banks, among them a Bahamas-based institute he renamed Banco Ambrosiano Overseas. The Ambrosiano had become a member of the seven-nation Inter Alpha Group of European banks in 1972. This group included the Kredietbank of Belgium, the BHF Bank of West Germany, the Royal Bank of Scotland, and the Crédit Commercial of France. All the members of the group owned controlling shares in each other's banks. Calvi further expanded, because of his close connections with Archbishop Marčinkus and Sindona, into new acquisitions in Italy, thus consolidating his empire.

Calvi was now working in close association with Archbishop Marčinkus and the Vatican's IRA, which took minority equity in several offshore banks that Calvi opened. The Vatican's *uomini di fiducia* were now intimately linked with the Ambrosiano: Carlo Pesenti became a major stockholder; Alessandro Mennini, son of Luigi Mennini, was appointed to a senior executive position. Archbishop Marčinkus joined the board of Calvi's Bahamian bank.

In November 1975 Calvi became head and chairman of the Ambrosiano. From the bank's pale-yellow building on Via Clerici, around the corner from La Scala opera house, he surveyed his realm. He was now head of the biggest investment bank in Italy.

Calvi was just about reaching his height as an international banker, in 1974, when Sindona's Franklin National Bank collapsed. It was the biggest bank collapse in U.S. history. That same year, Sindona's European banks were declared insolvent. His reign was at an end. When the dust had cleared away, the investigative commission appointed by Guido Carli, director of the Bank of Italy, and headed by Giorgio Ambrosoli as liquidator of Sindona's empire, reported that in one of the financier's banks the net losses through Sindona's unrecorded foreign exchange contracts and irregular fiduciary contracts were in excess of $500 million. If the remaining losses in Sindona's other banks were added, the total sum that disappeared was astronomical. The investigators discovered a morass of other irregularities, many of them involving the Vatican's IRA.

Informed sources placed the losses sustained by Sindona's banking associates in the Vatican finance agencies in the region of $1 billion. This has been denied, of course, and there is at present no documentary proof one way or the other. But the estimated figure remains plausible.

The disaster seriously damaged the economy of Long Island because of the profound losses suffered by all the prime shareholders living in that area. It also had a very adverse effect on the health of Pope Paul VI, who never really recovered from the shock of it all. Through it all, however, the financial health of the Vatican continued to be extremely robust.

Four days before Franklin National Bank was declared insolvent, on October 4, 1974, Sindona fled Switzerland, where he had taken refuge from the Italian police. He traveled to the United States via Asia, and settled in New York. He moved around freely, gave public lectures, and endeavored to pick up the pieces of his lost power. By indirect means, Roberto Calvi would supply him with funds. By January 1979, three former officers of the Franklin National were convicted of conspiracy to falsify Franklin's earnings, and were sentenced to prison. Two months later, Sindona was indicted on ninety-nine counts of fraud, perjury, and misappropriation of funds. On March 27, 1980, he was convicted of sixty-eight counts of misappropriation of funds, perjury, and fraud. Sindona was fined $207,000 and sentenced to twenty-five years in prison. An additional two and a half years' imprisonment was added for bail-jumping and perjury.[3] As late as January 1982, he was indicted in Palermo, together with

seventy-five members of Mafia families, for operating a $600 mil-
lion-plus heroin trade between Sicily and the United States. By the
time Sindona was convicted, there had been at least four assassinations[4]
of men engaged in the extensive inquiries surrounding his case and
one attempted assassination.[5]

From 1975 onward, Calvi started to locate substantial funds in
Latin America. He had the Ambrosiano's stockbrokerage affiliate
pick up some hundreds of millions of dollars' worth of Ambrosiano
stock. The funds to buy this stock were borrowed on the Euromarket.
The stock was located in roughly a dozen companies in Liechtenstein and Panama; these companies were for the most part "ghostly"
partners. The move gave Calvi a steel grip over 20 percent of the
Ambrosiano's stock. He was thus master of all that the Ambrosiano
commanded by way of funds and credit. In those years he drew
closer to Licio Gelli, head of P–2, and Gelli's close collaborator,
Umberto Ortolani. They were years when the political situation in
Italy was dominated by the terrorism rampant on the streets of its
major cities. Somebody was endeavoring to liquidate the last vestiges
of democracy in Italy, someone with large supplies of funds, access
to armaments, and a superlative degree of impunity.

But Treasury and fiscal authorities in Italy were now eyeing Calvi's
Ambrosiano. An inspection began in 1978. The inquiry dragged
on, impeded by the assassination of the investigating prosecutor,
Emilio Alessandrini, in January 1979, and the disgrace of Paolo
Baffi, the incumbent director of the Bank of Italy, and Mario Sa-
ranelli, both of whom were implicated in the Ambrosiano inquiry
(they were reinstated later). With the investigation finally concluded,
Calvi continued business with his offshore network of banks in
Switzerland and Latin America. There is very little doubt that the
interests of Licio Gelli and his P–2 were a dominant factor guiding
Calvi's moves. Calvi set up a central banking center for the Ambrosiano in Latin America in Lima, Peru: The Banco Ambrosiano
Andino had a balance sheet of $600 million, with many South
American banks as minority shareholders including the Banco de
la Nación of Lima. In Buenos Aires he opened the Banco Ambrosiano de America del Sud in 1980. What observers remarked about
both Ambrosiano branches was that they did practically no con-
ventional bank business. But the movement of "paper money" within
their precincts was continuous and involved huge sums.

Despite the resumption of the Italian State inquiry in June 1980,
Calvi's financing of various causes through his Latin American

subsidiaries continued at an astonishing pace. In April 1981 he acquired 40 percent control over Rizzoli Editore, Italy's largest publishing company, which also owned the nation's most prestigious newspaper, *Il Corriere della Sera*. The step had a fatal touch to it. For, unknown to Calvi, in March the police had raided Licio Gelli's estate at Villa Arezzo, coming away with 33,000 individual dossiers of the most prominent Italians of the day. They also found a list of names of about 900 members of the ultra-secret P–2, including those of Michele Sindona, Roberto Calvi, and the leading men at Rizzoli—Angelo Rizzoli, Bruno Tassan Din (the paper's general manager), and editor Franco di Bella. (Back in 1978, Andrea Rizzoli had sought financial help from Umberto Ortolani and Licio Gelli.)

On May 21, 1981, Roberto Calvi was arrested in his office and charged with malfeasance as chairman of the Ambrosiano. On May 21, also, the list of P–2 names was published. Clearly, these 900 people had been involved in blackmail, espionage, illegal currency deals, and probably in a plan to establish a junta-type government in Italy.

Up to now the Vatican's IRA had continued to vouch for the financial respectability and viability of Calvi's Panamanian finance houses.

In July 1981, Roberto Calvi was convicted of exporting $27 million illegally out of Italy, and was sentenced to four years in jail and a $13.7 million fine. He was out on bail a few days later and back as chairman at the Banco Ambrosiano. To defend his foreign operations he used "letters of patronage" supplied him by the Vatican's IRA and its head, Archbishop Marčinkus, stating that the Ambrosiano's Panamanian subsidiaries were "Vatican-related."

But every attempt Calvi made for the next nine months to shore up the hidden losses of the Ambrosiano failed. By May 1982, the Bank of Italy asked him finally to explain the foreign exposure of his bank—the investigators reckoned it to be at least $1.4 billion. Calvi was at the end of his tether. The IRA could not, for its own sake, intervene to help him; anyway, it already stood to lose a substantial sum. Holding in his hand a document that released the IRA from all connection with the earlier "letters of patronage," Archbishop Marčinkus, IRA's head, declined to help the Ambrosiano or its chairman.

At this point, Calvi seems to have been inclined to go to the authorities and tell all he knew. But he was induced by unknown persons to flee Rome secretly on June 10. On June 17, Calvi's secretary, Graziella Corrocher, committed suicide by jumping from the fourth floor of the Banco Ambrosiano, leaving behind her a note execrating Calvi for what he had done "to the group and to all of us, who were at one time so proud of it." On June 18, Calvi's body was found hanging from Blackfriars Bridge in London. There were twelve pounds of bricks and stones in his pocket as well as $20,000 in currency and a false passport. Murder or suicide? It would be 1983 before the London police would finally declare the cause of his death as unknown.

Subsequent inquiries showed an inexplicable "hole" of over $1.4 billion in the Ambrosiano's funds. As of 1980–81, Calvi's foreign subsidiaries had been put under very heavy strain. They had raised funds in the Euromarket from more than two hundred international banks. The Liechtenstein and Panama houses had bought Ambrosiano stock with dollar debt. The lira had sunk in value against the strong dollar by 1980. The dividend paid on Ambrosiano stock was not sufficient to cover the interest on outstanding loans. Those finance houses suffered therefore from an unwieldy imbalance between their lira-based assets and their dollar-based liabilities; U.S. interest rates were at an all-time high.

Following Calvi's demise, the Bank of Italy appointed a three-man commission to run the Ambrosiano. The real victims in the Ambrosiano collapse were the 40,000 shareholders and some hundreds of creditors. Whether the Vatican's IRA lost any money at all has never been revealed, because it has never been clearly established what the IRA's participation was—if any—in Calvi's Latin American network of finance houses.

Of all those who set out to make a bid for partnership in the worldwide arena of finance, two—Pope Paul VI and Roberto Calvi—are now dead. One, Michele Sindona, is in prison. One, Licio Gelli, is in hiding, having been imprisoned and escaped. Paradoxically, Gelli's disappearance from a Swiss jail is a relief to Swiss authorities. No longer burdened with his presence and the problem of what to do about him, they now possess invaluable information about his use of Ambrosiano money. Gelli's P–2 seems to be reduced to impotency.

Only Archbishop Paul Marčinkus has flourished. The Archbishop and two other IRA officials did, however, receive a "judicial communication" from the authorities alerting them that they were under investigation by a Milanese magistrate. The letter was a mistake, for the IRA is an agency of an independent state—the Vatican. It was sent back unopened with a request that it be submitted to the

Vatican through the normal diplomatic channels. Nevertheless, Treasury Minister Andreatta stated categorically that "the government is waiting for a clear assumption of responsibility on the part of the IRA because [the IRA acted as] a de facto partner of Ambrosiano" in many business matters. What answer Andreatta received from the Vatican on this point is not clear.

Pope John Paul II, through Cardinal Secretary of State Agostino Casaroli, appointed a three-man commission to investigate the IRA's relations with the Ambrosiano.[6] By October 1982, the commission reported that "from a strictly legal point of view" the IRA could not be held responsible for debts of the Banco Ambrosiano. The foreign subsidiaries of the Ambrosiano, they said, were never "under the direction of the IRA." Furthermore, it claimed that all loans made by the Ambrosiano Group to those foreign subsidiaries were made before Archbishop Marčinkus issued the "letters of patronage" to Roberto Calvi.

At a meeting of fifteen cardinals—including two from the United States[7] and one from Canada[8]—held October 19–22, 1982, in the Vatican, John Paul II established the name of this three-man commission: Pontifical Institute for the Study of Financial and Administrative Questions of the Holy See. One must remember that the IRA, by its papal charter, is not part of the administrative structure of the Holy See. The group of fifteen cardinals, therefore, had no jurisdiction over the IRA.

The three-man report was discussed in all its ramifications. A follow-up meeting of 123 cardinals was held on November 23 at which Cardinal Secretary Casaroli communicated the report of the three-man investigative commission. Contradicting one conclusion in the three-man commission's report, a former Ambrosiano official, Roberto Rosone, stated that the IRA owned indirectly 16 percent of the Banco Ambrosiano.[9] Casaroli did not address this point. A restructuring of the Roman Curia was also discussed at this general assembly of cardinals. John Paul II issued a document containing instructions to Casaroli. "The Vatican State," John Paul declared, "does not possess all the ordinary characteristics of a political community." Therefore, "the Apostolic See does not develop, nor can it develop, the economic activity that is characteristic of a state; and the production of economic goods and enrichment of its revenues are excluded from its institutional aims." The general conclusion among the cardinals was, as Krol of Philadelphia put it, that the IRA had been exploited by Roberto Calvi.

The assembly of cardinals on November 25 (now reduced to 92)

had the presence of John Paul II himself. Discussion centered around
the links between the IRA and the Banco Ambrosiano. Cardinal
Martin Höffner of Cologne read a report on the nature and the aims
of the IRA.

The final document of the assembly was issued on November
26. It described the current operating Vatican budget deficit as in
the region of $28 million. The 1981 income of the Vatican was
put at $99 million, expenditures at $95 million. Again, it must be
remembered: The IRA is not included in this administrative assessment, since its accounts are separate. The document also revealed that the IRA had unknowingly become a shareholder in those
ten Latin-American holding companies set up by Roberto Calvi.
Archbishop Marčinkus and other IRA officials had only become
aware of this in July 1981. "It resulted that the name of the IRA
was used for the realization of an occult project which, unknown
to the IRA itself, connected operations which, if considered individually, had the appearance of being regular and normal."

In his closing address to the cardinals on November 26, John
Paul II declared his Vatican was "willing to take all steps" so that
"the entire truth" be known about the relationship between the
Vatican's IRA and the bankrupt Banco Ambrosiano. He promised
the Vatican would publicly report on its financial situation because
"individuals and Catholics need to be sensibly informed both of the
needs and the uses of their offerings." To some Belgian journalists
he made the same promise.

The most significant move by John Paul was his agreement with
Italian banking and Treasury officials to join in a second and joint
investigation into the Ambrosiano scandal. Since then, an Italian
magistrate has frozen the assets of two Vatican *uomini di fiducia*,
Luigi Mennini and Pellegrino di Strobel, two close aides of Arch-
bishop Marčinkus. The magistrate, Renato Brichetti, has stated that
the Archbishop would undergo the same measures if he were an
Italian citizen. Brichetti holds that the "letters of patronage" helped
Calvi bilk the Ambrosiano of millions. Marčinkus and the IRA,
Brichetti says, are as guilty as Calvi.

At the special urging of American and German bankers, John
Paul agreed to set up a new panel of three lay bankers as a permanent
watchdog committee to monitor the IRA. Almost immediately there
was controversy about the leading member of this committee. He
was Herman Abs, a Catholic, former head of Deutsche Bank. In
January 1983, the Simon Wiesenthal Center for Holocaust Studies

denounced Abs as a former Nazi.[10] The Vatican's Casaroli immediately promised an investigation. Since then, another member has
been added to the committee, but no final judgment has been made
about Abs. Cardinal Höffner of Cologne has since publicly recommended putting all the operations of the IRA in the hands of
laymen.

But two new factors had already cropped up to complicate the
attempts of the Italian government and the Vatican to settle the
Ambrosiano affair once and for all to the satisfaction of all parties—
including the creditors of Ambrosiano. One was the renegotiation
of the Lateran Concordat signed in 1929 by Benito Mussolini's
government and the Holy See. The other was the proposal to
establish formal diplomatic relations between the U.S. and the Holy
See.

Negotiations for the revision of the Lateran Concordat had been
going on for fifteen years between the legal experts on both sides.
Doing most of the spadework were Guido Gonella, a democratic
politician (who died in 1983), and sixty-year-old Archbishop Achille
Silvestrini, secretary of the Holy See's Council for the Public Affairs
of the Church. The Lateran Concordat had made possible the
rebirth of the papal State, albeit in reduced form, and it had also
conceded to the Holy See the status which allowed it to accumulate
its assets. So the revision was no light affair.

The revision of the Concordat went through six drafts, and by
the end of the process in 1983 had reduced the original 45 Articles
of the 1929 Concordat to 14. But the Ambrosiano affair very nearly
halted the finalizing of the text, its protocollary signing and approval,
and its passage into Italian law.

Once the Ambrosiano affair broke and some facts became known,
especially the Holy See's involvement—innocent or guilty—the
Italian government put pressure on the Holy See to make at least
some token restitution. And the government had, after all, some
leverage. In the revised text of the Concordat, the tax-exempt status
and other privileges of the Holy See were maintained. That valuable
status and the privileges could be challenged, the Holy See's representatives were reminded by the ministers of Socialist Prime Minister Bettino Craxi's government. This was thus the most favorable
moment to get a revised text of the Concordat signed and passed
into law.

In the meantime, the issue of diplomatic relations between the
Holy See and the U.S. had arisen. The question of such formal

relations had remained dormant and untouched from 1867 until Franklin Roosevelt's presidency. American isolationism and native American Protestant anti-Catholic prejudice made the country permanently opposed to any connection with "that accursed Red Lady of the Mediterranean," as the Holy See was described.

But when World War II broke out, a very sensible President Roosevelt dispatched Myron Taylor on Christmas Eve 1939 as his personal envoy to the Holy See. It would be sheer madness to have neglected the valuable intelligence and cooperation of the pope and the Vatican in a world war. Myron Taylor remained there until 1951. That year, Harry Truman proposed establishing diplomatic relations, but the hurricane of demonstrations and recriminations made even that tough president withdraw in confusion. Presidents Eisenhower and Johnson sent no envoy because they could not buck the still virulent anti-Catholicism in the U.S.; President Kennedy sent none because he was the first Catholic president and needed to appear more independent of the Holy See than any Protestant. President Nixon resumed the practice in 1970, sending Henry Cabot Lodge as his personal envoy, and President Ford retained Lodge in the position. President Carter was the first president to choose a Catholic, David Walters, for the job; and, after Walters, he sent former Mayor Robert F. Wagner, Jr., of New York City, to the post. President Reagan sent his own choice, a Catholic Californian millionaire rancher friend, William A. Wilson.

The need to establish formal diplomatic relations became more acute in the aftermath of the Polish crisis in 1981–82, which taught the Reagan administration that for middle and eastern Europe there was no source of intelligence or influence to match the Vatican of Pope John Paul II. Mindful of the native prejudice in the U.S., President Reagan early in 1983 requested the Reverend Billy Graham, who was himself cool to the idea, confidentially to sound out the likely reactions of evangelical Protestant leaders—the Reverend Jerry Falwell, head of the Moral Majority; the Reverend Pat Robertson; the Reverend Billy Marvin, executive secretary of the National Association of Evangelicals; the Reverend David Hubbard, president of Fuller Theological Seminary in Pasadena; and the Reverend Gilbert Beers, editor of *Christianity Today*. None of the evangelical leaders could honestly see a logical reason against the step, but they were wary of how their congregations and sympathizers would respond. Graham summed up the reactions he met with in a letter to the President's adviser, Judge William Clark: "If anyone can do it and get away with it, it is Mr. Reagan."

Toward the autumn of 1983, the negotiations over the revision of the Concordat had become stuck over the Holy See's "good-will remuneration" of the Ambrosiano creditors. The liquidators of what remained of the Ambrosiano threatened to take legal action within Italy and at the International Court of the Hague against the Holy See. More publicity was the last thing the Holy See needed. Around the same time, the Reagan administration went public with its intention of establishing diplomatic relations and submitted the name of William A. Wilson to the U.S. Senate for confirmation as the U.S. ambassador. The administration's arguments were simple. As did the 106 other nations already having full diplomatic relations with the Holy See, the U.S. needed that relationship with the government of one of the most powerful men alive and the most influential religious organization on the face of the globe.

There now followed a short but intense passage of time during which Pope John Paul II and his Cardinal Secretary of State, Agostino Casaroli, were held down on the anvil of hard circumstances by the two claws of a pincers: the need to get a suitably revised Concordat text signed and the desirability of establishing diplomatic relations with the U.S. John Paul II needed that access to the U.S. government as much to control his rambunctious American Catholic bishops as for other, standard political reasons. The hammer that kept striking them was the Italian government's insistence that the Holy See make some "goodwill remuneration." It has been suggested that some of those Ambrosiano creditors had a voice not only with the Italian government but in Washington as well.

In any case, it looked as if the revision of the Concordat with Italy and the establishment of diplomatic relations with the U.S. would both be put off indefinitely. The Holy See would not do anything in the aftermath of the Ambrosiano affair which could be construed as an admission of complicity; and in the U.S. a storm arose over the sending of an ambassador. The National Council of Churches and the World Council of Churches started·a public campaign against the proposal. They were joined by the Reverend Jerry Falwell, the National Association of Laity, the Americans United for the Separation of Church and State, and a variety of other groups and individuals. Dr. James Dunn, speaking for the Baptist Joint Committee on Public Affairs, of which he is executive director, said the appointment of an ambassador to the Holy See would be "a terrible precedent." Archbishop Iakovos, supreme Greek Orthodox prelate of North and South America, said at a news conference that the proposal "was a mistake on both sides," and

added his voice to the protests. Monsignor George Higgins, retired
director of social relations for the Catholic Church in America,
admitted to one reporter that "in a secret ballot, without any pressure
from the Vatican, not 10% of the [U.S. Catholic] bishops would
vote for it." The reason for the bishops' opposition is clear. The
establishment of diplomatic relations would mean that in Washington there would reside an emissary of the pope with direct access
to the State Department and to the president, and who therefore
would have a stronger and more effective voice than the bishops in
the U.S. It would be an automatic curb on the bishops' tendency
in the last few years to enter political and even military disputes on
their own.

The main argument nationwide against establishing formal relations was that the Holy See was a "church," a theocracy, as one
Protestant bishop put it. Maintaining diplomatic relations would
"establish" Catholicism in a way forbidden by the Constitution.
Curiously, none of the many and varied protesters who crowded
the Senate hearing room or who spoke out in print and on television
had ever objected to the U.S. having diplomatic relations with the
only real theocracy in the world, Saudi Arabia. And as one listened
to the lay arguments against the Reagan proposal, it was evident
that behind them all floated that still virulent American prejudice:
anti-Catholicism. Archbishop Iakovos's attitude and childlike ignorance of facts were surprising, for no one acquainted with the
facts would have stated as he did that the National Council of
Churches and the World Council of Churches "are as deeply involved in the political affairs of the world as is the Vatican." No
prelate in the United States, Catholic or Protestant, has been and
is more involved in marshaling the political power of others to
further his views than Iakovos, whether concerning the Turkish
invasion of Cyprus, the plight of Patriarch Demetrios in Istanbul,
or the archbishop's personal career—which has been marked by an
assiduous cultivation of political power-brokers and the prestige derived from associating with them.

Caught in this triple crisis, the Holy See, after much negotiation
with the Italian government, finally consented to make some "goodwill remuneration" to the Ambrosiano creditors. On February 14,
1984, Italian treasury minister Giovanni Goria, himself a Democristian in Bettino Craxi's Socialist Cabinet, made two surprising
statements to the Italian Senate in Rome. The Holy See, he said,
was willing to make some remuneration—a formula had been found

that avoided any implication of guilt; and Goria publicly asked that the Holy See put all Italian business dealings of the IRA under Italian law and fiscal controls. He proposed, "on the initiative of the Vatican, the creation of an Italian branch" of the IRA. The "goodwill remuneration" was put into effect, but the Italian controls over the Italian business of the IRA remain up in the air. But the way was cleared for the Concordat.

On February 18, in the Villa Madama, a Renaissance palace belonging to the Italian government, the revised text of the Concordat was signed. Bettino Craxi on behalf of the government— and with the approval of all political parties, including the Communists—and Cardinal Secretary Casaroli for the Holy See put their signatures to the new draft. The new 14-Article text left intact the tax-exempt status of the Holy See. It dropped the description of Rome as "sacred," omitted the claim that Catholicism was the "State religion of Italy," made Catholic instruction in schools optional, permitted civil magistrates to review all Church marriage annulments, removed the Jewish catacombs of Rome and southern Italy from Vatican control, and declared the Church and the Italian State to be independent of each other and sovereign in their own right.

Early in March, the U.S. Senate confirmed William A. Wilson as ambassador to the Holy See by a 81–13 vote, the most notable negative vote being cast by Senator Jesse Helms of North Carolina. Helms was facing a tough reelection campaign in an area largely dominated by anti-papal Baptists. The State Department informed the relevant House Appropriation subcommittee that it needed $351,000 in order to administer the new Roman diplomatic mission. This sum was to be added to the $482,000 already earmarked in the 1984 budget for the office of the president's personal envoy. The total cost of the new embassy would be $833,000. Representative Neal Smith (D-Iowa), chairman of that subcommittee, vowed to block the request. But Smith would eventually fall into line. Three weeks after the Senate's confirmation of Wilson, Pope John Paul II made sixty-two-year-old Archbishop Pio Laghi the first papal ambassador to Washington with the title of Pro-Nuncio.

The previous week, the Holy See made known the extent of its "goodwill remuneration" to the Ambrosiano creditors. The Pope authorized the payment of $250 million from the funds of the Holy See, in agreement with the representatives of 120 banks owed money by the Ambrosiano.

To raise the $250 million, it is reported, the Holy See would sell part of its stock portfolio on European stock markets, on the Paris Bourse, and on the New York Stock Exchange. It had already in February sold its equity in Italy's largest construction company, thus realizing $20 million. It would also reportedly sell its controlling interest in the Banco Roma Svizzera of Rome, and thus acquire another $100 million. To make up the remainder of the $250 million "goodwill remuneration," loans might be sought, or some of the Holy See's real estate holdings might be sold off.

The position of the Ambrosiano creditors was thus bettered, but not restored. Swiss and Italian police recovered about $200 million in assets that had been secreted in Swiss bank accounts by Roberto Calvi and his associates. The bulk of the remuneration, $320 million, will be given to the 88 main creditors of Ambrosiano's Luxembourg-based holding company, BAH, who together lost about $600 million in the Ambrosiano debacle. Swiss, Italian, and Peruvian creditors will receive another $100 million.

Meanwhile, the announced deficit of Vatican central administrative operations in 1984 will be $31 million. This is up from the 1981 $28 million deficit, when the total budget for the Vatican central administration was in the region of $100 million.

The new report of the Vatican–Italy joint investigation committee is ready, but it may never be published. The way is opening out little by little, and painfully, for a restructuring of Vatican financial agencies. But it is fraught with dangers—economic, religious, and even physical—for all concerned, especially for Pope John Paul II.

Before considering any proposals about that needed restructuring, we need to understand how the papacy came to be involved in the recent scandals, and to fashion some rational norms whereby the Church's situation can be judged. Something more than a printed financial fact-sheet is required. For several other considerations must be weighed. All of them together form a *framework of power* and bear directly on an objective judgment about the Catholic Church and the Vatican, and on the kind of restructuring that is practical.

Foremost among these other considerations is the nature of the Catholic Church's identity, as well as the origin and nature of power, responsibility, and government in the Church. "Who speaks of money, speaks of power," stated Gerson Bleichröder, one of the great financial geniuses of the last century.

Then there is (for the Church) the ugly fact that a fundamental shift has occurred in this century. Examining the situation of the Church caught in the middle of that awesome shift, one's first impression is of profound pathos. For this institution that has lasted for over nineteen hundred years is now in exile, fundamentally at variance with the dominant trend in the human family. That re-alization of exile doubtless explains the desperation with which the Church's financial officials acted in the sixties and seventies.

But even after taking all these facts into consideration, how can one appreciate and appraise the forces that led the Church along these paths, unless one assesses the origin, progress, and develop-ment of Church finances from the time that the popes in Rome started to exercise veritable monetary and fiscal policies? What is necessary here is to show the line of development from ancient times that carried on over the centuries and reached down to the Vatican's present financial agencies. Some approximation is needed of the varying levels of wealth and poverty reached by the papacy over the centuries, so that what happened in the twentieth century be seen in proper perspective.

PART TWO

THE FRAMEWORK OF POWER

CATHOLIC IDENTITY

The visible structure of the Catholic Church has four essential visible elements. There is the head of the Church—a single man who, it is claimed, is the divinely approved successor to St. Peter, the Apostle; is the sole living representative of God among men; is endowed with absolute authority to teach God's salvation as revealed through his son, Jesus Christ, who was and is God himself made man. There is, secondly, the geographical association of that one man with one particular place on this earth, Rome. From the beginning and to this day, the head of the Catholic Church is the Bishop of Rome. The third element is the Church, namely the body of those men and women who depend on that one man in that one place for receiving this salvation of God. And, finally, there is a group of official collaborators with that one man, appointed and approved by him, a greater or lesser number of clerics, called bishops, who supervise the dispensation of that salvation according to the norms laid down by that one man.

This is the "Roman fact," as theologians have frequently called it: the pope in Rome, as head of the Church and of its bishops.

Catholic teaching is adamant on one point: There is but one Catholic Church in the whole world. There are no branches of Catholicism. There cannot be an authentic French Catholic Church, Chinese Catholic Church, Anglican Catholic Church, and so on. There are bishops and priests of the Catholic Church in France, in China, in England, and elsewhere; but the Catholic Church is a supranational entity with representatives and members in various countries and its center in Rome, Italy.[1]

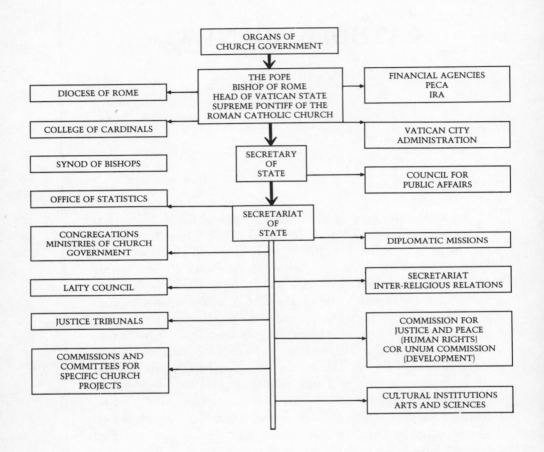

FIGURE 1

What that one man in Rome teaches in the name of Jesus Christ does not concern mere "mind" and "will" or even "aspiration" and "faith." For all those so-called qualitative factors have in themselves nothing to do directly with God and his salvation, belonging as they do to this material cosmos. The salvation taught by that one man comes gratuitously from outside the cosmos—not spatially, as if God dwelt out beyond the reaches of space, but existentially. The salvation proffered by the Bishop of Rome comes from a totally different dimension of existence, the supernatural, which is utterly unattainable by any force, qualitative or quantitative, originating in this cosmos of man. That one man in that one place holds the keys to that salvation. He is the Keeper of the Keys of the Kingdom of Heaven.

Catholic teaching holds that any Roman Catholic, any non-Catholic Christian, or any non-Christian of whatever other religion who receives God's salvation receives it through the spiritual office of that one man in Rome and the merits of his Church of believers.

The egregiously un-Catholic mentality and heretical opinions of modern theologians in this matter can be gauged from, say, the conclusions of Hans Küng and several prominent Catholics gathered in 1982 after Pentecost. The future of theology, Küng is reported as stating, "lies in its becoming a universal way of thinking which rises from the reflection and God-experience unique to each community of faith . . . its immediate spokespeople will be faith-filled communities committed to the struggle for a new society . . ." This is about as far from Catholic reality as an Eskimo igloo is from the Taj Mahal.

The essential note, therefore, of the Catholic Church is absoluteness. The triple claim is absolute: the pope as God's only official representative, Rome as the only place in which that pope is found as its bishop, the dependence of all who are saved on that one man and his sacred office. All else that the human eye and mind can associate with the Catholic Church is a temporary addition—cardinals, monsignors, patriarchs, legates, nuncios, ambassadors, clerical organizations of religious orders and congregations, clerical institutions (parochial schools, cathedrals, churches, convents, monasteries, orphanages, clinics, universities), Vatican City State and all it contains (newspapers, books, magazines, libraries, museums, political lobbies, social pressure groups, cultural projects, liquid assets, gold deposits, corporate participation). Nothing of all that belongs essentially to the visible structure of the Catholic Church.

Yet there is an enormous and cumbersome infrastructure to that essential core structure.

The Catholic Church is organized along two principal lines. Its adherents are divided into dioceses,[2] and each diocese is divided into parishes. Each diocese is headed by a bishop who is called the "Ordinary" of the diocese.[3] Each parish is headed by a priest aided or not by other priests. Each parish administers its own spiritual and temporal affairs in conjunction and alignment with its diocese. Through its chancery—a mainly clerical bureaucracy—each diocese administers its own spiritual and temporal affairs in conjunction and alignment with Rome.

The pope is residential bishop of the diocese of Rome, and that diocese has its own bureaucratic chancery to deal with the spiritual and temporal affairs of Rome. As pope he has an additional bureaucracy, mainly clerical. That clerical bureaucracy is commonly described as "the Vatican."[4] But this is really a misnomer, being a shortened form for the State of Vatican City. The pope is its absolute ruler. As a fully sovereign state, it has its own borders, police, judiciary, jails, taxes, stamps, coinage, newspapers, press office, fire department, security services, civil service, banking system, ambassadors, and accredited diplomatic corps. However, because it is surrounded by Rome and the State of Italy, its municipal services necessarily work in conjunction with those of Rome.

The bureaucracy of the Vatican is the pope's executive right arm, and, under his command, it has a double function: to administer the temporal affairs of the State of Vatican City and to administer the spiritual and temporal affairs of the entire Church. The Vatican bureaucracy—called the Curia[5]—is organized into sections corresponding to the ministries, offices, and services of a normal government. In Rome, the more important ones are called congregations, tribunals, secretariats, and commissions.[6]

In principle and, very largely, in practice, each diocese is independent of Rome in its fiscal and monetary administration. Each bishop has complete power in his territory; as the official representative of the Church there, he holds in trust and controls the property of the Church—liquid assets, real estate, and so on. He must, of course, visit the Vatican every five years in order to give an account of how his diocese is doing; and he must maintain friendly relations with the pope's representative in his country—in the United States this is the pro-Nuncio who lives in Washington. In the final count, the bishop is the business manager of his diocese.

The largest amount of money that goes to the Vatican from the dioceses is Peter's Pence, an annual collection made throughout the Church. From time to time, the Vatican will require additional contributions and "quotas." Within a diocese, the bishop endeavors to control the finances of each parish, utilizing surplus funds and the overall credit rating of the diocese in order to get a favorable interest rate from investment houses. But between Rome and dioceses, the business connection is not very tight. Each diocese is, in effect, autonomous.

Since 1942, both religious orders as well as dioceses have made use of the Vatican's financial agencies in order to obtain the best investment possible for their funds.

According to Catholic belief and traditional practice, all power to govern, to teach, to administer the temporal and spiritual affairs of the Catholic Church whether in Rome or elsewhere originates in the pope as Christ's representative. The pope is the first source and the ultimate recourse in the power structure. That one man as pope is given the plenitude of power. All others merely share in it. This is why all positions of power, except that of pope, are appointive: Power is given them by the pope. Only the position of pope is attained by election.

But the man elected pope does not receive his papal power from the cardinal-electors who vote him in. They do not possess that power. Catholic belief and dogma is that if a man is validly elected by the authorized electors, the cardinals, then God automatically confers the plenitude of power directly on the pope-elect.

From that point onward in the structure, all power is received by appointment. The new pope either confirms all previous appointments or he withdraws some; and, in any case, he makes new ones. His most immediate collaborators in the Curia are the cardinals. Other appointments—other sharings of power—in the Curia are either made directly by the pope or by the cardinals if they are empowered by the pope to do so. All authority to wield power and to confer power at any echelon depends on the power of the pope to grant that authority.

The same fundamental process normally takes place for the appointment of bishops throughout the Church. The power and responsibility of a bishop can be conferred on a man only by the authority of the pope or by those the pope authorizes to do so. The pope, as always, has the plenitude of power and responsibility. A bishop merely shares in that power as a subordinate.

In all analyses of power and responsibility in the Catholic Church,

we are led back to the earthly source of that power: the pope; and
to the manner in which he receives his power: the votes in conclave.
As the central cog in the mechanism of institutional Catholicism,
the secret conclave of cardinals has been of paramount importance
for about seven hundred years. As conclave goes, so goes the entire
Church—this used to be a Roman saying.

This may not be true any longer. Some mysterious extra dimension of power is producing profound changes and generating new
energies in the Church. That dimension of power always resided
within the entire community of believers everywhere as members
of Christ's mystical body; and Christ, according to Catholics, ordained that it be wielded actively by one man, his vicar among
believers and non-believers. All any conclave could do was provide
yet another occasion for its workings; the rest was mystery and the
mood of Spirit which "breathes where it chooses to breathe." Today,
that breathing resembles a high wind blowing relentlessly and de-
structively at the entrenched bureaucracy of the Church—if for no
other reason than that the bureaucracy may now have become a
crass obstacle to the divine designs of Christ. The pope is given
supreme power and responsibility, but he relegates the government
of the Church to his bureaucracy.

The bureaucracy may now be out of control. But ultimate responsibility for irregularities and for the financial scandals of recent
decades has to be laid at the door of the Roman Curial officials
engaged in the Vatican financial agencies and of the Pope himself.
For authority and government emanates primarily from him and is
preeminently shared by these officials.

He and they, however, are caught—like all of us today—in a
vast shift of forces and power. Neither he nor they would be true
Romans if they did not take that awesome shift into account. To
be genuinely Roman is to regard the cosmos as one's arena of activity
and all eternity at one's disposal.

THE SHIFT IN HUMAN AFFAIRS

Over a period of nearly sixteen hundred years, a systematization of human life and of all human society was started by Christians. It was developed by them, spreading through all the landmass of Europe, the two continents of the American hemisphere, South Africa, Australia, and New Zealand. For the first twelve hundred years, the system developed and spread chiefly under the tutelage of the Catholic Church. Together with a few isolated areas such as Ethiopia in northeastern Africa, and the Philippine Islands in the Pacific, this was the area that came to be called Christendom— Christian civilization.

When we examine that civilization as a whole, seeking to isolate what made it such a distinctive thing, we find one operative change the first Christians introduced into their world, a simple change but one with profound results. Their new religion, Christianity, was held to be true for all men and all time. They said that what their new religion taught them to believe was something that really happened in history. This was revolutionary: to claim one's religion to be universally true.

Before Christianity, there were many religions. Each one of them consisted of a series of ritual acts which had to be performed and of other acts that had to be avoided. Do's and don'ts. Each religion also had a mythology, sometimes quite vast and intricate. Some religions developed a theosophy: an esoteric collection of myths and folk wisdom and pseudohistory and adage and moralization. But none ever developed a theology, for they had no dogmas to be believed, and they never claimed or pretended that they were relating true, historical events.

When they produced a philosophy—Confucius in China, Plato and Aristotle in Greece, the Stoics in Rome, the Gnostics in Egypt—they did claim that philosophy to be true, to reflect reality. Yet since philosophy was a rational effort to understand reality, it was therefore alien to their religion. Nevertheless, they had no difficulty in performing the required acts of their religion that their philosophy rejected as based on invention and fable—because they never claimed their religion to be "true." Nor did their religion produce a system of morality, a theology-based ethos. There was no intimate or essential connection between a man's religious beliefs and the way he treated his friends, his family, his enemies, his rulers, his debtors, his inferiors, his dependents, his land, his possessions, his life, his death.

In religious matters, the pre-Christian world was ecumenical, tolerant. "Everybody is right. Nobody is wrong," was one message of the Delphic Oracle. "Whatever be the region of the earth where you find yourself," went the Roman principle, "that region's religion is your religion." In men's minds and in the way they conducted their affairs, there was no connection between religion and truth. Religion was not considered a true thing. Hence, prior to Christianity, there were no religious wars and no religious persecutions. There were no religious martyrs for their faith. No one tried to impose religion as such on anyone else. Only the Christians produced such wars, persecutions, and martyrs.

From their beginnings, Christians insisted that their religion was true, that it did speak about reality. They drew the logical conclusion from that: that it was universally true. That there could be only one true religion. Theirs. Hence all philosophy and all knowledge—any branch of human activity that dealt with the truth—had to be, would be reconcilable with the true religion, Christianity. Otherwise, it was a false philosophy, a false knowledge. Automatically, an all-embracing morality emerged from this Christianity. It permeated all aspects of temporal life: economics, politics, finance, the arts, education, social structures. Religion and politics, religion and wealth, religion and government, religion and art, religion and learning—between these there was no irreconcilable opposition. They were not separate or to be kept separate. Military matters, matters of politics, wealth, art, government—all became dominated by religion. For Christianity was true, universally true. On the strength of that new belief, and uplifted by its claim to tell men the truth about their historical origins and their living and dying, Christians built a new city of man: Christendom, the life-force of Western civilization. They created the first all-encompassing philosophy of reality which made possible the development of science and technology as we know it.

By the middle of the seventeenth century, however, the first cracks appeared in what had long been the solid masonry of that civilization. The original religious unity of Catholicism was shattered by breakaway Protestant groups. According to the Treaty of Westphalia (1648) that ended the Thirty Years' War—the most horrible war men had known up to that time—Christian states agreed in principle to separate their religious beliefs from politics. There would never again be a religious war in Europe, but the price of that achievement was the loosening of the bonds between Christianity and the civilization it had spawned.

With the American and French revolutions of the eighteenth century, religion and civil life, religion and parliamentary life, religion and culture were separated. In the mid-1800s, the first proponents of a deliberate and systematic atheism and irreligion organized themselves in Russia. By then it was clear that all over what used to be called Christendom there was a slow reversal to the state of affairs that reigned prior to the birth of Christianity: Religion was again being assigned to the realm of the unreal.

A fateful shift had taken place. It was not merely in the lives of individuals, social groups, and individual nations. The significant locus of that shift was in the relations between nations. It would be impossible to assign that shift to one year or one event as its cause, mainly because such historical changes are prepared and fomented over a long period by myriads of events and minor changes at different times, all coalescing, each one contributing one more weight to the logic of history, until at a given moment a critical threshold is reached and crossed.

At the end of World War II and with the slow formation of the international world we now inhabit, the affairs of the nations were organized around two values only: economic advantage and technological advances. Formal religions such as Christianity no longer had any say whatever. Christ no longer sat at the green-topped tables of power.

That shift has radically affected the ordinary populations of the world. Today, for vast numbers of Catholics and other Christians, religion is no longer an assent to the truth, to reality. They conduct their economic, political, financial, and artistic affairs on the open assumption that these departments of life are distinct and separate from religion because they deal with "reality." Very few people today have any inclination to oppose religion provided it does not claim to be true. The modern mind is ecumenical in this one sense: Being irreligious and therefore maintaining that religion has nothing to do with truth, it has no difficulty—no more than the ancients had—in admitting whatever religious practices society feels inclined to follow. Anyone's right to do so privately will be defended. Today adherence to a religion may be considered an aberration, a form of mild eccentricity, even insanity. But it is perfectly allowable. "America is a religious nation," one editorial in the *New York Times* stated,[1] "but only because it is religiously tolerant and lets every citizen pray, or not pray, in his own way."

Indeed, religion as a set of do's and don'ts is very practicable and useful. For there has evolved a new outlook based on the brotherhood of man, on all humans as passengers on the spaceship Earth, on the community of nations sharing a finite ecology, and suchlike "human" themes. It finds expression in a number of social acts—Olympic Games, international meets, international prizes for science, for peace, for literature, for art. This modern outlook and its consequent social acts constitute what is accurately called "secular religion." The basic tenet of this secular religion is that no religion is universally "true" in the old and traditional Catholic sense of that word.

With that difference, the theme of the new outlook is the same as under the old Christian regime: salvation. But this time salvation is presented as "the good life"—plentiful food, modern hygiene and medicine, the labor-saving devices of modern technology from cars and computers to microwave ovens and toasters. Freedom is interpreted as the ability to achieve that "good life" by money earned or, in the case of the disadvantaged and the Third World, by money given in the form of handouts or loans, whether to individual persons or individual nations.

Evidently, the outlines of a totally new civilization are already quite visible. They can be traced in two sets of changes.

First, a whole gamut of concepts and their concrete implementation have emerged, affecting our personal and social lives: sexual equality of men and women, death with dignity, the unacceptable character of the death penalty, single parenthood, reverse discrimination, a woman's right to her own body, homosexual rights, wombs-for-hire, fetal vivisection and experimentation, euthanasia, mercy-killing, legalized suicide, and population control—the latter by forced abortions and sterilization in modern China and India, elsewhere by stiffly promoted birth-control methods on which, for example, the U.S. government spends up to half a billion of the taxpayers' dollars every year. But these socio-personal changes must be seen in the context of the greater change which now promises to mold the world of man within the foreseeable future.

This is the escalating power of the managerial system in the day-to-day, year-to-year running of international life as well as the lives of single nations. There can be no doubt about the shape it is giving our world in the near future.

The managerial system, just emerging after World War II, passed into rapid development by the beginning of the eighties. It promises to reach a full-blown status by the turn of this century. Wherever that system takes over, decisions about the all-important elements in the economic and social lives of nations are not made primarily according to the political will, ethical consensus, traditional morality, or social trends of those nations. They are reached more and more according to the pragmatic judgment of non-political men who occupy managerial positions within diverse but interlocking organizational groups. These groups transcend the boundaries of city and state as well as the boundaries of the nation. The professional occupation of these managers is primarily economics, industry, and finance. Their primary loyalties and interests are in those spheres.

The system produces ten basic categories of managers: monetary, fiscal, communications, scientific, technological, manufactured goods, living services, food-supply, armaments, legislative.

Given the economic and political tensions that have strained and continue to strain nations individually and as members of the world community, the rise of such a managerial class seems to have been the inevitable result of rational efforts to ease those tensions. There is no doubt that the emergence of the system and the rise of its managers has been facilitated by the enormous steps taken to set up a global network of communications. But no one man or group of men deliberately set out to do this. It is an organic development within the lives of nations since the early days after World War II when the rearrangement and realignment of nations and international politics divided the world community between two superpowers, each one with vast influence over its own zones of influence.

That the basic elements of the managerial system are in place today is evident even from a cursory examination of the global scene: the International Monetary Fund; the Comecon; the multinational conglomerates; the international banking system in its present rudimentary condition; the international "rationalization" of manufactured goods; the increasing adoption of national industrial policies by elected governments; and those agencies of the United Nations Organization that are working effectively.

Decisions in the managerial system are taken according to no laws of individual nations, nor according to any system of morality we know of. The basic laws governing those decisions refer to the balance needed between the supply and demand of goods and services and the movement of liquid assets so as to diminish sociopolitical tensions, obviate collisions of differing national interests, and homogenize the production of goods and services all over the world. The managerial system is beginning to transcend political and ideological boundaries: more than one Soviet satellite is submitting to the rigorous conditions of the IMF; more than one Third World dictatorship is likewise submitting. Both kinds of states do so from economic and social need.

In the full-blown form of the managerial system, we can expect by the year 2000 local politics, political freedoms, and civil rights of each nation could be totally subordinated to the norms, rules, and decisions taken by these managers with a view to the welfare of the whole system.

As more and more vital elements in the social and economic life of the individual are decided according to the mentality and aims of the system's managers, it is not merely the individual's liberty that must be affected. (One could make some dire projections as to what could happen to his political rights.) But his personal morality as well as the morality of groups and nations will certainly be affected.

What he values in life, what is "good" and "bad," the very focus of meaningfulness in life must shift away from its traditional locus, namely something that transcended the entire human scene and was identified with the God of religion, the laws and demands and the promises of that God. The individual's regard for family, and ethical consensus—all hitherto colored by his religion—must be profoundly affected.

Thus, the inherent tendency of our ongoing managerial system is bound to lead to a completely new horizon for all men and women. The movement of the managerial system is toward complete collectivism in order to "protect" the average citizen and average nation "in their best interest." There is arising already a powerful bureaucracy to direct and control every citizen and every nation for "the good of all." No modern economist-banker has expressed this imminent reality more clearly and more simply than Paul M. Mazur:[2]

> . . . finally, the large number of governmental bureaus that will have their orbits in the atmosphere of our planet cannot be allowed the freedom to compete and collide with one another. So, in order to control the diverse bureaucracies required, a politburo will develop, and over this group organization there is likely to arise the final and single arbiter—the master of the order, the total dictator . . .

It is to be noted that Mazur was speaking exclusively from his view as an economist banker. He had in no way an "apocalyptic" attitude to human affairs, nor did he believe in "the End of Days" and the arrival on the human scene of "the Man" whom Christians traditionally call the Antichrist.

We who have never lived within such a tightly centralized, vast collectivist system cannot know its details. But those who sit at the governing center of the Catholic Church and are the beneficiaries of their age-old chancery's long experience have an eye and ear attuned to the shape and sound of things to come that must escape the man in the street as much as it escapes many neophyte governments and thinkers who presently direct human affairs from within.

Quite obviously, that managerial system would find most incompatible with its most valued principles any organization that fought bitterly against basing human society on economics and technology, at the same time claiming to be independent of this managerial control and to be supranational in character. Such an organization would be the managerial system's ultimate enemy.

That, by definition, is the Catholic Church.

THE PATHOS OF THE
CATHOLIC CHURCH

Ironically, the institution today most deserving of understanding, compassion, and moral support is the very one that runs the highest risk of total misunderstanding, contempt, and rejection: the Catholic Church.

Quite recently in history—and quite suddenly—came that fundamental shift in human affairs, with the world now spinning between the two poles of economics and technology. The orbit that it now traces is constantly widening out from its old accustomed tracks, out into wild stretches of uncharted space that some anticipate as the meadows of the millennium, and others fear as the desert wastes of self-destruction. The Catholic Church has not yet adjusted to that shift. The poles that determine its movement are still its original ones—good, which connotes Jesus and his salvation; evil, which connotes Satan and eternal damnation. The orbit it follows still swings between the long-established ellipsis points of God's heaven and God's earth, as it did in the fateful year 33 A.D.

Too vast, too experienced, the Catholic Church could not—would not—automatically synchronize with that sudden fundamental shift. In the uncertain decades since 1945, all else around the Catholic Church—political institutions, power centers, church bodies—is of recent vintage, unanchored in the culture, lacking ultimate definition, still in transition, still seeking permanence.

The structure of the Catholic Church was built on a principle of permanence all its own. It was not satisfied with the social, cultural, or political conditions obtaining at the time of its birth. So it set out to create a new entity, its own civilization. It succeeded because of its commitment to the idea of permanence. We moderns and all we signify are the products of that civilization in its glory and its decadence. Until 1945, nothing the Church encountered was new to it. Its history was long and varied, its mentality mature. Everything was a repetition, an echo, a recurrence of something it had already met and dealt with, and survived.

Until, in the postwar years, the axis of human affairs underwent a fatal shift. Today, the Church is just beginning to examine that shift, eyeing it with the hoary memory of millennial experience, refusing today's compromise because it foresees tomorrow's crisis. Its efforts are tentative, its movements agonizing, the policies from pope to pope sometimes contradictory, the sprawling body of its members vibrating under the strain of control, as it steers a tremulous and uncertain course.

It has not even begun to adapt to the new circumstances. The shift to irreligion is a passing phase. The Church must wait, suffer losses by the faithless, revolts by the impatient, and damage by the sins of its leaders as well as its followers. But, at all costs, it must wait. It has never merely reacted to history. It makes history. Nor has it ever simply followed human events, even when overpowered by brute force. It has always molded events to its own kilter. It either destroys its enemies or converts them. In any case, it lives on after they are dead and their empires gone. It cannot be likened to any other existing institution on our earth.

On today's horizon, the Catholic Church sees only one shape for the future: a world governed by money managers and technocrats. In the present interim period, it sees two competing ideologies: Marxism and capitalism. Merely considering their principles and concrete actions, it must conclude that neither is finally favorable to its spiritual mission of communicating supernatural salvation to all men and women. Both ideologies are based exclusively on a materialism that is terminal, that sets the limits of human endeavor at the material limits of this cosmos.

It may appear unjust to equate capitalism with Marxism in this fundamental respect, but the basic presumption of capitalism is the same as Marxism: The spiritual and supernatural have no function in the socio-economic and political development of men and women. According to capitalists, their power and the authority to wield it do not originate in a source outside the cosmos of man. At its crassest, capitalism maintains that power and authority originate in economic sinews. Marxism also asserts this. At its most "spiritual," capitalism will concede that power and authority have their source in the "qualities" and the "will" of the people. For people as the source of power and as the ultimate ideal of human endeavor form the core of capitalism's humanistic secular religion.

The one real advantage the Church can see in capitalism over Marxism is that democratic capitalists have no interest in inhibiting religious preferences. Marxism in its sociopolitical version, Communism, aims emphatically at the opposite: the total destruction of all religion and its practitioners. Catholicism nevertheless flourishes under attack by Marxism and Communism. Paradoxically, it tends to be corrupted, weakened, diluted, and finally choked by the professed liberalism and freedom of capitalism. Capitalism's exclusion of the spiritual and supernatural and its mandate to all and sundry to seek the "good life"—these are far more effective enemies of religion than the whips of commissars and the threat of isolation on the Gulag. Thus capitalism's basic prejudice against Catholicism is no less lethal than Marxism's.

Whichever of the competing ideologies ultimately wins, the Church can opt for neither capitalism, Communism, nor that other determining force in the world today, the managerial system that is swamping everything.

The managerial revolution, once installed in a full-blown condition, would be the cruelest, most baleful adversary the Church has ever faced. The Church is therefore in a holding pattern. It is passively anticipating the dénouement in the conflict between capitalism and Communism or the advent of a managerially run world. The Church awaits the logic of history to lead it to the appointed crossroads where once again it can take the initiative and mold its own civilization. Then the Church will be ready to make a radical change in its functional structure.

Cunctando regitur mundus is an old and tried principle of the Vatican chancery. He who can wait long enough will rule the world finally.

Many may be surprised at the imperious nature of this attitude. But that is because they have never understood or assessed correctly the Catholic Church's position in this world. The world today cannot know itself unless it knows the Catholic Church. The Church provides the sole continuing connection between the present and the ancient world of Greece and Rome and Judaism from which sprang the two bases—science and democracy—of the only true civilization we can find in 8,000 years of human history. The

Church has been the repository of that civilization as well as the matrix from which was born all we claim as art and literature, as law and decency, as gracious living.

But the really imperative reason for knowing and understanding the Catholic Church with compassion is the Church's centrality to the human condition: Were the Church to drop out of all human ken today, the ensuing vacuum would immediately suck the remnant forces for peace and hope and inspiration and courage and love down into a bottomless vortex. This is true not because Catholics number three quarters of 1 billion out of the present world population of 4.7 billion but because the Catholic Church is a focus of religious sentiment and reaction for the remaining 600 million Christians (who usually define themselves by their proximity to or distance from the Catholic Church) as well as for Islam's 700 million and the 1.2 billion Buddhists and Hindus. It provides a constant counterpoint to every new secular *ism*, be it social theory, political system, or intellectual fad. Ultimately, these are, each one in its day, defined by comparison and contrast with Catholicism's stance; frequently the Catholic Church has been the only institution around with sufficient strength and prestige and resources to confront and examine an innovation; and the Church claims to have something vitally important to say about all men's initiatives. Without the presence of Catholic Christianity, civilization as we know it would collapse.

There are indications today that many secular statesmen as well as political thinkers are scrutinizing the slowly evolving policies of the Catholic Church, precisely because it is viewed more and more as a reliable bellwether for the clouded future of the nations. No computer technology, no massive war preparations can supply what only mature instinct and honed experience provide. Once the Church has adjusted in its own good time and in its own way to the vast shift in the world of man, it will emerge at least as the most powerful and dynamic partner on the human scene, if not the deciding force in some fateful decision the nations must soon take at the crossroads of history.

In the meantime, the Church cannot and will not allow any tampering with its structure of permanence, either from within by its children who may be panicky or hasty or unfaithful, or from without by those who object to its presence. From outside as well as from inside the Church, the insistent clamor today reduces itself to one demand: Transform the visible essential structure of the

Church in order to bring it into conformity with the new structures
of human relations that are rapidly transforming the world.

But the difference between Catholicism and all other institutions
makes that demand impertinent. Society is constantly subject to
irregularly occurring cyclical changes in the economy; no expert
has ever claimed to understand their origin, and their course is
impossible to control. They simply have to be lived through. But
their puzzle remains. These changes modify and sometimes liquidate the structures of society and of nations. They frequently evoke
fresh political theories and new sociopolitical frameworks in the
wake of the turmoil, revolutions, and wars they bring on. Karl Marx
perceived this irregular and disruptive recurrence of economic cycles,
but his crass materialism and lack of historical sense propelled him
toward impracticable market theories and a metaphysics of matter
that had no foundation in reality.

The cause of cyclical economic changes escapes detection and
identification. Neither the principles of capitalism—rigid or democratic—nor the theories of Marxism offer any genuine clue to the
puzzle. For both of these rely on quantitative data, indeed are by
their natures limited to such data. At its very best, democratic
capitalism can temporarily allow itself the passing validity of some
apparently qualitative factors, a luxury Marxism must forbid itself
absolutely. These qualitative factors stem not from computers and
arithmetic but from the minds of men—faith in the potential and
growth of a dynamic body of people, faith in the future, confidence
of borrowers, desire to spend and make use of credit—the needs,
aspirations, and actions of men. These seem at first blush to be
genuinely qualitative factors. "There is a higher order of existence,"
wrote Horatio W. Dresser,[1] "where all quantitative explanations fail,
where thought must turn from the measurable to the qualitative
and from what merely is to what ought to be."

This is a momentary illusion. These factors are fathered by a
secular ethic, one in which "mind" and "will" and "faith" and
"hope" refer to quite measurable things. The "faith" of the creditor,
for example, is carefully measured by the debtor's collateral.

The reaction of the Catholic Church to these cyclical changes is
different.

It, too, is subject to the chaos induced by those changes. Like
other institutions, it has to grapple with the difficulties and ride out
the periodic upheavals characteristic of economic variations. It has
no inclination or instinct to revamp its structure on account of

them—first, because it claims to know why these changes occur, and secondly, because its structure was not dictated by economic conditions originally. It claims that it can and will outlive all the stresses and strains, including the economic ones, of this mortal existence. It also claims to understand the true causes of these disturbances.

All of nature—the material world as well as material forces in that world—was created by God to work in harmony with man. But, at the very dawn of his existence, because of vanity and pride, man committed the Original Sin, introducing a disorder into the very innards of the material world. That disharmony means that we will suffer at the hands of material forces no longer working in complete harmony for human good, afflicted with the same curse— the same proclivity to weakness, disease, death, and corruption— that befell Adam and Eve and all who followed them. "For creation was made subject to vanity," St. Paul wrote to the Romans, "and the whole of nature groans and suffers in pain together to this day . . . until it shall be delivered from the slavery of corruption."

The ability to perceive such a root cause of disruptive economic cycles and social changes is found only beyond the limited horizons that both capitalism and Marxism have set themselves. It is found in the Catholic Church. The Catholic Church claims that its structure is God-given, that this is a matter of firm faith, that it was not devised by man's brain working in a context of given economic or sociopolitical conditions.

The pathos of the Church's position emerges at this point. As her leaders now see it, there is something fundamentally askew with the financial agencies of the Church. The scandals of the sixties, seventies, and eighties made that quite clear. At the same time, the Church is awash in the sea-change that is overtaking the society of nations. How can it safely make fundamental changes in such a period of upheaval?

Many of the good works the Church has rendered in this century alone have been possible because the Church was self-financing, had a diplomatic corps, and retained its independence. At least 1.2 million Jews owe their lives to its financial and diplomatic efforts during World War II. Judge, then, the hesitation of the Church when faced by its detractors with the urgent call to a complete structural change in a world racked by change.

It is safe to say that no cleric of any rank has become a millionaire or retired to live handsomely and happily ever after because he built a fortune out of Vatican finances. The Vatican's wealth is corporate. No Vatican executive earns a salary of six figures; a small minority is paid in the low five figures. No politburo, no oligarchy, no junta, no single group of cardinals, bishops, or priests sits at the top of the heap enjoying the expenditure of millions for its own delectation or the enrichment of its successors. By contrast, the Church's past is full of examples of papal greed, cardinalitial fortune-building, episcopal power-grabbing, and the feckless disbursement of Church monies by clerics in search of individual pleasure.

The pursuit of pleasure and self-indulgence are among the least worrisome effects of power. To be sure, these produce a faulty degeneration of a certain gracefulness; but they ensure a certain balanced autonomy that men and women have always ranked as prime and valuable goals in themselves. Power has another effect that is far more dehumanizing and ugly: The use of power, the approximation to those who wield power—both have a subjugating effect on the spirit of the individual. There is no inherent beauty in power, nor any nourishment for human love; nor is truth the ultimate concern of power.

Power can be used to defend and further truth, to make human love possible, and to enhance the human condition with beauty. But the wielders of power and their close neighbors are often the last to enjoy beauty or to be smiled on by love or to yield to truth and its exigencies. This is because power, to be wielded, excludes anything resembling the childlike, the trusting, the truly loving. Such essential human traits are incompatible with the calculating coolness of power's proficiency. Yet beauty in human things and love between persons and the frank light of truth require exactly that—trust and childlikeness. If the Catholic bureaucracy has sinned through the use of power afforded it by its financial sinews, its sins are to be found in a deficiency of that trust and innocence.

Some solution must be found for the management of the Church's wealth.

Corporate wealth has become an end in itself; and the message of the Catholic Church is obscured, falsified, rendered ridiculous and open to the charge of hypocrisy, to be considered as merely a more successful version of what in America is often called "the billion-dollar religion business." There must be structural changes in the Catholic Church. But the Church is not like a run-of-the-mill corporation or even like a long-reigning dynasty of kings and queens. The structure it has today, together with the very principle of its economic viability and financial health, is the product of a long history and of the Great Experiment that lasted for the better part of fifteen hundred years. No one should speak of either structural change or total reform in the Catholic Church who is not deeply acquainted with that Great Experiment.

PART THREE
THE GREAT EXPERIMENT

THE FORMULA

The formula for the Great Experiment, besides being simple, was all-inclusive. According to the principles of Christianity, everything about human life was under its aegis. For Christianity was universally true, according to Christians, and therefore obligatory on all men and women. Not only the private lives of individuals but the social and political lives of nations, as well as the relations between nations, were to be modified by Christianity. They should conform to Christian principles as enunciated and taught by the Catholic Church, should be supervised by the head of Christians, the pope, who lived in Rome as his divinely appointed place on earth. His Christianity should affect everything. The pope, in sum, was to be the legitimizer of civil and political life, nationally and internationally. For he represented Christ; and Christians held that everything men and women did had to be according to Christ's will as interpreted by the pope and his Church.

The formula, then, implied a plenitude of power and authority within the office and persona of the pope. Difficulties arose from the mentality of ancient times, when men knew no other way for authority to be visible and palpable and vibrant except when embodied in a ruler decked out in the glory of sovereignty, and provided with all the trappings of sovereignty. One all-important element of those trappings was economic independence; and economic independence meant, ultimately, one thing: money and the freedom of living and action that only money confers. Historically, men knew no other way to give concrete expression to such supreme, central authority.

This, then, was the Great Experiment: that the pope, over a period of ten centuries, should assume the highest rung on the ladder of sovereign power, and that the exercise of his spiritual and moral authority would be directed not merely for the supernatural benefit of men and women, but also and most systematically to ensure that the most important element in the trappings of power—money—would be assured his papal throne.

It did develop a worldwide institution that must be seen as unique. That institutional form of Christianity, over a period of one thousand years, was the chief and, in many respects, the only nourisher of the education, the learning, the literature, the law, the architecture, the philosophy, the scientific progress, the exploration, and the performing and decorative arts which formed the flesh and bones and blood of Western civilization.

At a few intermediate points in this Great Experiment, it almost seemed that the goal had been attained. But the impression was illusory. Yet the effort continued, for in the minds of churchmen and lay folk there was no other viable way of ensuring the physical well-being of religious ministers of God's word and Christ's grace, and therefore of their supreme source of moral authority. The matching of the spiritual treasure with the earthly was the delicate spine of the Experiment.

The accumulation of that earthly treasure and the principle behind it made possible the financial structure of the Vatican today, and opened it up directly to the scandals of our century. To appreciate this strict line of origin, it is necessary to learn how the first Christian community started, how the Great Experiment was launched, what its apogee and its decline were like. That the Catholic Church of the twentieth century then had recourse to another way of renewing the Great Experiment—this emerges as an obvious if lugubrious conclusion.

THE PROTO-PERIOD

The proto-period of Christianity lasted from the late spring of the year 32 A.D. until the last decades of the fourth century. By 32 A.D., the Christians—mainly practicing Jews—were a cohesive body. By the last decades of the first century, they had made one of their first big sociopolitical decisions. But in the intervening time, they had a special attitude to money and worldly possessions, as is related in one of the Church's earliest extant records, the Acts of the Apostles.

It is quite clear from this document that the first community of believers in Jerusalem and elsewhere had a simple economic law: Once you joined up, the community could become possessor of all your worldly goods. Or of as much of them as you decided to hand over.

"No member had anything of his own. All things were held in common . . . owners of lands or houses sold them and handed over the proceeds to the Apostles—and whatever each one needed was given to him . . ."

The first Christians had a specific reason for this: They thought there was very little time left before Christ returned to Earth in his divine glory, gave a judgment about human conduct, ended the existence of the world, and took his faithful believers to Heaven, condemning the faithless and the sinners to eternal torment in "the Hell of the Damned." Consequently, Christians were to be in the world, but not of the world. Apocalypse was at hand.

There was no point, then, in accumulating worldly possessions. The only preoccupation in life was to prepare for that second coming of Christ. The goods of the community were managed by overseers appointed by the Apostles and ultimately under the personal control of Peter himself. Private ownership and possession, while not forbidden, did not fit in with the ideals of the community, which aimed at a total and voluntary sharing of all possessions by the members and by their leaders.

Peter's central authority in the matter is clear, and his control over the goods of the community was enshrined later in the consecrated phrase "the patrimony of St. Peter," meaning the possessions of the papacy and the pope's church in Rome. Theoretically, at least, the pope of today has as autocratic an authority over the present "patrimony of St. Peter" as Peter had over the goods and chattels of his church in Jerusalem.

The community-of-goods arrangement could not last. Gradually, because Christ did not return immediately, the realization of permanency in the human condition became current. We find St. Paul writing to his Greek converts that neither he nor anyone else knew exactly when that all-finalizing event of Apocalypse would take place and that they should not count on its proximity. They should settle down with their families and their work, and lead normal human lives. It was a fateful decision to be an active part of the social and political life around them.

By the late sixties and midseventies of that first century, there was no longer any substantive trace of the initial apocalyptic outlook nor any widespread application of the community-of-goods principle. Past the turn of the century, instead, we find individual Christians as well as local churches acquiring land and real estate needed for worship and for burial purposes. What economic participation the members of the Church exercised within their local communities was limited to voluntary contributions for the upkeep of churches and cemeteries, works of charity, and the support of their clergy—bishops, priests, and deacons. Between the churches in different cities and towns there was always a flow of contributions.

Because of Christianity's always uncertain status in the Roman Empire for the following two hundred years, Church organization remained at the simplest of levels. These conditions allowed the young Church no real opportunities for economic expansion. Static funds were established in each community for self-sustainment and for contributions to less fortunate communities. Legally, the Christian churches were under a tight ban; there could be no real accumulation of capital.

Nevertheless, the Christian population kept increasing. The peoples living in the lands surrounding the Mediterranean, from Gibraltar to the Levant, numbered about 4.5 million close to the end of the third century. Fully one-quarter of these were Christian by about the same time. It was from this period that the term "pagan" comes, meaning "village-dweller" or "country person." The Christians were in large part urban dwellers; outside the urban centers, the old religion clung on among the "pagans."

Surprisingly, one of their strongholds was the entire North African shore country from what today we call Morocco (then Roman Mauretania) to the land of modern Israel (then Roman Palestina and Syria).

The North African churches as well as those in the other littoral areas were in constant, if not frequent, communication with the head of the Church in Rome. For he, whoever he was, was the successor to Blessed Peter. And, from the beginning, it was Peter and Peter's teachings that decided the inevitable disputes that arose about beliefs and moral practice. The letter of Pope Clement I (88–97 A.D.) to the Christians in Corinth makes this leadership and authority of the Roman bishop quite clear.

Between the death of Peter in approximately 64 A.D. and the year 312 A.D., there were thirty-one Roman bishops. Of them, at least fifteen were put to violent death, and at least seven died in exile. Few died in their beds.

The Great Experiment was launched by one man and one man only: Emperor Constantine. In gratitude for a supreme military victory in the year 312 over his worst enemy, Maxentius—a victory Constantine ascribed directly to Christ, the God of the Christians—Constantine showered material favors on what had been up to that point an obscure and sometimes hated religious sect headed by a cleric living in Rome.

Constantine richly endowed the Church in Rome and down south in Calabria and Sicily. He passed new laws legalizing bequests to the Church and according the Bishop of Rome and his dependent bishops civil, judicial, and military privileges. He established a papal treasury, amply furnished with funds in the Lateran Palace—the new Roman residence of the popes. And he made the pope his own official representative in the West.

Constantine also exempted the clergy from taxation. He allowed them to be named heirs to landed property, and gave them pre-

cedence over the officials of his empire. At the end of the fourth
century, the Church owned about one-tenth of the real estate in
Rome and its province. Through legacies, bequests, purchase, and
outright grant by the government, the pope at the end of the fifth
century was the biggest landowner in the Western Roman empire.

By the end of the sixth century, the pope was landlord of extensive
land holdings in and around Rome, and exercised considerable
judicial power in civil affairs. This cluster of real estate, rents, and
rights formed the material foundation of the papacy. As the landed
possessions of the papacy increased, they were called "the Lands of
St. Peter," "the Papal States," or, more accurately, "the papal State,"
for all was ruled by the central government of the papacy in Rome.

In the beginning these "Lands of St. Peter" formed a triangular
piece of territory, its base running along the western coast of Italy
from Civitavecchia in the north to Terracina in the south—a distance of approximately 100 miles, its two sides meeting in rough
apex at Rieti some 90 miles inland. It included the Tuscan, Sabine,
and Maritime provinces. As time passed, other lands originally
donated to the Church passed out of papal control, among them
territories in Dalmatia (modern Yugoslavia), North Africa, Sicily,
and France.

The main source of papal revenue lay in the rents and tribute
from the lands. For the early period, it is difficult to fix any exact
figure for the revenues from these estates. But by the time Gregory
I was pope (590–604 A.D.), we have a very approximate idea: The
papacy had by then over 400 farms in Sicily, which continued to
be the granary for Rome as it had been in more ancient times.
From Sicily and Calabria alone, the papacy derived an annual
income of 25,200 gold *soldi*.[1] From the other possessions in Italy,
France, North Africa, and Dalmatia, the annual total revenue hovered around 500,000 *soldi*, which in modern terms would certainly
put the income somewhere over $1 million. The bequests and gifts
from emperor, kings, and princes must be added to this figure,
bringing the sum up perhaps by another $100,000 or $200,000.

The monies were not merely rental. Fishing and hunting rights,
the marriage of a daughter, water rights, for example—all cost extra.
There was a general accounting office in Rome at the pope's palace,
staffed with papal bookkeepers and accountants. There was also a
team of inspectors and rent-collectors. There were papal farms on
which work animals were bred, slaves to be cared for, tenants,
security forces, hospices for the poor and the sick, and the usual
year-round keeping of books and tallying of accounts.

But papal administration and papal revenues became vastly expanded as of 756 A.D., when the power of the Byzantine emperors ceased all over Italy except in a small diamond of land northeast of the Apennine Mountains and around the lagoons of Venice.

In order to expel the Lombards, a Germanic race of barbarians who were threatening the safety and the existence of the papacy, Pope Stephen II (752–757) wrote an urgent letter to King Pippin of the Franks, on February 23 of that year. The Franks, living in what we now know as France, had already been converted to Christianity at the end of the sixth century. Pippin regarded himself as the God-appointed protector of the Church and its pope.

Stephen's letter displays that trait which later popes would also show: the use of spiritual authority and supreme religious status in order to obtain temporal results. Having invoked Pippin's protection in the name of God, Stephen concludes his letter on a vigorous note:

> Should you, which we cannot believe, be guilty of delay or evasion, or fail to obey our exhortations in coming to the rescue of this, my city of Rome, its inhabitants, and the Apostolic Church, entrusted to me by God and its chief priest, know that, by the power of the Holy Trinity, by the grace of the Apostolic office confided to me by the Lord Christ, on account of your disobedience to my summons, you shall be declared to have forfeited the Kingdom of God and Eternal Life.

Pippin descended into Italy and crushed the Lombards. His next step was fateful. He drew up a document, a "deed of gift," in which he handed over to the pope possession of the Italian cities he had conquered, along with their territories. Pope Stephen thus became ruler of two large northeastern areas of Italy. One, comprising some 4,542 square miles, centered around Ravenna. It was later called the Romagna. The other, comprising 3,692 square miles, lay below Ravenna and stretched down to the center of Italy. It came to be called the March of Ancona.

Pippin then chose as his official emissary a certain Abbot Folrad from the Abbey of St. Denis. The abbot traveled around to all the cities in the ceded territories. He took all the keys of the cities, went down to Rome, and symbolically placed them in the shrine of St. Peter.

Rome was now a thoroughly ecclesiastical city, the governing center of a state. And the pope, from being a supreme episcopal authority, became, in addition, a temporal ruler with lands to govern, taxes to impose, wars to wage, diplomacy to exercise, fiscal and monetary matters to regulate. There was a moment in that same eighth century when the citizens of Rome gathered in a true parliament and conferred upon the pope supreme authority over them. This historic act took place in the year 787.

From now on until 1870, it would be a categoric principle of the papacy that the pope had to be a temporal ruler in his own right if he was to discharge his sacred office as supreme pastor. The papal State had been founded. It was about 16,000 square miles in extent, and was divided into *patrimonia*—the patrimony of Tuscany, the patrimony of Perugia, the patrimony of the March of Ancona, the patrimony of the Romagna, the patrimony of Bologna, and so on.

The center of this papal State was "the duchy of Rome." Under the pope, a duke governed the papal State, flanked by the cavalry of nobles and their foot soldiers. This was called "the Most Blessed Army." The duke was counseled by a senate of distinguished Romans, and aided by "Elders"—deacons and cardinal-priests—together with the lower ranks of employees. All this new panoply of state power culminated in the person who at his papal consecration was hailed as "the Apostolic Lord, the Vicar of St. Peter, the High Priest of the Roman Sanctuary, the Primate of the Bishops of the Whole World, and Teacher of the Church Universal." It was an attempt to unite the spiritual and the temporal in one system. And it was the basic arm of the Great Experiment. "Let us work for St. Peter," Pope Gregory III wrote to Charles Martel, leader of the warlike Franks, "and then we shall prosper in this world and in the next."

It is very difficult to calculate what amounts of revenue accrued to the papacy at that time from its territories and those others that it continually acquired, all the more so because over the space of the ensuing six centuries, the papacy lost, regained, and lost again several of these possessions. We know some details: Sicily, for instance, produced revenues of 31,000 gold *soldi*; the papacy received 16,000 of that sum. From the duchy of Rome, the papacy on the average earned up to 70,000 *soldi* annually.

Nevertheless, it is certain that the Apostolic Camera or papal Treasury[2] was in an ample condition. It received all rents from ecclesiastical estates, together with what seems an endless list of taxes—on roads, bridges, meadows, quarries, wells, rivers, woods, markets, harbors, grassland, gates. There were also monies from fines and judicial exactions, as well as tithes, collections, gifts, custom and excise charges, and bequests. Only the papal government had the right to issue coinage, and the papal mint had already become an essential bureau of the papal administration.

Naturally, as papal acquisitions increased,[3] revenues increased, and the greater was the papacy's involvement in temporal affairs. The papal court and administration now grew to full proportion. Around the pope was grouped his Curia, the papal ecclesiastical bureaucracy composed of cardinals, priests, deacons, and sub-deacons.

By the middle of the ninth century, there existed and flourished a true papal State, ecclesiastical in all the upper echelons of its administrators, which enjoyed spiritual prestige and authority and was economically independent of all other powers on earth. We can still read today the letter Pope John VIII (872–882) wrote to the Empress Engelberga telling her of the papal fleet he had built and positioned in the harbor of Pontus. He speaks of our "men-of-war," of the "combustibles" and "projectiles" on board each ship.[4] "We can defend ourselves and Holy Mother Church," the pope concluded in a satisfied tone.

The Great Experiment was on its way, and it was to continue in high gear six centuries more, through the early feudalism of Europe, past the Middle Ages into the Renaissance, while slowly the world of western nations was being formed. The leaven of that world was Christianity as taught and championed by the Church. Through it all, the Great Experiment was tried. The Roman popes pursued their cherished ideal of a temporal framework in which to house what they considered to be the supreme source of religious enlightenment and of all authority on earth. The success of this sustained effort was enormous, so enormous that we moderns find it almost impossible to realize its full extent.

It is difficult in today's secular age to believe that it mattered so much to the secular governments of all Europe who was pope. But the fact was that at this stage of European culture and civilization all political and civil life together with its commerce and culture depended intimately on the existence of a papal authority, clearly defined, concretized by a valid election, embodied in one man who wore the triple tiara. Without that figure, political life had no focus, commercial life had no direction, and the social life of nations had no center of moral gravity.

Strange as it may seem to us now, the peerless position of religious prestige and moral jurisdiction the papacy had achieved by the dawn of the European Renaissance is an eloquent tribute to the depth and solidity of the hold Catholicism and "the Roman fact" had achieved in the civilization and cultures of that age. Europe as an assembly of nations had found the gravamen of its authority and the source of its authenticity. The popes and their churchly institution as we find it toward the end of the fifteenth and the beginning of the sixteenth century represent the utmost achievement of the Great Experiment begun in 313 A.D., when Emperor Constantine placed the pope and his religious office on a pinnacle of social prestige and political power. Their formula of total Christianization seemed to have been successfully applied.

What we need in the present context is an accurate idea of the concrete application of that formula at the opening of the sixteenth century. For once that century closed, historical Christianity would never be the same again, and the Catholic Church would start its slow descent into the pit in which it would find itself in the last quarter of the twentieth century.

THE FORMULA APPLIED

If one had visited Rome in the autumn of the year 1450, one would have found it to be a city exclusively preoccupied with the pope, with his court and papal business. The population was not more than 35,000. The city was the center of the Roman district which contained 366 towns, villages, and castles. It was surrounded by the old Aurelian wall and fed by one aqueduct, the Acqua Vergine,[1] which produced the bubbling water of the Trevi Fountain.

The majority of Rome's citizens were *bovatieri*, people engaged in stock-farming on the papal farms around the city. As autumn wore on and winter set in, these *bovatieri* drove their flocks of sheep, goats, and cattle down from the surrounding high ground and into the city pastures for the winter.

The remainder of Rome's citizens were merchants, textile workers, money-changers, artisans, and hoteliers. Rome had many inns as well as hospices belonging to the various nations of Europe—German, Spanish, French, Sicilian, English. There were also palatial households, some belonging to the old Roman families, some to the cardinals and high officials of the papal court, others to bankers, mainly Florentines—the Medici, for example, or Roman bankers such as the famous Astalli. The grand residences provided employment for thousands as servants, as house guards, couriers, maintenance staff. But in one way or another, all of Rome's citizens were connected in their work with the venerated man who reigned as sovereign lord, political head, and vicar of Christ on Earth for all men, including Romans.

The Pope.

The ruins of imperial Rome lay in every direction, much of it overgrown with grass and weeds or buried in landfill. Still dominating the skyline, however, were certain insuppressible monuments of the Caesars—the Capitol, the Colosseum, the Pantheon (now a Roman Catholic church), the Baths of Diocletian, side by side with the Basilica of St. Peter up on Vatican Hill, two or three other basilicas and churches around the city, and finally, somewhat southeast of Vatican Hill, the Lateran Palace where the great humanist pope, Nicholas V, resided and from where the papal State was governed.

Before one headed for the Lateran, one would note everywhere the indubitable signs of revival and restoration under Nicholas's glorious reign (1447–55): City thoroughfares, blocked with ruins and debris for centuries, were now open; forty churches had been restored—pilgrims were obliged to visit each of them, pray for the pope's intentions, and make a cash contribution; sculptors' studios and painters' workshops were on every street, for the redecoration of papal Rome had begun and would go on for two hundred years more.

At the palace of the pope, one might be tempted to dally in the library, where His Holiness employed literally hundreds of copyists to reproduce old and battered manuscripts. Hundreds more collated the pope's own collection of manuscripts, and filed the mountain of registers, records, correspondence, and chronicles. This mass of material would form the nucleus of the later Vatican Library.

But, rapidly, one's interest would be drawn to the offices of papal government. There was first and foremost that cluster of buildings where the pope and his household resided. Close by it was a building where the College of Cardinals had their offices; they themselves, for the most part, resided in their own palaces throughout the city. Behind the pope's residence were rooms and offices housing papal agencies, including his penitentiary (which dealt with ecclesiastical penances) and the courts that dealt with marriage cases. But one would want to make one's way in particular to what officials called the Camera,[2] the nerve-center of papal financial administration.

In the courtyard of the Camera, at its doors, and throughout its corridors, one passed armed guards, doorkeepers, couriers, and maintenance personnel. Inside, one's interest would be directed to the main conference room, which was used for full meetings of the Camera.

Presiding over these meetings was the all-powerful Camerarius in his official robes. Close beside him sat a man holding a leather pouch, the Keeper of the Cameral Seal. The imprint of the Great Seal meant fortune or bankruptcy, freedom or prison, civil rights or loss of all rights, the sinews of war or the defense of peace, the creation of beautiful works of art, the working of metal mines and salt mines, capital punishment for criminals and sinners, municipal freedom of cities all over the world, the safety of traveling merchants, the escort of merchant marine ships, the good standing of princes, the legality of kings. With the waxen imprint of the Great Seal on a document, all and anything could be achieved. And it always cost money to have that imprint. The Camerarius was the only one authorized to use it or command its use. After His Holiness, he was the most powerful man in God's Church and in Christendom.

The Camerarius supervised an operation that covered all countries in Christendom. He supervised all the papal household in all its arrangements. The various bureaus of the Camera dealt with the receipting and disbursement of funds, accounting, year-end reports, loans, money transfers, mercantile investment, provisioning of papal armies and papal fleets, financing of papal envoys and missions, and bank deposits at home and abroad.

Under the Camerarius was an army of tax-collectors, revenue-officers, couriers, ambassadors, emissaries, and agents who fanned out through the world, for by this time funds poured in continuously from kingdoms, princes, bishops, monasteries, convents, dioceses, and parishes. The job of the Camerarius was to make sure all monies owed to the pope were collected, deposited safely, and finally transferred to Rome either in specie or by solid promissory notes between international bankers.

In any meeting of the Camera, he would have seated around him his Cameral subordinates, the two most important to his right and left. One was the treasurer, who had personal responsibility for that room at the heart of the building where two armed guards sat night and day watching over the chests of monies and valuables. The other was the Datary—a new official, always clashing with the Camerarius because the Datary now controlled the pope's Privy Purse, a function the Camerarius used to have. The Datary, who disbursed at the pope's private command, knew the intimate plans of His Holiness. That knowledge was power.

Listening and taking part in these discussions were four main groups of Cameral officials. The legal department was made up of attorneys in the employ of the Camera for the multitude of civil and criminal suits relating to fiscal matters. They were headed by the Fiscal Proctor, an expert in Church and civil law in Rome and in every country where papal interests were at stake. The accounting department consisted of seven clerical types: They knew papal finances down to the last Italian mancuse[3] and English penny, for they were in charge of all receipts, disbursements, account balances, treasury deficits, outstanding loans, the monetary value of each depositor in the papal treasury, and the assets of the two dozen banking firms—mainly Italian and predominantly Florentine—with headquarters in Rome. They also ran the Registry Bureau and the Sealing Bureau, as well as the Bureau of Audits.

The hypothetical visitor to the Camera would have found the law officers sitting in one corner waiting their turn to speak about current difficulties in securing convictions of offenders. The scribes and notaries would be sitting in another corner; their contribution was their intimate acquaintance with the filing system of tax registers, fiscal documents, and correspondence.

Such subordinate Cameral officials always emerge in any complex bureaucracy. Similar to the permanent under-secretaries of British government offices, they were the middle-echelon officers who remained at their posts through changes of administration, thus assuring an uninterrupted tradition in fiscal and monetary matters.

Two other groups of Cameral officials always attended plenary sessions of the Camera. One group, consisting of six clerics, formed the Cameral Bureau of Collectorates. These men supervised the worldwide collection of papal revenues from all over the known world. The other group, composed of three laymen, represented the secular bank with which the Camera normally conducted its business of currency exchange, depository facilities, money transfers, loans, and mortgages. The Cameral banker was one of the most knowledgeable laymen in the Church.

This, then, was the Apostolic Camera; without its cooperation, the day-to-day functioning of pope and Church would grind to a halt. Indeed, the functioning of civil life for millions would stop. For His Holiness wielded temporal power as the encasement of his spiritual authority.

The Camera was the most important financial office in the papal administration but not the only one. By the year 1450, in the Curia, the cardinals had organized their own financial camera, so that they too could be sharers in papal revenues. All the monies that the

Cardinalitial Camera received came through the efforts of the Apostolic Camera; the cardinals, however, could participate only in those levies of taxes paid directly to the papal court. They had their own Camerarius and a complete staff of subordinates—a treasurer, accountants, and auditors. The internal politics of the papal Curia revolved around this Cardinalitial Camera and the middle-echelon bureaucrats in the Apostolic Camera. The cardinals depended on their friendships and contacts among those bureaucrats in order to keep abreast of the extent of papal revenues.

Though the Apostolic Camera was heavily involved in the papal financial administration, about half its time was devoted to judicial proceedings, because there were interminable lawsuits and claims. The Camerarius and his clerks had judicial power over the entire papal State and over every member of the clergy anywhere. Their law-enforcement methods were mainly ecclesiastical—censures (you were declared to be not in good standing), interdictions (you were forbidden to receive the Sacraments), and excommunication (you were expelled from the Church, regarded as already damned to Hell fire, and if you died in this condition your body could not be buried with any religious ceremony or in consecrated ground. It would probably be burned, cast into the sea, or thrown into a shallow grave in the local Potters' Field). The Camera also disposed of corporal punishments: flogging, imprisonment with or without hard labor, exile, torture, and death by hanging (which usually implied drawing and quartering), burning, or the sword.

We moderns must remember that this judicial power and its stiff sanctions were used to enforce papal fiscal and monetary law. In order to obtain the funds deemed owing to the Holy See, not only physical coercion was used, but also spiritual penalties of the extremest kind. Only those who firmly believed that all things temporal—including civil jurisdiction and political power and the material sinews of economic well-being—were penetrated by the spiritual could have developed such a system. This was precisely the outlook of Catholic Christianity.

We must remember, too, that the Camera was evolved within the economic and financial framework of the feudal Middle Ages. Capitalism had not yet been born, and the business ethics taught by the unique teacher of that time—the Catholic Church—created obstacles to both the capitalist ideology and its implementation in society. There was an official and deep-seated hostility in Catholic doctrine to wealth, be it moderate or egregious. "Mammonism" derived its undesirability from the Gospels, and this attitude was enshrined in moral teachings.

"A rich man is either a thief or the son of a thief," St. Jerome declared. "Trading in goods shifts the soul's attention from divine things," St. Augustine wrote. Primitive banking and commerce were held to be necessary evils, the worst aspects of which—like moneylending—should be left to non-Christians such as Jews and Chinese. The Church, and the various governments under the tutelage of the Church, had strict laws against interest on loans (usury). The medievalists had a very strict doctrine about what was called "the just price," and there was no place in medieval law and theology for the business speculation and profit-making on which capitalism was later built.

Even in these early times, however, there was production of wealth, and therefore a "social surplus." After taking care of basic needs, and catering to the trappings of one's station in life within the social hierarchy, one was supposed to devote any "social surplus" to the support of the Church and the pope. The development of worldwide papal revenues was based on this primary supposition of medieval Catholic social teaching.

Lest we regard the judicial punishments and financial coercion of these times as entirely reprehensible, it must be acknowledged that this already vast institution, fueled by the funds thus gathered, was proceeding to spread its message of salvation and to create the flower of Western civilization known as the Renaissance. It was nourishing sanctity and piety and good works that eased the misery of thousands everywhere. It was educating and elevating the minds of men and women, stimulating exploration and scientific research, while evolving the most comprehensive philosophy of human life in recorded history. There is no doubt that the Church carried out her mission, spiritual and humanistic.

By the middle of the fifteenth century, there had been modifications in the various *patrimonia* of the papal State. The head of each *patrimonium*, originally called a rector, had now become a provincial governor with a chancery and an exchequer complete with treasurer. Many districts were leased on feudal, instead of rental, terms, a goodly number to towns; and some cities were generous to the inhabitants who paid an annual fixed sum. All the fees and tollages of the feudal system—agricultural, municipal, military—were imposed.

Revenues from the Papal State

From the various *patrimonia*, via the provincial governors' offices, the central office in Rome collected the annual payments, rents, fees, toll and custom and excise monies, as well as property and defense taxes. From the Roman district, an annual sum of approximately 150,000 florins[4] passed to the Cameral Treasury. The discovery of alum at Tolfa and the papal monopoly on the mine yielded another 100,000 florins annually. Naturally, some *patrimonia* yielded less, some more.[5] The registers show a continuing variation in the annual income of the *patrimonia* and therefore of the papal Camera. In addition to Tolfa alum and the yields from some other mines owned by the papacy, income in the *patrimonia* derived mainly from wines, grain, fish, pasture, timber, fustian[6] and woolen cloths, cattle, pigs, olives, and fruits. These were subject to the vagaries of weather and the warlike or peaceful conditions of the countryside. All official expenses for the upkeep of provincial installations and public services were deducted first, before the remainder was remitted to the Apostolic Camera.

And before the Camera actually received the income, the sums owing to it were deposited with one special official who acted as banker for the province. Agents from the Camera would come out and do an accounting of provincial affairs, thus determining what was actually owed to the Camera.

The collection of revenues owing to the pope from outside "the Lands of St. Peter" required a totally different collection system. Before describing that system, one must review the non-Statal revenues in question.

Other Revenues

Besides Statal revenues, the Holy See had nine other major sources of income together with eleven comparatively minor sources.

Two ready sources of income were the religious houses (monasteries, convents) and temporal rulers. In both cases, the process was the same. A monastery in England would need protection from a rapacious baron or a greedy bishop; a temporal ruler—prince, king—would need to be protected against rebellious tenants and opposing rulers. Both monastery and temporal ruler made over their possessions nominally to the pope for an annual sum of money. In return, they then could use all ecclesiastical weapons against their enemies. The temporal ruler need not assemble a small army to defend himself; he could get his attackers excommunicated and banned under ecclesiastical law. He could also add a surcharge to the rents his tenants paid him, passing on the extra sums to Rome.

There were, then, a series of lucrative taxes the Holy See imposed on its Catholic subjects. For a long time, the most lucrative of these was the tax on benefices and dignities. Originally a voluntary contribution, it became a compulsory tax. Every parish, diocese, priory, monastery, and cathedral was reckoned to be a benefice. Ecclesiastical dignities ran from simple parish priest to archpriest, bishop, archbishop, patriarch, abbot, prior, and cardinal. The theory was that all benefices and dignities belonged to the pope and were his to give away as he wished. Those who wished to possess a benefice or acquire an ecclesiastical dignity had to pay for it.

In two ways. There was one principal sum—usually one-third of the annual income the future possessor of the benefice expected. This was divided—unevenly—between the Apostolic Camera and the Cardinalitial Camera. Violators who did not pay this tax were excommunicated. A number of other small fees were attached to the tax—for preparation of documents, reinstatement after excommunication, dispensations, exemptions—and these fees were given to the servants and officials of both Cameras.

Connected with the benefice tax, there was the annate tax: One-tenth of the first year's revenue derived from the benefice was due to the Camera. When one recalls the enormous number of benefices in, say, the fifteenth century, some idea of the revenues from them can be formed. It meant a constant supply of money to the pope.

Another lucrative tax was on income and chattels. After an assessment and yearly valuation, the sum—one-tenth of total value—was determined.

The spiritual entered in here too: Penitents who had been enjoined with a stiff and costly penance could mitigate the severity of the penance by increasing the tax they paid. It worked both ways. Penalties for default were primarily spiritual, but could be expiated by extra tax payment. Ostensibly this income tax was for charitable or philanthropic purposes.

A third tax was laid on all ecclesiastical dignitaries who were required to come to Rome to visit the pope. The practice, at first limited to bishops living near Rome, was gradually extended to all visiting dignitaries. On arriving they were supposed to make a gift of cash and/or valuables to the Holy See. Penalties for noncompliance included excommunication. The tax was shared by the two Cameras.

By far the most lucrative source of money during a certain critical period of papal history was provided by indulgences. The first traces of the use of indulgences is in the third-century Africa of St. Cyprian, when the heroic acts of those who suffered for their beliefs were held to be a means of obtaining indulgence or pardon from God for sins committed. Each sin involved two elements: guilt and consequent punishment. Even if forgiven the guilt, one was still liable for punishment. As time went on, it became a widespread practice to undertake certain penances in order to mitigate the punishment due. Very often, the penance took the form of money—sinners deprived themselves of a certain sum and what it could buy them, so that the punishment might be mitigated. Hence the practice of granting "indulgences" as remission of punishment, consequent on one's performing certain penances. But the Church never taught that by performing the required indulgence penance, the punishment was surely remitted, for it held that such an eventuality depended on God's mercy. Originally an indulgence was a simple affair: A penance was enjoined on a person for having committed sins. The sin was forgiven by a priest, but some portion of the guilt remained. The penance lasted a year and forty days, one hundred days, or a year and two quarantines. If an indulgence was granted by the Church, it meant that to one's spiritual "credit" was added the spiritual effect that would have accrued to one if one were to perform an actual year's penance or one hundred days' penance or a penance lasting one year and two quarantines.

As long as the indulgences given by the Church remitted only part of the enjoined penance, indulgences never came into great vogue. But the moment it was decided to grant "plenary" indulgences—full remission of all penance and, with it, forgiveness of punishment due, the real vogue of indulgences started.

At first, it was merely a question of making an offering of some money, but rather quickly concrete prices were fixed on each type of indulgence. In each parish, there was a triple-locked chest, the keys in the possession of three different people, in which indulgence monies were kept until they could be transferred to Rome. Bulls of indulgences were issued by the pope and proclaimed throughout Christendom. No matter what tariff was set on an indulgence, a person had to be "truly penitent and have confessed his sins" before benefiting spiritually from the indulgence.

The real abuses had started under the mercenary Pope Boniface
IX (1389–1404). He conceived of another step in the indulgence
procedure. Every so often the popes declare what is called a Jubilee
year. In that year, if the faithful visit Rome, say a certain amount
of prayers, make a pilgrimage on foot to certain churches, they are
believed to obtain an indulgence and remission of guilt. Boniface
IX made one small adjustment: You needn't come to Rome—the
majority of Catholics couldn't anyway—to get this plenary indulgence. Stay at home. Say certain prayers. Visit certain designated
churches in your area. Pay a fixed sum. And you receive the Jubilee
indulgence.

The price of such indulgences was one-half or one-third of what
it would have cost a person to make the journey to Rome. If the
sin was having broken a solemn oath, one was required to make a
pilgrimage to Jerusalem's Holy Places; guilt and penance could be
commuted by an indulgence in the form of a payment in pure gold.

In fourteenth- and fifteenth-century Rome, there was a team of
people called *quaestores*, promoters or commissioners of indulgences, who fanned out over Christendom selling official Roman
indulgences and returning to the Roman Camera with the monies
so obtained. The great humanist pope, Nicholas V (1447–55), was
enthusiastic for the sale of indulgences.

The whole practice was open to abuse, and led ultimately to a
catastrophic rupture in the Church: It was the arrival in the German
town of Wittenberg of the Dominican priest Johann Tetzel in October of 1517 that sparked the first Lutheran revolt and the defection
of nobles and commoners alike.

Tetzel was to all intents and purposes a traveling salesman. His
boss: Pope Leo X (1513–21), who had devised a new sales campaign
to get funds for refurbishing St. Peter's Basilica in Rome. His wares:
indulgences. His prices: exact monetary value for the forgiveness of
every imaginable sin of the already dead. His sales technique: a
cardinal red booth, a receipt box, and a marvelous gift for mimicking
the pleas of the dead who suffered in Purgatory and craved the
monetary help of the living so that they might escape the punishment
of eternal fire. His sales pitch: a memorable jingle—"As soon as
the coin in the coffer rings, the soul from Purgatory springs."

Nearly fifty years would elapse before the abusive sale of indulgences was condemned at the Council of Trent (1562). Five years
later, Pope Pius V abolished and revoked all indulgences for which
money payments of any kind had been prescribed.

Besides some minor sources of revenue,[7] monies came in an irregular but never quite failing stream from bequests and legacies willed to the Church and to the pope. A network of intricate laws governed papal participation in such monies; it was found necessary to legislate matters minutely because of claims by local churches against papal claims of priority and seniority. Subsidies were also asked for by the papal court; refusal to make these one-time contributions for a specific purpose—the war against the Turks, for example, subsidies for missionary friars, or for the rebuilding of a cathedral—could bring on papal displeasure.

Once the New World opened up with Columbus's historic voyage in 1492, the increase in certain papal revenues was quite noticeable after five or six years. But as a sample year, 1492 will serve to illustrate the ordinary revenues of the papal State. The official inventory in gold florins makes significant reading:

Spiritual dues	60,000
Stamping and sealing	36,000
Matrimonial cases	12,000
Venal offices	15,000
Indulgences	10,000
Livestock custom & excise	16,000
Salt taxes	18,000
Contributions from the treasuries of Ancona and Romagna provinces	12,000
Perugia taxes	6,000
Roman taxes	4,000
Ascoli taxes	3,000
Bologna wine tax	4,000
Ferrara and Bagnacavallo taxes	4,000
Urbino taxes	1,400
Faenza taxes	1,000
Pesaro taxes	750
Forlì taxes	1,000
Imola taxes	300
Tribute from squires	500
Direct contributions	1,500
Riverine taxes	16,000
Sales taxes	1,000
Pasture fees	6,000
Secretarial and ceremonial fees	6,000

Special fees from Ancona, Romagna, and
Foligno 10,000

Total: 245,450

In that same year, for the true picture of total revenues entering
the Camera Apostolica, we must add some 350,000 to 400,000 gold
florins coming in from international revenues.

A comparison of papal revenues with the revenues (again in gold
florins) of the chief city-states and principalities of Italy in 1492
gives some idea of the financial status of the papal territory. The
papal revenues are exceeded only by Venice, Naples, Milan, and
Florence:

Asti 12,000
Bologna 60,000
Camerino 10,000
Carpi & Correggio 15,000
Faenza 12,000
Ferrara 20,000
Florence 300,000
Genoa 100,000
Imola & Forlì 30,000
Lucca 20,000
Mantua 60,000
Milan 600,000
Montferrat 50,000
Naples 600,000
Colonna & Orsini 25,000
Pesaro 15,000
Piombino 20,000
Rimini 10,000
Saluzzo 10,000
Savoy 100,000
Siena 60,000
Urbino 50,000
Venice 100,000,000

Toward the end of the Middle Ages, chancery fees and taxes,
along with the sale of positions within the papal bureaucracy, brought
an increase in revenue to popes who were usually living beyond
their means. Chancery charges were nominally for whatever labor
the ordinary personnel put into the rough drafting and engrossment

of a needed document, the placing of the Camera's seal imprint, or the registering of the document in the official archives. Each step commanded what amounted to a gratuity calculated sometimes on the number of words, sometimes on the hours of work. What one paid as gratuity had nothing to do with the cost of the document itself. The revenues from such chancery fees never ceased to be substantial, and always kept growing.

The sale of offices, which had always existed, took on a grand scale with Pope Boniface IX. Every job of scribe and minor clerk had a price. Higher positions, including that of cardinal, were priced and sold. One pope simply created 71 new collectors' jobs and realized 20,000 florins immediately. All told, at the end of the fifteenth century, the sale of offices brought in an approximate annual sum of 35,000 ducats. Receipts from the sale of offices went mainly into the papal Privy Purse. The Camera saw very little of those sums.

A document dated July 20, 1514 and now preserved in the Vatican Archives[8] gives us a concrete idea of what those sales of offices brought in. Prices are in ducats:

CAMERAL POSITION SOLD	PRICE
7 Clerks	10,000
1 Auditor	10,000
1 Fiscal Lawyer	1,200
1 Fiscal Proctor	1,200
9 Notaries	2,500
101 Scribes	2,700
101 Solicitors	1,100
104 Collectors of the Seal	1,400
101 Archivists	3,000
141 Security Guards	650
48 Shared Notaries	1,500
5 Subdeacons	3,000
8 Acolytes	500
10 Auditor Notaries	1,400
81 Writers of Protocol Documents	1,300
3 Masters of the Seal	6,000

Offerings ("oblations") laid on the altar of St. Peter's and other churches sometimes ran to the thousands of ducats. The bullion always went to the Camera; the remainder was divided among the canons (or the priests) of the church. From earliest times and down to the present day, the Church has been left legacies and gifts. Then as now, the papal administration was quite efficient in dealing with these monies and properties. They have always been a source of ready funds.

Collection and Banking

The Catholic world of the fifteenth century—all the world known to Western nations—was divided by Cameral planners into a distinct number of collection districts or collectorates throughout which monies owing to the papal Camera had to be regularly collected and conveyed to the Camera's possession in Rome. One particular bureau in the Camera supervised the collectorates and their operations.

Over each one of these Church collectorates there was one General Collector appointed by the Camera. Usually a cleric—archdeacon, prior, abbot, rector, canon—and very rarely a layman, the General Collector was never domiciled in his collectorate. The reasons are obvious: On his appointment, he came to Rome, was sworn into office, and promised "to exact and receive the fruits, rights, and revenues owed the Apostolic Camera, and to transfer such fruits, rights, and revenues to the said Camera according to the appointed times."

He pledged his own personal property plus a possible forfeit or bond of at least 500 gold florins, as guarantee and sign of his good faith and correct intentions. He then received a formal commission signed and sealed by the pope and the Camerarius; a series of letters of credence addressed to the lay rulers and ecclesiastical authorities within his collectorate; the Cameral lists of those owing money to the papal authorities; and the accounts of his predecessor.

He then went to his collectorate and established a central residence, usually at a monastery but sometimes in a house of his own if it was well protected. He appointed and swore in as many deputy collectors as were necessary to cover his district. He had a daily stipend from the Camera, could demand travel, lodging, and work expenses from local rulers and ecclesiastics, and charged to the Camera all his out-of-pocket expenses for horses, mules, parchment, armed escorts, sacking for the monies, chests for storing the monies, messengers, servants, notaries, and scribes.

The General Collector's first job was to take the lists of revenue-payers and assess each one for each tax owing. A monastery or a bishop might owe the Camera several kinds of taxes. The collector determined all exemptions from taxes as well as the penalties for those in arrears. He finally chose some place—his own house sometimes, but usually a monastery or the dwelling of a trusted banker—where he could safely deposit the monies he collected. All this done, he set out with his deputy collectors to perform the collection.

He traveled with the equivalent dignity and privilege of a papal nuncio and was everywhere the guest of his taxpayers. He had complete discretionary powers to remit debts temporarily, to issue receipts, to lower or raise taxes—although every two years he had to justify all his decisions in person to the Camera. In addition, the Camera demanded chits and vouchers for all out-of-pocket expenses, lists of taxpayers, and all his receipts.

He was totally immune from all local jurisdictions of any prelate. To enforce taxes, he could issue excommunications, suspend all clerics so that they could perform none of their ecclesiastical functions, and finally call on the secular arm to seize and imprison defaulters, cite them to court, or sequestrate and expropriate all their property. The use of the secular arm was not always necessary; the ecclesiastical sanctions of excommunication and suspension meant that a cleric could not perform his clerical functions. Since he lived off the monies earned from performing these functions, either of those two penalties meant abject poverty and usually loss of his ecclesiastical benefice. In all this, the collector acted with severity. For he himself and his livelihood were at stake. The Camera did not brook weakling collectors.

The General Collector was permitted to keep ready and at hand for his disposal a large sum of money, allowed to act as a banker to make loans, and—despite rigid Church law—allowed to obtain interest on those loans. Eventually, he had to effect the transfer of the due and collected monies to the Apostolic Camera in Rome. He either conveyed it in specie himself, or deposited the sums with a local Cameral banker who then issued bills of exchange or promissory notes honored by his associates in Rome.

At the end of his stewardship, provided he was certified as owing no money to the Camera, he was usually rewarded with a benefice—a bishopric, canonry, monastery, or oratory. His deputies were paid off with a lump sum.

Integral to this highly efficient collection system was the element of international banking, monies in various currencies—ducats, florins, pounds, shillings, pence, *grossi*, *julhatis*, marks, mancuses, *carlini*, black crowns, Venne pence, old Aquileia pence, money of Graz, pounds of Tours.

The papal Camera by the fifteenth century had begun to rely on agents outside the ecclesiastical structure for the deposit, transfer, and currency exchange of the collected monies, as well as for contracting loans. The worldwide financial activity of Cameral collectors was an essential stimulus for the beginning of what we moderns call banking. But, even by the thirteenth century, a banker (or an "exchanger," as he was called) was a functionary at the papal court. And in that early time, the Church relied on the Knights Templar for the deposit and safe transfer of monies. The Knights were a military order, lived in military strongholds, and could take care of themselves and anyone or anything assigned to their care. Their downfall in such terrible circumstances[9] was doubtlessly due to their eminent position as the proto-bankers and armed escort for papal revenues.

As we have seen, the Apostolic Camera of the fifteenth century had a permanent in-house bureau of bankers. Cameral bankers received deposits from Cameral collectors and issued receipts. They undertook all risks of deposit and transfer of funds, were allowed to retain the deposits for quite a while, could use the deposits to make interest-bearing loans, could invest the deposits in their own commercial ventures, and even made loans to the Camera.

Eventually, they had to transfer the deposits in specie or by bills of exchange or through their representatives in the Camera (account transfers). The Cameral bankers acted on behalf of the treasuries in the papal *patrimonia*. In fact, at the opening of the sixteenth century, the Apostolic Camera and the financial existence of the papacy depended on the Cameral bankers. When the Buonsignori banking house collapsed in the fourteenth century, the Camera lost 64,000 florins. The Cameral bankers and merchants were also accredited by the papacy to kings and princes, thus increasing their business. They also were recommended to all ecclesiastics coming to Rome with money problems. In order to recall the loans they made, Cameral bankers could employ the very effective ecclesiastical censures of excommunication and suspension as well as the judicial power of papal prisons.

The papal Curia and international banking have a long historical association. But this entire financial system, which evolved over a period of six hundred years, reached the apogee of its efficiency as the economic nature of European society was starting to change. Between 1200 and 1500 A.D., the volume of long-distance trade between centers of primitive capitalism grew. For a long time, the cloth and woolen trades as developed in England, Flanders, and Florence were the only truly capitalist industries creating capitalist techniques and specialized ancillary industries. The orientation of medieval times to feudal serfdom was interrupted.

The old market economy ensured that farmers, artisans, and workmen alike were certain of their money returns either in their home market place or, if they transported their goods some distance, in outside market places. The processes of exchange which depended on predetermined routes and conditions of terrain and society were unchanging; all the pricing differentials were known in advance. As commerce expanded, however, new economic realities confronted the old theology. Long-distance commerce and trade by ships, intermediate storing of perishable (wheat, grain) and imperishable goods (gold, spices, precious stones, silk, valuable woods, tar), and varying social conditions (revolutions, plagues, wars, and famines along the routes of the transported goods) created a series of new concepts that moral theologians started to play with. A chief one was *damnum emergens*—possible loss of the transported goods through "the hand of God or accidents of nature." There arose the idea of permissible "interest" as distinct from the forbidden "usury." When I charged you a fee for merely using my money, that was "usury." When you, in using my money, risked losing it altogether, I ran the risk that my money would perish. I could therefore charge you a fee for risking that perishment. The word "interest" derives from the Latin "to perish," "to be ended."

In practice, long before they did so in spirit, the Cameral authorities as well as Catholic bankers and merchants were adapting the medieval rules of trading and money-making to new conditions. They were engaged in a banking system and profit-making that were essentially capitalistic. The alliance of the Apostolic Camera with Italian bankers in particular, but also with northern European and English bankers, was an accomplished fact long before genuine capitalism flourished in the world of Christendom.

As feudalism declined, [10] Europe witnessed an intermediate stage on the road to capitalism. This was the mercantilism of 1500–1750. The rise of strong national states made mercantilism possible. The profits of mercantilism spurred on the growth of those same states.

The old feudal system of government in the papal State took a forked road at this point. The ordinary molds in which the social and political life of its inhabitants continued were feudal. But as time passed, the pope became more a constitutional monarch and less an absolute ruler. The papal State benefited little directly from mercantilism. By 1500, the papal authorities had no means of creating a mercantile marine. Nor could papal troops be sent out to Africa and Asia to colonize new territories. Nor did the papal State ever have even a beginning of the industrial power needed for mercantilist exchange. Fundamentally, the economy in the papal State was agrarian. It remained so until 1870.

However, this lack of participation in mercantilism did not mean impoverishment for the papacy or its State. Impoverishment was to come only much later, long after mercantilism had grown into capitalism. And before all that happened, the papal State had to live through the violent changeover that altered the world it had molded and dominated.

The Changeover

At the opening of the sixteenth century, the papacy had a relatively short time to go before the world in which it had achieved its greatest success passed away violently. The religious unity of that world under the umbrella of Catholicism was doomed: In England, Germany, France, and Austria, the men who would lead the Reformation were already born, most of them already thinking actively of reform. Moreover, the economic and political structure of that world was about to change radically: Capitalism would develop within the bosom of democracy. The papacy and the Catholicism it taught men and women for over ten centuries had made capitalism and democracy both possible and inevitable. But, strangely enough, neither the papacy nor Catholicism would participate in the changeover—at least in the beginning.

In order to understand the fateful decisions taken by Vatican financial managers after World War II, one has to understand what happened to the papacy when it did not participate actively in the huge economic and political changeover that took place between 1500 and 1700. Vatican memories are long: Its managers in the twentieth century did not wish to see the same mistake repeated.

PART FOUR

CAPITALISM AND CATHOLICISM

CAPITALISM AND DEMOCRACY

It is clear that the development of capitalism in western Europe and the Americas was made possible largely by the rise of participative democracy. We need to inquire why the papacy and the papal State did not enter into the mainstream of international development that resulted in the capitalism of the eighteenth century, and whether the Catholic Church was alien to participative democracy. The answer to several questions is intimately connected with this inquiry: Was the papacy inimical to capitalism? Did the Church make any contribution to the rise of capitalism?

Three important traits of the Church in the last centuries of the Middle Ages prepared the way for capitalism and democracy. There was the vast and intricate revenue-collection system developed by the Church throughout all of Europe. There was the Church's drive to evangelize, to spread the good news which fueled the first explorations of Asia, Africa, and the Americas, giving rise to mercantilism, the forerunner of capitalism. And there was the idea of participative government and republican representation of the people which the Catholic Church was the first in history to nourish. Without participative representational government, democracy would never have been born. Without democracy, classical capitalism would never have flourished. We may conclude, therefore, that capitalism can claim to have been made possible by Catholic tutelage.

The revenue-collection system of the Church necessitated the rise of international banking, and by the middle of the fifteenth

century, definite steps had been taken in that direction. It was quite
distinct from the "clearinghouse" function of the Champagne fairs,
and from the warehouse trade and local banking systems that developed among the northern cities of Italy and among the German, Scandinavian, and English cities of the Hanseatic League.
These systems remained localized.

Another type of banker lived off the finances of the international
wool trade and the collection and transmission of papal revenues:
He was the prototype of our modern banker.

At the beginning, these international bankers were mainly Italians
from the chief cities of Lombardy. Hence the name of the chief
financial street in London—Lombardy Street. Those Italians set
out to challenge the monopoly exercised by Jewish bankers in the
early part of the Middle Ages. The Jews had specialized in this field
because they were not allowed by law to possess land and they were
not bound by the Christian laws against usury. Christian bankers
from Piacenza were the first to enter international banking in a big
way, followed by those of Lucca, Siena, Genoa, Venice, and Florence.

The Apostolic Camera used bankers of the stature of Sir William
de la Pole, the Cely family in England, Jacques Cœur in France,
the House of Fugger in Germany. But it was the Italians who came
to dominate the scene, and particularly the Florentines. They accepted deposits, transferred money between accounts in payment of
debts, had a primitive mortgage system, made loans, engaged in
credit transfers, and granted credit on the basis of some collateral.
For a long time their most creditable and profitable client was the
Apostolic Camera and the papal Privy Purse.

Florentine bankers, after a bad period in the late thirteenth and
fourteenth centuries, had a new period of prosperity in the fifteenth
and early sixteenth centuries. Among them, the Medici family gave
the Church more than one pope and cardinal. The rivalries between
such Cameral bankers as the Medici and the Pazzi had all the
violence, cruelty, jealousy, and enmity that was to appear again
during the twentieth-century Vatican scandals.

From the medieval Church's drive to evangelize—its first big
manifestation was the Crusades—was born the mercantilism of European states. Evangelization and exploration went hand in hand.
What fired the explorations and their organizers—incredible though
it may seem for moderners accustomed to the separation of Church

and State—was Catholicism. A sovereign such as Louis IX of France considered his throne and power only as a means of spreading Catholicism. To be sure, the desire for gold and new sources of wealth was a powerful motive for conquistadors and explorers. But we cannot dissociate from that desire the evangelizing drive that Catholicism created in those people. For them, for Louis and the other sovereigns, this did not exclude national rivalries; and shipping, the basis of mercantilism, was that rivalry's chief weapon.

Long-distance transport of goods and a method of financing and profiting from such risk investment of capital spawned energies in the late medieval and Renaissance world that would make the blossoming of classical capitalism possible. No other institution in the Western world was as instrumental for the channeling of those energies as the Church by its very size, prestige, power, and by the activities it promoted and supported.

However, the forces—above all the social overhead surplus—that molded the logic of history and ultimately made capitalism inevitable, were to be born of democracy itself as it flowered in the seventeenth century. Now democracy was the direct child of medieval Catholicism. The mentality and the sociopolitical institutions we claim today as hallmarks of our democracy were directly conveyed to us by the Catholic Church.

Participative governing assembly of the governed was first nourished by the councils and conventions of clerics and lay folk that operated in France, England, Spain, and Portugal from the seventh century onward under the patronage and organization of the Church. At stake always were not merely spiritual questions but social conditions and political action, the correction of injustices, the provision of local amenities for living, traveling, and working. The process was always deliberative and by vote, ending in an accepted pact and agreement. Those conventions were known as *communia*, gatherings of the people. The *communia* were the forerunners not merely of the European communes of today, but of the municipalities of the Renaissance. It was the *communia*, the "Commons" of England, that wrested the Magna Carta from King John in 1215.

From the beginning, these conventions or councils were attended by delegates or elected representatives. By the eleventh century and into the twelfth, we find parliaments of such elected representatives from towns and municipalities operating as single deliberative and executive bodies in Spain, Sicily, and France. The biggest contribution here came from the Dominican friars who during a long period were the only intellectual force in Europe. The Dominicans taught and put into practice their own constitutional principles. Enshrined in that constitution of the Dominicans were the three basic operating principles of democracy: All authority is confided in those the local communities choose by a free vote; each community enjoys self-determination; the various communities through their elected representatives can meet and take decisions by vote that affect all the communities. That system of direct democratic vote by the people was introduced into parts of Switzerland in the thirteenth century, and it is still the rule in the Catholic cantons of today.

In those times, one of the main functions of the local assemblies was to protect the communities against the depredations of local feudal lords and king, if necessary. Thus the Franciscan cleric William of Ockham (1280–1329) could write:[1]

> The king is superior to the whole kingdom, and yet in certain cases he is inferior to it, for in case of necessity the kingdom can depose and imprison him . . . every people, community or body which can legislate for itself without the consent or authority of an outsider can without further authorization elect members to represent the whole community or body . . .

It was left to a cardinal, Nicholas of Cusa (1401–1464), to enunciate a principle that would be dear to the hearts of the Americans in 1776:[2]

> Every constitution is rooted in natural law and cannot be valid if it contradicts it . . . Since all are free by nature, all government, whether by written law or a prince, is based solely on the agreement and consent of the subject. For if by nature men are equally powerful and free, true and ordered power in the hands of one can be established only by the election and consent of the others, just as law also is established by consent . . . It is clear, therefore, that the binding validity of all constitutions is based on tacit or express agreement and consent.

And it was Ockham who formulated the basis of all true republicanism. His words might have been those of the men who framed the American Declaration of Independence five centuries later as well as those who fought the American Revolution: "Every people, community or body," Ockham declared,[3] "which can legislate for itself without the consent or authority of any outsider, can, without further authorization, elect members to represent the whole community or body."

These principles were enunciated in an age of kings and feudal lords, when international economics was based on an incipient mercantilism and a rather primitive international banking system. Within some hundreds of years later, systems of long-range financing and venture-capital had been developed. The first of many inventions revolutionized work habits, production schedules, and the quantity of products. Religious laws no longer required believers to surrender their surplus of revenue to religious purposes. That surplus became instead the overhead financing for industrial and social development. The medieval philosophic principles enunciated by thinkers like Ockham and Nicholas of Cusa became rules of social and political behavior and organization. Thus was created the social overhead surplus that economists and sociologists speak of as essential to classical capitalism.

By the fifteenth century, the age of states had arrived. England, France, Spain, Germany, Portugal, and Italy had by now their own separate vernacular languages. Each, too, had its own organized legal system which knitted together the various *communia* composed of the people. For nearly five hundred years previously, it was the continuing, sometimes acrid, always polemical discussions about the structure and the government of the Catholic Church that had molded and fashioned men's minds to thinking of participative government and republican representationalism. The various national groups started by organizing themselves on the only model they had—the Church, with its cathedral chapters, its consultative assemblies of clerics and lay folk, the authority of bishops and priests mitigated and restrained by the mass will of their subjects. It was all a protracted lesson in self-government. The Renaissance Prince that Machiavelli pictured and the king with a divine right that the Anglo-Saxons preferred were but interruptions in a development that was bound to continue and bear fruit. But, at least, by the early 1400s, the idea of statehood had been born. It was still the time for princes, however.

The Pope as Prince

By this time also, the popes exercised a temporal power not only over the papal State but virtually over all the lands of Europe. That temporal power had its vicissitudes, but Europe as a whole had never repudiated it.

The pope's character as worldly princeling and potentate was further emphasized because of the reign between 1450 and 1550 of a series of popes who were, with few exceptions, quite venal, and used their power as a vehicle for their ambition and greed—just as their contemporaries on the various thrones of Europe. The pope became a sovereign surrounded by princes—his cardinals. Conclave, the sacrosanct means of choosing the Vicar of Christ on earth, became the sport of those "princes." In at least one conclave— that which elevated Cardinal Giovanni Battista Cibò to the title of Pope Innocent VIII—the papacy was actually bought.[4] During his eight years as pope (1484–92), Innocent granted full honors at papal functions to Franceschetto, one of the illegitimate sons he had fathered before he took orders.

Morals apart, the "princes" became quite rambunctious, as would the powerful members of any European sovereign's court. The Cardinalitial Camera had always been at loggerheads with the pope's Apostolic Camera over the issues of the division of the Church's universal revenues and the appointment to high posts in the Curia.

Faced with popes who claimed to be temporal princes as well as spiritual leaders, the cardinals organized themselves, refusing to elect a pope until they were granted a charter of their own princely rights—particularly concerning revenue sharing and the appointments to key posts in the Curia.

That Curia was the most massive bureaucracy the world had ever seen since the time of Emperor Diocletian, who had reigned for just over twenty years (284–305 A.D.) over the Roman Empire and was the only ruler in history who succeeded in totally reforming a government bureaucracy. The Curia was now almost completely Italian in personnel, organized along the lines of interlocking directorates which members of the great Italian families strove to control, and it disposed of massive funds—but seemingly never enough to subsidize the pageantry of their religious ceremonies, the luxury of their lifestyles, or their indulgence in art and music.

Most Curial business had nothing to do with religion directly. It was primarily legal, fiscal, and monetary. However, it touched on religion closely in one sense: Much of its revenues came from the traffic in ecclesiastical benefices, the sale of indulgences, the granting of canonical dispensations and exemptions, and taxation imposed in the name of Christ. Gradually a burning resentment built up throughout Christendom.

By the end of the fifteenth century, the papacy was incredibly wealthy and enjoyed the highest prestige. It was now no longer a power among the peoples of its world—it was an *authority*, and its papal State was regarded as an Italian polity, no longer as "the Lands of St. Peter." Popes still received the "obedience" of new rulers and they still ratified treaties between nations as the universal authority. But the worldly aspect predominated.

So thoroughly did some popes work at their status and image as princes of a local principate that Machiavelli could find the models for his Prince in Boniface VIII, Martin V, and Sixtus IV. With them, "reasons of State" justified any action they thought necessary—including the use of the old spiritual weapons of excommunication and censure—in order to further their princely power, status, and wealth.

The wealth that poured into Europe from newly discovered lands—and the Apostolic Camera was one beneficiary—created the social and political conditions that cumulatively and within only two centuries introduced economic changes into European lands. Not only was the "social surplus" augmented, but the new prosperity made possible the unique seed-bed of genuine and classical capitalism. Private and individual wealth increased enormously during the mercantilist period, as did that of sovereign governments, the Apostolic Camera and the papacy included.

A portrait of the first genuine Renaissance pope, Nicholas V (1447–55), will give a very accurate view of papal ideals at the beginning of this period.

In order to put his papal house in order, Nicholas V reformed the government of Rome, placing all judicial and municipal appointments and decisions in the hands of four prominent citizens. He refurbished the system of taxation throughout the various provinces and appointed Cameral collectors, who saw to it that due revenues came in on time. Much money accrued to the Cameral Treasury in the Jubilee Year of 1450; estimates place the total offerings somewhere beyond two million gold florins. Nicholas employed the services of multiple banks—about seven in all, on the principle that if one went bankrupt, the others would hold; but the Medici bank was his favorite; he deposited there a minimum of 100,000 gold florins after the Jubilee Year. Nicholas's control over taxes and monies was so extensive and so well known that it provoked much criticism among those who saw the need for deep reform of the Church's attitude to temporal goods. "If Christ were again on earth," the celebrated Carthusian monk Jakob von Jüterbogk wrote about his time, "and occupied the Apostolic See, would he approve the present practice of that See in regard to benefices and to the Sacraments of the Church, the many *reservations, collations, annates, provisions, expectancies, benefices* which are given for money, the *revocations, annulments, nonobstantia?* . . ."[5]

Nicholas V was the Renaissance pope par excellence, and his expenditures—apart from the sums devoted to defense—went to the elaboration of humanism which by now was in full vogue.

He assembled a regular army of calligraphers, translators, scribes, scholars, linguists, geographers, chemists, astronomers, historians, geologists, tapestry makers, mosaic workers, painters, and sculptors in order to foment and nourish the studies and researches that fascinated him, spending continually large sums on everything— except artists, whom he paid miserably.[6]

Nicholas spent liberally on translations: 10,000 gold florins for a translation of Homer; for the ten books of Strabo, 1,000 scudi; for Polybius, 500 ducats. By the end of his life he had spent over 70,000 scudi on books alone; the Vatican Library by then had five thousand volumes. He lavished 60,000 ducats on a papal reception for King Frederick III in Rome, and always carried around on his person a leather purse with some hundreds of florins—for chance purchases, for charity, and small loans.

He had the most grandiose plans for a total rebuilding of Rome and of every building in the Vatican. If he had succeeded, his contemporaries said, he would have beggared the Church, but he would have created the eighth wonder of the world. Nicholas planned to build a new Basilica of St. Peter, a new Apostolic Palace, a whole new ecclesiastical city for the residence of his cardinals and bishops as well as for his papal government offices. His new walls and towers enclosing Rome were to be impregnable.

When one examines those plans today, one marvels at the genius behind them. But death intervened, and all that remains substantially of his vast plans and achievements is the present Tower of Nicholas V inside the Gate of Santa Anna in Vatican City. Perhaps fittingly, the Vatican Bank and its offices are today housed in that tower.

When he died, in spite of his heavy expenditures, Nicholas left 20,000 ducats in the Treasury. His own dying words are often quoted to indicate the amplitude of his outlook and the self-conscious mission he had fulfilled:

> I have so reformed and so confirmed the Holy Roman Church which I found devastated by war and oppressed by debts, that I have eradicated schism and won back her cities and castles. I have not only freed her from her debts, but erected magnificent fortresses for her defense, as, for instance, at Gualdo, Assisi, Fabriano, Civita Castellana, at Narni, Orvieto, Spoleto, and Viterbo; I have adorned her with glorious buildings and decked her with pearls and costly books, and tapestry, with gold and silver vessels, and splendid vestments. And I did not collect all these treasures by grasping avarice and simony. In all things I was liberal, in building, in the purchase of books, in the constant transcription of Latin and Greek manuscripts, and in the remuneration of learned men. All this has been bestowed upon me by the Divine grace, owing to the continued peace of the Church during my Pontificate.

In this profession of success, there is not one word that to our modern minds would indicate spiritual leadership and moral authority. Love of his Church is translated into magnificence of building and richness of endowment. Papal leadership is synonymous with secular leadership. That was the characteristic of the age and the principle of the Great Experiment: the identification of secular and spiritual power in the person of the pope.

The Protestant Reformation

It was in these conditions that the papacy and the Church were ushered into the Renaissance and the beginning of modern times totally unprepared to meet the onset of new forces. The nations of Europe were exiting from the world Catholicism had created in which all the "givens" were absolute. The fate both of papacy and Church would have been quite different if the popes had realized that willy-nilly their old Catholic world was heading out into the unknown; that the old could never be reinstated; and that the thousand-year-old grouping of the world around the temporal power of the pope was finished. Copernicus established that the sun, not the earth, was the center of earth's system. But, as R. G. Collingwood wrote,[7] ". . . the true significance of the Copernican revolution

consisted not so much in displacing the world's center from the
earth to the sun as in implicitly denying that the world has a center
at all." The center that the papacy had represented for its world was
doomed.

Catholic reaction to the Protestant Reformation was slow in coming. It took the Council of Trent from 1545 to 1563, with inter-
missions, to draw up plans for a Counter-Reformation. But when
this finally got under way, it did roll back many of the religious
conquests of Protestantism. It reinstated holiness in Rome and the
papacy. It evoked a whole new series of heroic and devoted men
and women, and it strengthened the centralized control of the pope
over the bishops of the universal Church.

The great advantage now for the Catholic Church was a succession of seven popes in the second half of the sixteenth century who
led blameless lives and devoted all their attention to the spiritual
renewal of the Church and the ecclesiastical efficiency of the Curia.
Under those popes, there were far-reaching changes in the papal
Curia. The former sources of papal revenues in the universal Church
had been cut off or were drying up. The Apostolic Camera was
losing its central importance and, with it, the Camera of the Cardinals was diminished. The long internal bureaucratic struggle
between pope and cardinals was decided in favor of the pope. In
the seventeenth century, a new figure started to play a key role in
papal affairs: the papal Secretary of State. Most probably the origin
of the Secretary's power is to be sought in the old office of the
Camerarius. For when a pope died and before a successor was
elected, the most powerful man in the Church was the cardinal
who controlled the purse-strings, the Camerarius. In the interreg-
num he was the Chamberlain of the Universal Church, the Cardinal
Camerlengo.

The number of cardinals was increased to seventy—no doubt,
originally, because of the high price paid into the pope's Privy Purse
by each aspiring candidate. But by the sixteenth century, the moral
quality of cardinals had improved; and, bureaucratically, they were
under stricter control. They were now organized into fifteen permanent congregations (or government ministries). In the Catholic
counter-reforms the centralized authority of the pope had increased
enormously. The power of pope and Secretary of State was also
enhanced by the new system of papal nuncios or diplomatic representatives that fanned out from Rome over Christendom.

The economic and financial well-being of the papal State was
consolidated. The bureaucracy organized taxation, the exploitation

of natural resources, and a very clever system of public loans—all this to replace the funds that used to come from the universal Church but were now drying up or already cut off.

The Sources of Democratic Capitalism

Outside the jurisdiction of the pope, in the new Protestantized nations of northern Europe, capitalism was aborning. But as long as the old medieval doctrines on the evil of wealth and avarice, the strictures against profit-making—even in principle—and the governing feudal mentality remained intact and preserved by an all-powerful, centralized Catholic Church, the seed-bed of capitalism could not be sown. New sources were needed for that, and the Protestant revolt with its new work ethic provided precisely those sources in the sixteenth and seventeenth centuries.

But first the Protestant nations had to abandon the sociopolitical principles of the men who made Protestantism possible. Nothing in the teachings of Martin Luther, John Calvin, or that master of the English Reformation, Thomas Cromwell, would justify what Protestants now aimed at: democracy.

Luther, at heart a despotic conservative, wrote and spoke the most bloody-minded exhortations to powerful lords and princes, urging them to crush any hostile movements in the people, any popular attempt to be free of feudal control. "Rulers," he laid down, "are to drive, beat, choke, hang, burn, behead, break upon the wheel the vulgar masses—*Herr Omnes*."[8] If they riot, then "anyone may act as judge and executioner . . . whoever can, should smite, strangle, stab, secretly or publicly."[9] Luther upheld the complete and absolute authority of rulers over the ruled. Nowhere in his works do we find anything but sheer contempt for the common people and their well-being. Democracy, certainly, could not be derived from Lutheran principles.

John Calvin was slightly less vitriolic against the people and the will of the people. There is one meager paragraph in all his works which can, with much imagination and good will, be stretched so as somehow or other to envisage democracy.[10] Where we learn the mind of Calvin on this question is in the form of government he established in Geneva: an oligarchic theocracy that took no account of what the people wanted but, with summary executions and torture as a commonplace of municipal administration, governed the Genevans until democracy reasserted itself in 1794. In the meanwhile, Calvin called for the assassination of his enemies and the shedding of "the blood of abominable idolators" (Catholics), and—of great interest to the women's liberation movement of our day—trumpeted continuously against "the monstrous regiment of women." Calvin's principles had to be abandoned by Calvinists themselves in order to found democratic assemblies.

The Reformation in England was chiefly and thoroughly effected in one decade, 1530–1540, by the tireless efforts and will of one man, Thomas Cromwell. Cromwell had one purpose in mind which was neither the purification of the Church, the advancement of religion, nor the propagation of biblical belief. His objective was, simply, "the consolidation of an absolute royal power under the form of a constitution, by the aid of a subservient parliament and a terrorized Church." What Cromwell founded was later perfected by Queen Elizabeth I and her minister, Baron Burleigh.

The anti-democratic teachings and mentality of the Protestant Reformers were in fact so pronounced that when the Scottish Covenanters, English Levellers, and American Puritans rose up against the despotism of the Protestant establishment, they had to look for antecedents in pre-Reformation thought among Catholic medieval thinkers. There they found all they needed, the basic ideas of national law, the sovereignty of the people, the freedoms of corporate bodies and municipalities. Scotland's George Buchanan (1506–82) has been touted by Protestant historians as having produced the principles that undoubtedly produced "the two great English, the American, and the first French revolutions."[12] But even Buchanan himself admitted that he merely wrote down all he learned from his Catholic mentor, John Major. Major, a sixteenth-century Scottish historian and philosopher, in turn was merely repeating the old thought of Aquinas, Antonius of Florence, Nicholas d'Onesme, William of Ockham, and others.

It was to this pre-Reformation womb of democracy that the men of 1776 turned—Covenanters, Presbyterians, Calvinists, Huguenots—when they wished to frame in a Constitution and a Declaration of Independence those principles of democracy that would make democratic capitalism a possibility and, in time, the dominant reality of our modern world. Out of the institutions of their democracy could come the social overhead surplus that capitalism needed.

But Protestantism did have its own particular contribution to the development of capitalism. This mainly lay in its work ethic.

According to this ethic, the accumulation of wealth was not sinful, and man's vocation was to work hard, live frugally, and perform efficiently. In the new Protestant nations, education of the middle, lower-middle, and lower classes advanced far more rapidly than in the old Catholic nations. Legal codes favorable to capitalist expansion were developed. Domestic markets were freed from unnecessary tariffs and tolls. Uniform monetary systems grew up. Physical facilities—roads, bridges, warehousing harbors—and merchant marines were developed.

When the first industrial inventions—the flying shuttle, the steam engine, the water frame, for example—arrived on the scene, all was set and ready for their exploitation. Accumulated capital in private hands made possible the exploitation of the new inventions. Foreign (colonialized) markets provided both capital and raw materials. The age of pure mercantilism was over; the transition was quickly made from sheer commerce to industry. Industrial capital was to dominate over commercial capital until the middle of the twentieth century, and eighteenth-century England led in that industrial revolution. The age of the commercial empires—British, French, Dutch, and German—was at hand.

The papal State remained largely untouched by all this. Partly because the papacy was locked in a life-and-death struggle with its Protestant enemies. Partly because the theology and sociopolitical doctrines of the Catholic Church at that time prevented the laying of that necessary seed-bed of capitalism within the papal State where feudal conditions of service and ownership persisted almost unchanged until well into the late nineteenth century. And partly because the once universal revenues of the Apostolic Camera had dried up.

Catholic Achievement

Ironically, it was during this very period of approximately two centuries (1550–1750) when capitalism was being born that some of the greatest achievements of the Catholic Church are to be found, and that the modern structure of the papacy took form. Rome and Vatican Hill were beautified and enriched with the buildings and art treasures we marvel at today. The Vatican Library was built up. Archeological researches on ancient Rome were begun. The rich art treasures now regarded by all men as part of our human heritage are the result of those popes' labor. The Gregorian calendar was fixed. The Vulgate text of the Bible was published. Art, drama, literature were promoted. John Milton, the pope-hating, pope-baiting, anti-royalist English Puritan, sat in the Roman palace of the Barberini popes among the red-robed cardinals and watched classical play after play. There was an intense scholarly activity— in philosophy, theology, languages, and cultural studies—and a sustained interest in nourishing and patronizing painters, sculptors, and other artists that in retrospect shows the papacy and its popes to have been the benefactors of all men.

The papal State and Rome might be outside the materialistic dynamic of the Protestant nations, but there was no doubting the vigor of Roman institutions and the intent of pope and Curia to reconquer the world for the Christ they claimed to represent. In the meantime, while the Protestant nations pressed on with the conquest of the physical world and the formation of capitalism, the Catholic Church under its popes assembled a legacy of humanistic treasures that would outlive the boldest commercial empires and end up worth millions more than all the gold and currency amassed by the new privateers of human society.

The only trail-blazing, peculiarly papal innovation with a slightly capitalistic aura was the once famous establishment known as Monte di Pietà ("mountain of mercy"). Properly speaking, it was an innovation of Franciscan friars rather than of popes; but, very rapidly, popes came to see its advantages and possibilities.

By the middle of the fifteenth century, interest rates on loans in the papal State and throughout Italy were exorbitant. In Florence, for instance, outside the circle of bankers who served the big commercial concerns as well as the nobility and the Apostolic Camera, the money-lending bankers to whom the ordinary people had recourse for their credit needs charged anything up to 32.5 percent interest. The situation was not much better in other cities, Rome included. Statutory rates of interest were rare in Italy and elsewhere at this time.

A group of Franciscan friars decided to do something in order to counteract the baneful hold of these high-interest money-lenders over the ordinary people. With papal license from Pope Pius II, they opened an incorporated establishment in Orvieto in 1460, and over its door stood the Latin lettering *Mons Pietatis*.[13] Its working capital was supplied by voluntary donations, collections, bequests, and gifts. Here, anyone in want of ready money could obtain it in modest sums, in exchange for some pledge. It resembled a pawnshop; but unlike contemporary pawnshops of the time which charged exorbitant interest, the Monte, as it was popularly called, charged no interest.

Within a year similar organizations arose in every major town and city in the papal State and throughout Italy. Pope Paul II opened one in Perugia in 1470. Sixtus IV established a Monte in his native city of Savona. A Franciscan friar, St. Bernardino da Feltre, traveled around Italy, preaching against usury and opening Monti wherever he went.

The Monte that opened in Florence found that to cope with the demands on its resources, it had to impose a small charge—it amounted to interest—on each loan. Immediately the Franciscans were attacked by the Dominicans in a bitter theological controversy, the Dominicans wishing to do away with all the Monti. But too many popes had already given their blessing to the whole idea: Pius II, Paul II, Sixtus IV, Innocent VIII, and Julius II had permitted their establishment.

Finally, in 1515, Leo X granted the Monti a privileged status, allowing them to charge that certain percentage on loans which would defray the expenses of carrying the account. Anyone who attacked this privilege would suffer excommunication. This statutory privilege of the Monti in Italy was a prime cause for the drop in interest rates during the sixteenth century. Leo had a vivid motive for supporting the Monti: He himself was always having recourse to one in order to pay his perpetual debts.

In time, the chief Monte in Rome became a bank in all but name, and it was used by successive popes to float state loans. But there was no way the papal State could join in the efflorescence of capitalism from 1750 onward. By the time Adam Smith published his *Inquiry into the Nature and Causes of the Wealth of Nations* in 1776, the papacy could not adhere to the laissez-faire doctrines of free-market competition and the regulating power of impersonal forces. For, to the traditional Catholic mind, a dangerous and ir-religious rationalism governed the new business mentality with its insistence on free trade, balanced budgets, little or no social welfare for the underprivileged, its social utilitarianism, its materialistic definitions of human quality and human success, its (at times almost visionary) reliance on progress in order to reach a new millennium, its subjection of nature to the demands of that progress, its godless principle of scientific inquiry ("everything real is verifiable by concrete experiment"). None of this was reconcilable with the old Catholic mentality. The Catholic Reform had enclosed that mentality in a bastioned strength that would be volatilized only in the second half of the twentieth century.

THE SLOW DECLINE

The eighteenth century history of the papacy, which opened with the long pontificate of Pope Clement XI (1700–21) was one of disaster for the papal State and for the seven popes who reigned after Clement's death to the opening of the next century.[1] It began with deep troubles of a political and economic nature in which the popes were embroiled *only* because they were heads of a temporal state with political, territorial, and financial interests. It closed with the total demise of the papal State.

The eighteenth century was one of historic contrasts. In this century, the Protestant nations were to take off into the full flight of classical capitalism. No one can state with any accuracy that the lot of peasants in the papal State was worse than that of peasants in Scotland, Holland, Prussia, Saxony, or Cornwall. For, in the first hundred years of capitalism, there still persisted the ancien régime, consisting of a dominant class of kings and aristocrats placed far above the masses of the people—shortly to be sanctified with the name of proletariat—with a bourgeois middle-class wedged in between those two extremes. That ancien régime would disappear only with the first great organized industrial slaughter of World War I.

But what can be stated with historical truth is that the Protestant nations developed both the education of the middle-class and the socioeconomic structures and instrumentalities that made capitalism possible. This development was precluded now from the papal State and, as a general rule, from the mainly Catholic southern nations of Europe.

A second and glaring contrast between the Catholic and Protestant nations concerned culture. Ironically, it was during this eighteenth century—as the papacy lost the battle for economic leadership to the Protestant nations—that the humanism of Rome achieved its greatest glory. What is now considered to be Rome's artistic and cultural heritage for all men and women—its architecture, its museums of archeology and painting and sculpture, its patronage of opera and of classical ballet—all that crowning of Rome's cultural glory took place in the century of its greatest troubles since the persecutions of Diocletian in the late third century A.D. There is a direct line of achievement running between the first efforts of the humanistic popes of the fifteenth century and the steady, dedicated cultural policies of all eight eighteenth-century popes. Nothing remotely like this magnificent humanism of papal Rome is to be found elsewhere in Europe, and certainly not in the newly formed United States of America.

A third contrast concerns religion. When the English and German reformers, with their religious allies, broke ranks with the Catholic Church in the sixteenth century, one insistent cry was that if they could do away with what they condemned as "the superstition, the intellectual oppression and ignorance, and the authoritarianism" of "the Red Lady of the Mediterranean"[2] they would once and for all spread the Good News of Christ's salvation to the ends of a world they were just beginning to explore and exploit. The Americas were still the "New World." Africa, Asia, and Oceania were either "dark" or "mysterious" or "terra incognita"—favorite expressions in the eighteenth century. By getting away from what they called the hocus-pocus of "Romish" rituals, the unnatural demands of celibacy in priest and nun, ridding the truth of Revelation of all its superstitions, the Protestants claimed they would fulfill Christ's injunction of "teaching all men in the name of the Father, the Son, and the Holy Spirit."

This is not how things worked out.

In that one century, those "cruik-shank celibates"—as Thomas Cromwell contemptuously described them earlier—succeeded in spreading Catholicism far wider than any of the splinter Protestant churches and sects of the day were able.

As of old, Catholic missionaries were often the first to contact unknown peoples in Africa, Asia, Oceania, and the Americas. This was mainly due to the efforts of those eight popes. The century saw the foundation of such missionary orders as the Missions Etrangères de Paris. The Jesuits also achieved their greatest glory in this century—prior to their sudden and total suppression in 1773.

The Catholic missionary effort was officially directed by the Congregation for the Propagation of the Faith, the "Propaganda Fide," in Rome. This was one Roman institution that was always running in debt. At mid-century, the average annual income of the Propaganda Fide was 3,321,940 scudi; its expenses ran to 3,852,309 scudi. This money was not spent on a vast missionary bureaucracy, however. It went to the education of missionary priests, brothers, and nuns, the building of mission stations, the interminable journeys that had to be undertaken in Latin America, in Canada, in Burma, in Tibet, in sub-Saharan Africa, in India and southeast Asia.

The Church's success in this century was quite extraordinary. If measured by the yardstick of numbers, it was the greatest missionary effort in human history. It ensured that the Catholic Church would be numerically the largest church of the twentieth century. It provided missionary models that even the Protestant missionaries finally adopted. And, of greater importance for us moderns, it gave Catholicism a place in what today is called the Third World, making papal policy in those countries a pivotal factor in the struggle between the two contending superpowers. Fully one-half of the world's 761 million Catholics live today between the southern borders of Texas and Patagonia at the tip of South America.

The only great failure of the Church's eighteenth-century missionary effort was in China.[3] The failure was due to the jealousy of Dominican and Franciscan missionaries in regard to the Jesuits, the myopia of Roman authorities, the mistakes of the Jesuits themselves. It was the greatest pastoral failure in the Church's long history. Today, China's near 1 billion and Japan's 110 million would most probably be Catholic Christians had it not been for the petty pride of those long-dead men and the provincial stupidity of their Roman superiors.

Against the backdrop of all this humanistic and religious success, we must place the complete failure of the papal State to function in an economically sound, progressive way during this fateful century. There was no compelling reason why it should have failed so dismally, but the course of events is quite clear: The papacy, being a temporal power and claiming at least tribute from many states, became necessarily embroiled in the politics and wars of those states. This has always been the price the Church has had to pay for its pursuit of temporal power.

The Catholic nations in that strange awakening world of the so-called Enlightenment were constantly at war or bickering with each other and with the papal State. This meant an interruption in the collection and conveyance to Rome of papal revenues. In certain areas—Spain, Sicily, Naples[4]—the papal revenues were coveted by local rulers.

From the beginning of the eighteenth century, the finances of the papal State were in deep trouble. Beginning with the reign of Clement XI, the national debt of the papal State stood at 15 million scudi: There was a sparse treasury of 80,000 scudi and a staggering economy which was mainly agricultural. By 1730, the debt was 60,000,000 scudi. In 1758, on the death of Benedict XIV, the debt hovered around 85,000,000 scudi.

The population of the papal State at this time was 2,036,747. There was starvation and beggary throughout the State. The northeastern provinces were still fairly well off, but the central and southern provinces were suffering from a lack of grain and oil, industrial stagnation, and inflationary prices. On top of all that, a series of bad harvests and bitterly prolonged winters made life utterly miserable for the vast majority of the inhabitants. Naples in 1763 was hit by a serious famine which crept toward Rome slowly. Civil order started to break down at a steady rate. One statistic is revealing: In the eleven years of Clement XIII's reign (1758–69), 10,000 murders were committed throughout the papal State, 4,000 of these in Rome itself.

Taxes were doubled—the taxable classes had diminished in numbers, and an effort to compel the large estate owners to cultivate more land for grain was futile.

Before Clement's death, papal revenues had practically ceased from Portugal, Spain, Naples, and Sicily. Clement had lost the papal estates at Avignon and the Comtat Venaissin in France as well as Benevento and Pontecorvo in Italy. He had lost control over the State deficit. His Privy Purse was practically empty, and the State debt had risen beyond the point that anything practicable could be done about it.

The contrast between the impoverished southern European countries and the flourishing northern European states at this time was a glaring one. Already Protestant England had become a world power and was on its way to founding one of the great commercial empires. Protestant Prussia was prosperous and powerful; Protestant Holland was already starting the overseas trade that in time would offer it the title of empire. A traveler passing from northern and central Europe down into France, the Iberian peninsula, and Italy would be struck by the contrast in economic well-being, standard of living, and general education of the people. The northern and central nations, predominantly Protestant, had none of the starvation and endemic poverty exhibited down south. Classical capitalism was off on its first flight and the Protestant nations were ready to take advantage of it.

The statesmen and kings in southern Europe held Rome and the papacy primarily responsible for that degrading difference between them and their Protestant counterparts. The difference was real, whatever the cause. But the solution of those kings and statesmen— to transform the Spanish, the Portuguese, the Italians, the French, into Britons and Prussians and Scandinavians—was fallacious. Tanucci, Charles III, and the other Catholic leaders failed to realize that. Even today, with all economic and political strangleholds by the Vatican reduced to nothing, the economies of southern European nations continue to lag behind the others.

This misapprehension of the Catholics must be placed in the wider context of general opposition to the papacy and the papal State. We are inclined to forget that the eighteenth century saw the flowering of a hitherto unknown element in Europe: organized and professional atheism. In France especially, but also in Austria, Spain, Portugal, Sicily, the Netherlands, and Prussia, a new breed of men and women arose who made it their profession in life to disprove and to eliminate Catholicism and its influence. The prime enemy for them was papal Rome. As long as the Catholic Church maintained a centralized government over the various segments of Catholics in the world, there was no way that abominable thing called formal religious belief could be done away with.

Among Rome's chief enemies at this time was the Gallican Church and a theory called Gallicanism. This was professed mainly by French ecclesiastics who claimed that the Catholic Church in France headed by its bishops should be free of papal control not merely in revenue matters but also (and more importantly) in matters of belief, ecclesiastical discipline, and the rules of morality.

Gallicanism went right to the root of the papacy: It denied the supremacy of the pope in ecclesiastical jurisdiction and in teaching doctrine. Without that supremacy, the pope was just another bishop among fellow bishops; he was subject to their judgment and their censure. He had no personal infallibility. The "Roman fact," the basis of Rome's greatness, was declared a fiction. In reality, it meant the end of Catholicism as all the popes had understood it.

On November 2, 1789, all Church property in France was declared by the National Assembly to be "at the disposal of the nation." On July 12, 1790, the Civil Constitution of the Clergy was enacted into law. Its basic principle was: "The Church is within the State, the State is not within the Church." The real purpose of the Constitution was to separate the Church in France from the greater unity of Catholicism, and make it a government-policed institution. Within three years, the French Church was stripped of all its financial resources.

There thus passed into the hands of the French Republic the vast and rich properties of the Church in France. There is no doubt that the wealth of this part of the Church has been exaggerated. But there are accurate estimates of it, and they have a place in this context with relation to papal finances.

Competent historians have calculated that Church property in France covered one-tenth of the country's surface. The Baron de Montesquieu placed the net value of the Church's real estate in 1746 at approximately 3 billion francs[5] which yielded about 85 million francs per year in revenue. Strictly ecclesiastical revenues—bishoprics, abbeys, tithes, monasteries—brought in 95 million. There was a total annual revenue of 180 million. The Church in France, it must be remembered, spent a goodly sum on the education of youth and charitable works.[6] Even so, a certain number of bishops and abbés spent enormous sums on self-indulgence and pageantry of a vainglorious kind.

The revenues paid to the Holy See per year by the churchmen of France were not negligible. At one moment in the papal State's history, the French quota was the single largest one in the universal Church. There are no exact figures, but reliable estimates place that quota somewhere between 10 and 20 million francs. By order of the Comité Ecclésiastique, which had been appointed by the National Assembly to implement the Civil Constitution of the Clergy, the Church in France was forbidden to contribute any revenues to the papacy.

Another blow was struck at the financial well-being of the papacy on June 29, 1790, when the Jacobins in Avignon and the Comtat Venaissin, papal territories in southern France, declared themselves absolved of allegiance to the papacy, and to be part of France. French troops were dispatched there in November. The rich revenues from these French properties was now sorely lacking.

A twenty-six-year-old Corsican, Napoleon Bonaparte, was given charge of the French army in October 1795, and instructed to defeat

France's enemies in Italy. "Consider the idea," his home superiors suggested, "of destroying Rome which is a scourge in the hands of fanaticism." Napoleon adopted the idea as an ambition. Reportedly, he said: "My name will live forever." His success was dazzling.

By May 21, 1796, Napoleon was victor in Milan. In quick succession, either by battle or the threat of battle, he took Ferrara, Bologna, Ancona, and the Romagna. "He is a man who breathes only blood and fire," was the report to Pius VI. Napoleon laid a tribute of 21,000,000 scudi on the papal State, to be paid in three installments over three months. In addition, 100 art objects and 500 manuscripts had to be given over to France. Napoleon sent a commission of French experts to Rome in order to do the choosing. The list was completed by mid-August. All art works of any value were confiscated and sent to France from Parma, Modena, Ferrara, and Verona. Milan's silver church ornaments, St. Mark's treasury in Venice, and ancient Bolognese manuscripts were likewise dispatched to Paris. Already, the wealth of the papal State was severely diminished.

Draconian measures were taken by the papacy. First, 700,000 scudi were extracted from the treasury of Sixtus V. (This sixteenth-century fund was kept for just such emergencies, and lasted about three hundred years.) The first installment of the 21,000,000 was thus paid. Then, by edict, everyone in the papal State, from cardinals to sharecroppers, had to send in a list of their valuables. If necessary, all would be taken in order to pay the final two installments.

But Napoleon wanted a signed armistice. Talks began that August. Discussion was derisory. Napoleon's agents handed the papal representatives a list of demands with these words: "Accept or reject."

Pius VI, after some waiting, rejected the armistice conditions. He suspended further payments of the tribute, and ordered unpacked the objects that had been chosen by the French experts and readied for transport to Paris. General mobilization was ordered. At the beginning of 1797, the papal army numbered 12,000. But by February, all resistance was judged futile. Papal emissaries signed the Peace of Tolentino on February 19.

The treaty had twenty-six articles. All chosen art objects and the manuscripts were to be delivered; money to be paid amounted to 46,000,000 scudi. Papal claims to Avignon and the Comtat Venaissin as well as to Bologna, Ferrara, and the Romagna were to be abandoned.

There was an additional list of demands. To pay the indemnity, everyone made sacrifices. Cardinal Doria-Pamfili gave 6,000,000 scudi of his own. The papal palaces and vestments were stripped of their pearls and diamonds. Subjects of the papal State surrendered their gold and silver valuables in return for paper money. Heavy taxes were laid upon the diocesan and religious clergy. Pius VI sold many valuable possessions of his own.

But Napoleon and the French government were bent on eviscerating the papacy. The accidental death of General Duphot on December 27 was seized as a provocation.[7] On January 11, 1798, general orders were given to the army to take Rome, expel the pope, and establish a Roman Republic. By February 10, the capitulation was signed. On February 15, French troops entered and occupied the city. The Roman Republic was declared to exist. The pope was deposed "forever" as temporal ruler and taken into protective custody, as the Vatican was occupied. On February 20, the eighty-year-old pontiff was placed in a horse-drawn carriage and left Rome, never to see it again. General Hallen, commandant in charge, removed the ring from the pope's hand at sword-point. By July 1799, the French had brought the pope to Grenoble. On July 14, he reached Valence, where he died the following month.

"The death of Pius VI," stated the Parisian newspaper *Courrier Universel* on September 8, 1799, "has, as it were, placed a seal on the glory of philosophy in modern times."

Meanwhile the depredation of the papal State, of Rome, and of the Vatican continued unabated. The policy of the French government was to turn Paris into the artistic capital of the world.

Every week large convoys of horse-drawn vehicles departed—in one day alone there were 500 vehicles—laden with sculptures, tapestries, paintings, gold and silver decorations, manuscripts, and ceramic treasures destined for Paris.[8]

All Rome's palaces, churches, and convents were stripped of gold, silver, and precious stones. The precious stones alone that were expedited to Paris in April were valued at 4,000,000 scudi.[9] The treasury in Castel Sant' Angelo, the funds of the Monte di Pietà, and the home treasuries of the cardinals and aristocrats amounted to 15,000,000 scudi in gold bars. By June all this booty was in Paris. And on July 15, a convoy of 1,000 horses was driven from Rome for the French army. There was systematic plundering of all Vatican offices, the proceeds being auctioned off. The possessions of the Holy Office, for instance, brought in 2,000,000 scudi.

By this time, the financial condition of Rome was at its nadir.

Food was scarce and expensive. There was little money, no commerce, and little hope of future betterment. The short-lived Roman Republic was on its last legs when the French troops left the city in the late autumn of 1799. Pius VI was dead. The papal State no longer existed. There were no funds in the papal treasury. Indeed, there was no treasury, nor any papal government. Pius VI's successor would come to Rome only in July 1800.

THE GREAT INJUSTICE

After the collapse of the Napoleonic Empire, the Congress of Vienna restored the original eighteen provinces of the papal territories. The papacy was now to have a short breathing spell before one final onslaught swept the papal State away for ever.

Financially, the papacy of Pope Pius VII (1800–23) was not in bad straits. The priceless booty taken from Rome by Napoleon was restored and indemnities were paid. Pius did renounce the valuable Church properties in France that Napoleon had expropriated and secularized, but what the pope received in return more than made up for these financial losses. The tendency of the French bishops to act independently of the pope was curbed. Pius VII had a more centralized church, and this meant that ecclesiastical revenues (taxation for Rome Curial services, for transmission of benefices, etc.) became more regular.

For the first five years after the Congress of Vienna (1815), the Camera Apostolica enjoyed an annual surplus after the budget was met. But the economy of the papal State went into a sharp decline in Pius VII's last two years. His successor, Leo XII (1823–29), reduced papal expenditures and thereby mitigated the rigors of papal taxation. But Leo, who had been elected by the majority vote of conservative Curial extremists (the *zelanti* as they were called), soon witnessed the papal State being infiltrated by new liberal ideas of nationalism and unification of the Italian peninsula into one nation.

Before his death in 1829, Leo XII promoted a very prominent and promising young cleric named Giovanni Maria Mastai-Ferretti to the post of archbishop of Spoleto, in the heart of the papal State.

There the young archbishop had to deal with nascent revolutionaries and the activities of the Carbonara, the famous Italian secret society that dealt in assassination and terrorism in order to promote Italian unification. The Carbonara—a strange mix of aristocrats, patriots, revolutionaries, and Mafiosi—would be the forefather of the Propaganda Due that was to bedevil Italy for the last thirty years of the twentieth century.

Leo's successor, Pius VIII, reigned only twenty months (1829–30) and was followed by Gregory XVI (1831–46). Revolts in the papal State had to be quelled by Austrian troops. The Joint Memorandum of May 21, 1831, from the Great Powers (England, Austria, Prussia, and Russia) recommended that the new pope introduce liberalizing reforms into the papal State so as to offset the growing tide of Italian nationalism. Both Gregory and the young archbishop, Mastai-Ferretti, thought that some concessions should be made to nationalism, but both realized they would probably signal the beginning of the end of the papal State. And, then, they asked themselves, on what would the papacy subsist? From where would it derive its needed revenues? Mastai-Ferretti later became archbishop of Imola, and he found there the same nationalist and revolutionary spirit that had greeted him in Spoleto.

Gregory XVI spent a great deal of treasury funds on missions to Africa and Asia. Indeed, he was the first pope to envision a native clergy and native bishops in those continents. In Europe, although disliking all forms of political liberalism, he did not hesitate to support the liberal stance of Catholics when this was necessary for gaining their civil rights and religious liberty.

When Gregory died in 1846, the papal State had undergone one of its worst years economically. The treasury was low in funds, and the papal Privy Purse was empty.

The Last Pope-King

With the election of Giovanni Maria Mastai-Ferretti as Pope Pius IX on June 16, 1846, the last phase of the 1500-year-old papal State began. The new pope, just 54 years of age, would be the last pontiff to be saluted as "the Pope-King" (*il Papa Re*). Already renowned as a "liberal," he was to sit on the throne of Peter for thirty-two years—longer than any one of his 257 predecessors—and preside over the total liquidation of the papal State and the temporal power of the papacy as a territorial sovereignty.

At this time, the total population of the papal State was 3,300,300 living in an area of 16,000 square miles. Its length ran for 635 kilometers from Terracina on the west Italian coast up to Ferrara in the northeast. Its breadth was 202 kilometers from the Maremma district in the west to the Esino coast on the Adriatic. This papal State was composed of four main territories: the Patrimony of St. Peter (still with the same borders as in the days of Gregory the Great around 600 A.D.); Umbria—the mid-Italian section; and two trans-Apennine Adriatic provinces, the Marches and the Romagna. The papacy owned small estates and some cities (Pontecorvo and Benevento) outside these territories.

The State was still divided administratively into eighteen provinces, each headed by a governor who was a cleric. Certain cities called the Legations were governed by bishops. All public positions in local government, savings banks, philanthropic organizations, and inter-province relations were filled by the upper classes and by clerics. Each province was further subdivided into communes.

It was in principle a theocratic state, its chief executive, legislative, and judicial offices being filled by clerics who administered strict Church laws concerning fasting, dress, church attendance, marriage, social contracts, and public profession of faith. The *prete politico*, the politician-cleric, was as familiar a figure as the congressman and senator of our day.

In spirit and in practice, the government of the papal State was feudal, and discontent with this old regime was so widespread— and the attitude of the Great Powers as expressed in the Joint Memorandum of 1831 so adamant—that the new pope set about liberalizing the papal regime throughout the State. Pius IX was not a convinced liberal, but he recognized the need for change if the papal State was to continue to exist. *"Tolerare per vivere"* (tolerate, in order to go on living) was an explicit principle of his and his Secretary of State, Cardinal Antonelli.

One month after his election, Pius declared amnesty for all political prisoners in papal jails. He reformed the procedures of papal criminal courts, ordered the gallows standing in all major cities and towns to be removed, and mitigated Church censorship rules of newspapers, pamphlets, and books.

He transformed the old State Council of Ministers, who all were ex officio clerics, into a regular cabinet staffed with heads of departments. Only the Secretary of State was to be a cleric. By 1848, there was a 24-man advisory council of elected deputies; but the

cardinals and the pope exercised full veto over its decisions. Elected
representatives were to govern the various municipalities and provinces. Pius IX made some slight adjustments in taxation, and modified the papal monopolies in salt and other basic commodities. But
all this merely opened the floodgates of popular revolution which
was already sweeping through the other Italian states. Insurrection
broke out in Milan on May 18, 1848. On May 22, Venice rebelled,
and the state of Piedmont declared war on Austria—which had
occupied both cities since 1815. On November 16, insurrection
took place in Rome. Pius IX fled for his life from Rome to Gaeta
(northwest of Naples); and, early the next year, the first Republic
of Rome was established. But Pius IX had protectors: France and
Austria brought military pressure to bear on the Roman Republic,
and by April of 1849, the Republic was dead, Rome was back in
papal hands, and a three-man commission (the "Red Triumvirate"
of three cardinals) took on the task of reorganizing Rome for the
pope's return.

The first part of this task was to remedy the financial confusion.
The short-lived Roman Republic had issued paper money in the
sum of 7 million scudi with an exchange rate of more than 20
percent. Pontifical bank notes amounting to 1.5 million scudi were
also in circulation. By order of the Red Triumvirate, 3.7 million
in Republican scudi notes were burned in public, as well as the
first bonds issued by the provincial Republican governors, totaling
82,215 scudi. An equal number of treasury bonds was deposited in
the Apostolic Camera's own safe. Another 3.3 million of the Republican scudi were left in circulation for some months but had to
be exchanged for new money by a certain date. Papal treasury bonds
and a new coinage of copper and silver were issued.

The paper money of the pontifical bank was recognized at par.
Some of it was replaced by treasury bonds. In compensation for a
bank loan of 300,000 scudi at 2½ percent to the government, the
bank was permitted to issue 400,000 gold and silver scudi annually.
Revenue certificates, each one for 50,000 scudi at 5 percent, and
payable at par in ten years, were issued.

Although they did not quite share the arrogant opinion of Cardinal Rivarola who remarked once that "laity in the papal State
should be only just tolerated by the generosity of clerics," the three
governing cardinals made sure that only clerics held positions of
public authority—the Ministers of War and of Police were both
priests—and that law and order was observed. "Any person found

wearing knives, daggers, stilettos, or any kind of lethal weapon, shall be instantly shot," was one public ordinance to the forces of order.

The Red Triumvirate resigned when Pius IX returned to Rome in April 1850. This time he was firmly convinced that even the smallest concession of his temporal power to popular demands could lead only to a total loss of his spiritual authority. It was not that the pope instituted a social and political tyranny; simply, he and his papal State blocked the road that led to the unification of the Italian peninsula into one sovereign nation since he could not envision how a pope could function if he lost his territory.

The monetary condition of the papal State was extremely precarious. The management of fiscal funds was antiquated and riddled with corruption. Four-fifths of all the territory belonging to the Vatican was tied up in mortmain. Most estates were run by agents who paid the owners a fixed quarterly sum. While papal rents and leases brought in a reasonable sum each year, papal taxations became merely reasons for one of the most flourishing contraband organizations in the whole of Europe; and black markets flourished in every major town and city, including Rome itself. Papal estates were tied up in trust deeds, and statutes of mortmain, which hindered any real development, encouraged absenteeism among the inalienable possessors, creating stagnant poverty among the rural peasant classes.

Almost immediately on the pope's return, a large discrepancy between receipts and projected outlays became evident. A new classification, divided into ten categories, was made of all taxpayers, individual and corporate. Special tax commissioners were appointed in each town and city, and they drew up lists of evaluated taxpayers. All in all, however, papal taxes were not oppressive. The normal rate of taxation between 1855 and 1870 was 1 scudo and 30 baiocchi[1] per every assessed 100 scudi of income and property. Wine, liquors, and all luxury goods had special taxes. Death duties were at 2 percent. But the economy of the papal State was largely undeveloped and mismanaged.

A feudal agriculture swung between plenty and scarcity. The main staples were wheat, barley, maize, cheese, wine, grapes, and vegetables. Periodic famines swept the provinces, due as much to government hoarding and contraband violence as to "accidents of nature and the hand of God."

Industries remained at a bare minimum. Silk at Perugia, Città di Castello, Senigallia, Jesi, Osimo, Terni. Cotton at Bologna.

Cloth manufacture at Bevagna, Cagli, Todi, Fossombrone. Paper at Subiaco, Guarcino, Fabriano. Sugar at Grottamare. Hemp rope at Cesena, Todi, Bologna, Ferrara. Oil, leather, copper, glass at Terni.

No attempt was made to develop a merchant marine, or to provide berthing and loading facilities along the two coastlines the papal State possessed. Fisheries were almost exclusively in the hands of privateers.

Export trade—which usually hovered around 6.6 million scudi in receipts and was severely diminished by the extensive contraband and smuggling organizations—was limited to small amounts of beef, hemp rope (this was much prized throughout Europe), silk, linen, art objects, sulphur, and wooden furniture. In 1857, the total number of export licenses for artworks issued by the Roman Ministry of Commerce reflects a value of a quarter of a million scudi. But it was a well known fact that at least five times that sum was earned by smugglers. Imports, some of which were heavily taxed, generally totalled about 8.2 million scudi annually; again, the import trade was the victim of the underground economy.

Poverty and want were so endemic that large sums were needed each year by the State to pay for welfare programs. Internal communication between the provinces was extremely difficult; roads were few—none at all in the mountainous central area. Although there were only two free ports, Ancona and Civitavecchia, commercial activity lucrative to the State in the other parts was at a minimum. The organized underground economy of contrabanders and smugglers, with the connivance of the local authorities everywhere, had perfected a system of covert warehousing and sale. It was a way of life among the inhabitants of the papal State. One papal inspector calculated the State's annual losses to be one and a half times the size of the State's annual income.

That income varied. In 1852, it was 10.5 million scudi. Public expenditures were 12.3 million scudi. The deficit was high. In 1859, income was nearly 14.7 million scudi, and there were expenditures of 14.5 million scudi. Surplus in any year was never much greater than that.

A flourishing system of savings banks had spread throughout the eighteen provinces. The banks raised capital by public subscription, paid no more than 4 percent interest, and had extremely limited liability. Exchange investments were common practice, as were mortgages. There was no technical control of these banks by the pontifical bank. The wealthy families of the papal State preferred to do all their banking abroad—in England and France, to a lesser degree in Switzerland and Germany.

The pontifical bank was reformed as of 1852. New capital was injected; and fresh managers, men of probity, were put in charge. But they lacked experience and anything like the profit-drive that had already made English and French banking enormously wealthy. Pontifical bankers couldn't compete even with the private banks in the papal State. They granted easy credit and unsecured loans. The losses were concealed by lower echelon officials in fictitious accounts and nonexistent inter-bank operations.

The pontifical bank was finally ruined by scandals. A severe scandal involving the embezzlement of 70,000 scudi and unauthorized loans of up to 1 million scudi shook Rome's Monte di Pietà in 1853, though it remained in vigor well into the 1870s and 1880s. In time, it made loans and outright gifts to the Apostolic Camera. Its name and some of its functions (as well as some of its evils) persist until our day.

The bare beginnings of modernization were introduced. Postage stamps came into use in 1851. The first telegraph system was inaugurated in 1854. Railways built by French and Spanish companies were much slower in being organized, as the general graft and corruption hindered the immediate success of public subscriptions.

The city of Rome itself was an egregious example of how not to organize a modern urban conglomerate. The census of 1857 gave the total population as a round 200,000. Of these, 110,000 contributed nothing to the economy; approximately 42,000 were children, and the rest were unemployed. The majority of Romans at this time lived on welfare of one kind or another. The papal government had charity commissaries that distributed food, clothing, and small sums of money in alms.

The city contained a quite abnormal amount of hospices, orphanages, shelters, refuges for the homeless and for reformed sinners, hospitals, and one-night lodging houses. Fully one-third of Rome's annual revenues (3.5 million scudi) was devoted to welfare. Parents of large families were exempt from taxation. Parochial charges for the services of the local priest were carefully graded according to one's place in Roman society. Princes (any of the aristocracy) were charged, say, 5.50 lire for a mass, prelates paid 2.75 lire, middle-class workers paid 1.50 lire, and all others were charged 50 cents.[2]

The working classes were organized on an inviolate patriarchal

rule. Sons succeeded fathers in their trade or occupation. The small
middle class gradually moved up the social ladder. The price of
food and rents was low, but the cost of maintaining the papal
government and papal court ate up revenues continually. The Apostolic Camera did engage the services of foreign bankers and brokers
to secure good investments, yet deficits were always creeping up on
the Camera's harried accountant-general. The availability of liquid
money was always a problem.

Sanitation in the city was effected only (and partially at that)
because of Rome's abundant water supply. Rome was reputedly one
of the dirtiest cities in Europe. A meager effort to distribute 131
trashcans throughout the city made no real improvement. At one
stage in the 1860s, over 28,000 scudi were spent on city lighting,
and sometime later an English company was paid handsomely to
install gas-lighting. But Roman streets continued to be badly lit until
well into the twentieth century.

In this disorganized and underdeveloped state of things, the monies at the disposal of the papacy were always limited. Between State
revenues from the provinces, the annual Peter's Pence collection
(never much greater than 10,000 scudi), taxation of Curial services
to the universal Church, legacies, bequests, and gifts, the equalized
annual income at the disposal of the Apostolic Camera was usually
slightly in excess of $3 million in modern terms. But annual ex-
penditures in those last twenty years of the temporal power of the
papacy ate up the greater portion of all that. The papal Privy Purse,
except at one very low moment, stayed at a normal $40–50,000.

The End of the Great Experiment

The leaders of the Italian unification movement marched inexorably
toward their ultimate goal of one country with its capital in Rome.
It was to use the phrase of Italy's most famed revolutionary leader,
Garibaldi, "Roma o morte!"—Rome or death. The papal State now
existed only because two European powers, France and Austria,
agreed to maintain its independence. The Austrians could guarantee
the northern provinces of the papal State beyond the Apennines;
France could guarantee Rome and its patrimony. When these two
guarantors fell out, as they did in 1859, the papal State was doomed.

In June 1859, rebellion flared in fifteen provinces of the papal
State. By 1860, papal rule no longer extended there. A papal army
which included the famous international brigade of *zouaves* fought

the last battle in papal history at Castelfidaro in September of 1860. The papal army was destroyed.

Meanwhile plebiscites held in the lost fifteen provinces yielded an overwhelming majority in favor of unification. Pius IX responded with a papal decree of excommunication against all persons in Italy or outside of Italy who had fomented, encouraged, taken part in, or accepted the results of the plebiscites. When Count Cavour, the chief architect of Italian unification plans, lay dying on June 6, 1861, and a good priest tended his last moments, granting him absolution from the excommunication, Pius was furious and excoriated the priest personally. "I helped a Christian to die," was the priest's answer. *"Qui tetigit papam, morietur,"* was Pius's answer. Whoever lays a hand on the pope will die. It was, once again, the use of spiritual weapons for temporal purposes. Without the papal State, Pius maintained, he could not govern the Church.

To his credit, Pius realized that, then as now, the real battle was for men's minds. Already the revolutionary ideas of France and the U.S. were sweeping Europe. A statute passed in 1867 by the American Congress prohibited expenditure of any funds for U.S. diplomatic relations with the Vatican. The U.S. representative in Rome packed his belongings and left. He was soon followed by other diplomatic missions. Everyone smelled the approaching death of the papal State.

The ideal of the new capitalist democracy was total separation of Church and State—something Pius IX and his successors necessarily rejected on doctrinal grounds. Karl Marx and Friedrich Engels published their *Communist Manifesto* in 1848, "the year of revolutions" in old Europe. Pius IX stood for the old Catholic idea of the "confessional" state, in which Catholicism would be acknowledged and honored in public as well as in private: no liberalization in politics, total freedom for the Church within the framework of a monarchy. Unfortunately it was too late for Pius IX. He could not dissociate the statal independence of the Church from the exercise of his papal mission. Hence his irredentist stand against Italian nationalism, and his military resistance to forceful annexation.

No amount of papal resentment or use of ecclesiastical censures could make up for the Vatican's financial losses. With the loss of the fifteen provinces, the total revenue entering the Camera Apostolica as of 1859 was $4,600,000. What straddled the Camera between impossible alternatives was the Statal debt of $3.9 million contracted by the Camera some years previously on behalf of all eighteen provinces. Those provinces by right should have been paying off $2.8 million of the debt plus interest. Appeals to Catholics in Belgium, England, and Spain did start a flow of contributions which never stopped during Pius IX's life, and long-term loans were negotiated with foreign banks, the last large one for $200,000 from the House of Rothschild in July 1870. But the financial losses to the treasury and to the papal Privy Purse were never repaired.

The pope was now sovereign only of "the Patrimony of St. Peter," the Roman province, that triangular-shaped territory that had been the papacy's first territory in 320 A.D. And Pius held that small patch only because of the French troops that defended him.

On August 19, 1870, the protecting French troops withdrew definitively. With the battle of Sedan on September 2, the empire of Napoleon III came to an end. The papacy had lost its last defender, and France, the "eldest daughter of the Church," was to have an astounding 99 governments between 1871 and 1940. Immediately the Italian nationalist troops marched on Rome. They encamped around the old Leonine walls of Rome on September 19. The following day, after some three hours of artillery barrage and sporadic hand-to-hand fighting, the pope ordered the white flag to be raised above the dome of St. Peter's at 9:30 A.M. Ten minutes later, all firing had ceased. The Italian troops entered the city and took possession of it all, leaving Vatican Hill untouched. The papal State had ceased to exist. Its 16,000 square miles were now reduced to the 480,000 square meters on and around Vatican Hill where St. Peter's, its adjoining buildings, and the Vatican gardens were clustered. The next day, September 21, Pius IX wrote a short note to his nephew:

Dear Nephew:
All is over. Without liberty, it is impossible to govern the Church. Pray for me, all of you. I bless you.

Pius P. IX

This was a faithful echo of the ancient voice of Rome's papal rulers who from the beginning had tied the performance of their spiritual mission to a framework of temporal power. The pope declared himself a prisoner in the Vatican, and refused to leave Vatican Hill even for a short absence. All his successors until 1922 followed suit, none of them even appearing on the front balcony of St. Peter's to give the papal blessing of a new pontiff. The confinement of the popes and their sovereign access to that hill in Rome—"the Roman Question"—was to fester in Italian national life until a later date in the twentieth century when a viable solution to the problem was found by other men with minds freed from the ancient persuasion about the pope-king's requirements.

The force of Italian unification, under the leadership of the House of Piedmont, attempted to present Pius IX with a list of acceptable compromises. He could be the head of a confederation of Italian states. Or he could be given ironclad guarantees by law as to territory and access to the outer world. There would be generous financial recompense for the loss of the papal State. An international committee would assign a quota of contributions to the Catholic powers so that the papacy could be amply subsidized. A Law of Guarantees passed by the Italian parliament on May 13, 1871 declared the pope's sovereignty to exist still.[3] His person and his office were deemed inviolate, and he was to receive the same honor and privileges as royalty. He was to receive monetary compensation for his loss of revenue—3,250,000 lire annually;[4] this was the amount set aside in the budget of the papal's State's last year for the support of the papal court and the maintenance of the papal diplomatic corps. The papacy would have Vatican Hill and certain territories in and outside Rome, even a nominal stretch of Roman territory as far as the west coast of Italy. The pope would be entitled to conduct Vatican diplomacy and sovereign affairs. Italy and the Vatican were to be separate states, the Vatican to have its own diplomatic corps and accept the accredited representatives of other countries.

Pius IX rejected all this. Rightly, he distrusted mere legal guarantees, and he had no faith in either the good intentions or the continued existence of the Catholic powers. On these two points, later history bore out his sound judgment.

With the abolition of the papal State in September 1870, the management structure of papal finances was thrown into a period of confusion. All statal offices—army, police, judiciary, municipal councils, provincial governments, customs and excise, agricultural councils, mining companies, railway and postal services, the pontifical bank and its various branches—immediately lost their purpose, and most of them simply ceased to exist forever.

The fiscal and monetary situation was stable for some years. Pius IX was a careful administrator, and the treasury was by no means empty. Indeed, its estimated contents at the fall of Rome in 1870 were in the neighborhood of $1.5 to $2 million (reckoned in 1983 dollars). Some wise investments had been made abroad on behalf of the Holy See, amounting to some $2 million. There was solvency, therefore, for immediate expenses and for the near future.

But the outlook was bleak. All revenues of any kind from the provinces ceased. The government of Italy made no overt or covert attempt to interfere with communications between the papal institution on Vatican Hill and the outside world. Some monies owing and others on deposit in provincial banks made their way to the Apostolic Camera. They were quite paltry. The main sources of revenue now were those arriving from abroad: the normal tariffs and prices charged by the Vatican bureaucracy for ecclesiastical services; land taxes on certain properties at Assisi, Padua, and Loreto that had remained in Vatican hands (these were of an annual value of 40,000 scudi); the customary donations on acceptance of benefices; legacies, gifts, and bequests; special collections as well as Peter's Pence (which still remained at its usual low figure of 6 million French francs). The demands of the annual budget were reduced to less than one-twelfth of the original State budget (approximately $1.3 million). The now reduced papacy had a roster of old employees who had flocked to Rome when the papal State had ceased to exist. All had to be pensioned. But for the remaining years of Pius IX's life, quite substantial sums were contributed yearly on a voluntary basis by Catholics outside Italy. The 1870 loan from the House of Rothschild was paid off, and annual income was sustained at the level of $70–100,000.

As we have seen already, the Apostolic Camera functioned in that last century both as finance ministry and principal justice tribunal. Overnight, the second of these two functions practically ceased: There were no more civil cases, for there were no more citizens of the papal State. The first function, the collection of revenues, ceased altogether. The all-powerful Camerlengo and the Camera were now overshadowed by the Secretary of State. A long period of bureaucratic infighting was about to start.

Pius died peacefully on February 7, 1878, at the age of 86, murmuring a favorite phrase of his from the Psalms: "*In domum Domini ibimus.*" We will go into the House of the Lord. The longest reigning pope in history, he had kept hammering away to the end at what came to be known in Catholic circles as "the Great Injustice." The earthly home of Christ's vicar had been forcibly and unjustly wrested from papal hands. In his view, it was a calamity that smacked of Apocalypse.

Pope Leo XIII, who succeeded Pius IX, decided on certain fiscal management measures. He placed what remained of "the patrimony of St. Peter" under the direct control of his Secretary of State, Cardinal Nina. Under Nina's personal administration, the payroll of Vatican employees was provided, and the upkeep of Vatican buildings was maintained. The Secretariat of State now superseded the Apostolic Camera. There was some bitter bureaucratic infighting between the Cameral officials and the Secretariat. The Camerlengo, head of the Apostolic Camera, and his associates were not happy with this arrangement. For the Camera was now, in practice, reduced to a tribunal for the trial of (mainly) canonical cases.

In order to begin to solve the impasse, Leo decided to create a consultative commission of three cardinals to aid Nina, granting them also the all-important function of governing the Church after the death of a pope and before the election of a new one. But this did not placate the Cameral group. The infighting continued.

The minimum sum now required to meet a pared-down annual budget was in the region of $1.6 million. If the Holy See of Leo XIII did nothing but live on its actual income, it would have been forced to neglect many of its customary, strictly religious activities, since that income did not exceed $110,000 yearly. But it was supplemented continuously by donations from pilgrims to Rome; by a certain portion of the monies contributed by pilgrims to the shrine of the Immaculate Mother at Lourdes, a portion voluntarily assigned to the papacy; by a steady stream of legacies; and by an increased sale of relics and mementos of the popes and saints in Rome itself. Now and again, the Apostolic Camera laid a special assessment on each Catholic diocese in the world, when funds sank too low.

In the meanwhile, some more aid in matters financial was coming to the papacy from the outside world.

When the papal State ceased to exist and its territories were incorporated in Italy, this happened with the consent of the overwhelming majority of Italians as well as a majority of papal State inhabitants. The mismanagement of statal affairs, the stagnation of the papal economy, the force of nascent Italian nationalism, and the violent anticlericalism of the intellectuals created an irresistible national will in favor of incorporation.

However, the strongest opposition to the merger of the papal State with Italy came from a group of aristocratic families who had always been attached to the Holy See. Some were against the absorption of the papal State for selfish reasons: They valued the old semifeudal conditions—mortmain, absenteeism, the ecclesiastical power of the papal State to back their privileges. Some opposed the absorption because they read the handwriting on the wall: The Italian revolution, the *risorgimento*, was one more manifestation of a new tendency throughout Europe which threatened the entire triple social structure of aristocracy, bourgeoisie, and proletariat. Some sided on religious grounds with the papacy in its refusal to accept the new regime: The vicar of Christ on Earth should be a sovereign, independent ruler enjoying complete immunity and honor within the traditional "Lands of St. Peter."

Whatever their motives or mixture of motives might have been, there was a definite ground swell of resentment against the new regime among the aristocracy. Because they supported clerical rule— that is to say, rule by those men who wore black cassocks—these aristocratic supporters of the papacy came to be called "the Black Nobility" (*i neri*), a name they gloried in. They were the inheritors of the Guelph tradition and their ideas were the same as the "Blacks" of Dante's time in fourteenth-century Florence and Pisa. Old patrician families like the Borghese, Torlonia, Patrizzi, Massimo, Sermoneta, Aldobrandini, Rospigliosi, Colonna, Salviati, Campara, Canino, Lancellotti rallied around the papacy, inveighed against "the Great Injustice," and set out to solve the basic problem now confronting the head of the Catholic Church.

That problem was independence and freedom of action for the pope and the Holy See. In the end, both independence and freedom to act were reduced to one need: income. To be and act as a sovereign ruler, the pope should not depend on any earthly power for financial viability. In Italy, the problem seemed much more acute than elsewhere in Europe and the Americas. The moment the Italian State was formed in 1870, all the major banks in the country were allied with that state. They were "secular" banks.

More often than not—and certainly when it was a question of the principal banks in Rome, Venice, Milan, Turin, Naples, or Genoa—the management was Masonic, its members active and prominent in the Italian branch of the Lodge of the Grand Orient. Between the Lodge and the papacy there was an undying hatred. By 1723, the Constitutions of the Grand Lodge were published in London. English Masonry spread quickly to the Continent. In April 1738, membership in the Lodge had been forbidden by Clement

XII to Catholics under the direst penalties—excommunication, refusal of burial in Catholic cemeteries, nullification of marriage. Clement had had good reason. From its starting years in the sixteenth century, the Lodge had required of its members "princypally to love God and holy churche and alle halowis," to be "trewe men to God and holy Churche and . . . vse no Errour nor heresye . . ." By 1738, the Rev. James Anderson in the second edition of his *Book of Constitutions* (a history of Masonry's founding) stated that "a Mason is oblig'd, by his Tenure, to obey the Moral Law . . . 'tis now thought more expedient only to oblige them [Masons] to that Religion in which all men agree . . . that is, to be good Men and true, or Men of Honour and Honesty . . ." The Protestant Reformation had happened.

By the middle of the eighteenth century, French, Spanish, Belgian, German, Dutch, Portuguese, and Italian lodges were openly and covertly hostile to Catholicism, maintaining that, instead of the revealed religion Rome preached, all men should be deists, and all human activity—commerce, learning, education, science, politics—should be purified of any ecclesiastical, clerical, or religious traits. Deism, in effect, denied the existence of any supernatural dimension. Masons were actively prominent in suppressing Church influence in academia, in political life, and in economic participation. In fact, Masonry became synonymous with anti-clericalism. There was—and still is—no way traditional Catholicism could be reconciled with this type of Freemasonry.

It is very difficult for many in England and America to understand the extreme hatred and hostility that reigned between the Catholic Church in Europe of the eighteenth to the twentieth century and the various lodges. In Italy, the hated *bagarozzi* became the targets of extended opposition. Now that the chief of the *bagarozzi* was relegated to his Vatican Hill, why not proceed to throttle the entire Church, beginning with its head? And it did seem a feasible proposition: The prestigious *Times of London* intoned majestically in one of its autumn editorials of 1870 that finally this ancient institution had passed away, after so long and so glorious a duration. The Church's enemies firmly believed that the papacy's lease on life had been foreclosed.

The "Black Nobility," with their allies in the Italian bourgeoisie, set out to remedy the Italian banking situation of the Church and the papacy. The strategy here was to compete: to found a series of "Catholic" banks in opposition to the "secular" banks, but to do so without violating the principles of Catholic business ethics. As the executive manager of one of the new "Catholic" banks wrote, they hoped "to demonstrate how . . . one can exercise the function of providing credit without offending the great ethical principles of Christian teaching . . ."[5] The Church and the papacy needed that credit, to meet the payroll and upkeep expenses of St. Peter's and the Vatican complex of buildings; to finance its diplomatic corps; to build or repair its schools, orphanages, convents, and universities; to keep Catholic presses rolling and Catholic literature in print. Funds kept coming in, but long-term loans at easy rates were essential. The much reduced budget for the Vatican was running to an annual average of $1.5 to $2 million. Liquid assets were limited and diminishing.

The "Catholic" banks project was a definite, if not a resounding, success. Between 1870 and 1885, a series of urban and rural "Catholic" banks were opened and flourished. One of those urban banks has had an interesting history. It was the Banco di Roma, founded in 1880, in order principally to buy up real estate in and around Rome. Several of the "Black Nobility" families contributed capital in specie to start the Banco di Roma. One of its acquisitions, two years after its foundation, was the English company which had been brought in by Pius IX to oversee the water supply of Rome. The water company became the Società dell'Acqua Pia Antica Marcia. In the 1930s, the Vatican itself bought out the company.[6] The Banco di Roma, in 1885, also acquired major equity in the company that ran Rome's transport system.[7]

But, in spite of their successes, within Italy itself the "Catholic" banks were agonizing in their movements because of the stranglehold the "secular" banks exercised. These had the supreme advantage of their alliance with the Italian State. Abroad it was a different story. In spite of the anti-clericalism and anti-papalism rampant in commercial circles, the papacy had toeholds that were invaluable. There still were strong layers of support for Church and papacy among the moneyed middle classes. The remnants of the old European aristocracy in France, and the imperial houses of Britain, Austria, Spain, Portugal, Russia, and Germany, had an attachment to the papacy: They foresaw their own downfall in the papacy's loss of temporal power. At the Congress of Vienna in 1815, when the victors against Napoleon gathered to rearrange Europe, it was the Protestant king of England, the Protestant emperor of Germany, and the Orthodox emperor of Russia who insisted on restoring the papal State to its pre-Napoleonic extent and privileges. The papacy was regarded as part and parcel of a European sociopolitical regime that all wished to restore and preserve.

Through all the bitterness of eighteenth- and nineteenth-century Catholic–Protestant struggles and mutual hate, papal Rome and the Vatican had been open ground for princes and kings. "Here, in Rome of the Popes," wrote one English Protestant observer in the 1860s, "a man is free to be what he likes. No sectarian prejudice, Catholic or Protestant, prevents him from participating in the full life and glorious events of papal Rome." It was always possible for papal representatives to obtain favorable loan terms for the papacy's needs, as it was quite feasible for them to aid Italy's "Catholic" banks in their foreign and overseas operations.

Over the space of those first fifteen years after the disappearance of the papal State, the tussle between "secular" and "Catholic" banks resulted in a much saner and, from the business point of view, much more profitable attitude. Simply put: Both sides found that it was mutually advantageous to avoid the extremes of hate and opposition. That, in sum, was bad business. The anticlericalism did not wane, however, much less disappear. The canonical strictures of the Catholic Church against Masonry remained in force.

But compromise at the more rarefied levels of fiscal and monetary matters was achieved. Besides, Masonry had made some adaptations. In order to facilitate the Lodge's access to the ministerial level of government as well as to the royal house of Piedmont which now gave Italy its kings and princes, the Italian Lodge created an in-between organization to which Italians could belong but which would not imply formal, full membership in the Lodge proper.[8] The king, the prime minister, and the ministers without portfolio could thus be *all'orecchio*, "within earshot," of any vital information to be received or to be passed on between the sectors of government and private business. It was always a presumption that certain prelates from the Vatican were detailed off to be members of this intermediate organization.

In view of the relaxation in enmity between "Catholic" and "secular" banks, Pope Leo XIII created an entirely new organism within his Vatican finance ministry. In 1887 he formally established an office called the Administration for the Agencies of Religion[9] which had its own juridical status and reported directly to the pontiff. Some such office was needed with sufficient independence from the old Camera Apostolica, set in its ways and now a pawn in the

inter-bureaucratic struggle of Curial members. For the monies administered and distributed by the AAR came from the expansion of
Vatican investments in the European economies (to very little extent
in the U.S.).

Leo finalized the structure of his finance ministry more definitively in 1891, when he detached the Camera Apostolica from all
control of the Secretariat of State, putting the Cameral Camerlengo
in full charge of ordinary revenues and upkeep of property, and—
an important step—leaving the newly formed AAR independent of
the Camerlengo. The Secretary of State would not, with few exceptions, occupy the very powerful position of Camerlengo. The
Pope's Privy Purse was held by the Datary.

Leo also confirmed the already age-old function of the Camerlengo and his Cameral College of Cardinals, clerics, and lay advisors
to govern the Vatican and the Church during that critical gap in
the papacy called *Sede Vacante*[10] after the death of a pope and
before the election of his successor. The Camerlengo, aided by his
Cameral colleagues, would be in charge at that time. They would
control the finances of the Vatican; and, of much more weighty
import, the Camerlengo would be in charge of the entire pre-
conclave and conclave proceedings by which a new pope is elected.

There is usually no possible doubt as to the strict legality of those
election proceedings, nor about the freedom of the cardinal-electors.
There the Camerlengo should not—would not—interfere. But, in
scores of ways, an intelligent and clever and determined Camerlengo
could influence mightily those conclave votes. For the cardinal-
electors vote, not on the strength of personalities—except as adjunct
and secondary issues—but on matters of policy. And, in the pre-
conclave proceedings, it is up to the Camerlengo to assemble an
impostazione for the electors, an analysis and projection of Church
conditions and needs in the world. Conclave discussions center
around this *impostazione*. In recent times, the only divergences
from discussion of the Camerlengo's *impostazione* arose when the
old Curial abuse had crept in: the Secretary of State—in this case,
Cardinal Jean Villot, Secretary of State for Pope Paul VI[11]—had
secured for himself the post of Camerlengo while retaining leadership of the Secretariat. But, on the death of Pope Paul VI, Villot's
subtle efforts to direct conclave proceedings so as to incline cardinalitial electoral votes toward the liberal candidate of his own choosing (a Latin American cardinal) ran up against stiff opposition. Out
of that conclave in August 1978 came the thirty-four-day reign of

the conservative Pope John Paul I. After the latter's sudden death, Villot was Camerlengo for the conclave of October 1978 at which once again his ideas were foiled, and Karol Wojtyla of Poland was elected John Paul II. Those who opened the locked and sealed doors of both conclaves and saw Camerlengo Villot emerge will never forget the look of frustration, anger, and impatient defeat that he displayed. Villot died suddenly a couple of months after that October conclave.

THE DECENT
COMPROMISE

The contrast is great between the financial condition, outlook and practice of the papacy during the last years of Pius IX and the reigns of all the popes until the outbreak of World War I. The outlook and practice of the Holy See was one of temporizing. No pope and no Curial official ever acquiesced in the loss of the papal State, although no one seemed to have a practical solution to this calamity. At the moment that the State had been wrested from the grasp of the papacy, its sociopolitical structure was a modified feudalism, and that determined its financial condition, outlook, and practice.

But the Europe of which that State had been a part was in the middle of a fully developing classical capitalism. Africa and Asia had been carved out into spheres of influence for the European empires—British, French, Spanish, Portuguese, Belgian, German, Dutch, and, a little later than the others, Italian.

The capitalism of these European empires and the other countries associated with them was built on the principles of free trade, home industrialization, balanced budgets, private ownership of resources and assets, the gold standard (which provided a needed two-way market for gold in the currencies of countries engaged in import-export relations), a minimum of government intervention in the individual's efforts—either to limit those efforts or to supplement their wants. The fundamental element of that capitalism, however, was ownership of resources and, more particularly, of the means of production. In fact, this was a sacred tenet of that capitalism. It had come from the old Catholic ethical teaching about *jus proprium*[1] that English philosopher John Locke had translated into "the right of a man to the labor of his body and the work of his hands." Material things became a man's property when he "mixed his labor with it."

Those empires of Europe and their capitalism dominated all international trade. Europe, with Britain in the lead, became the banker for the world—including the papacy.[2]

The papacy never took part in that flowering of capitalism, yet it benefited from capitalism's successes because of the contributions that flowed into its treasury from countries where capitalism flourished. It was able to entrust its savings for investment in capitalism's enterprises by European and American banks. But it was never an active member of the international commercial and financial markets.

Doubtless the reputation the Catholic Church had for a long time into the twentieth century as a reliable supporter of capitalism and the status quo of privileged social classes was due as much to its own long semifeudal tradition in the papal State as to its dependence on capitalism's achievements for its economic life-blood. Yet, the other side of this coin was that only a pope, Leo XIII, could issue a solemn warning to the capitalist states of his day, telling them that workers had rights that could not be violated with impunity. Lenin, the leader of the Soviet Revolution of 1917, was to steal phrases from that well-known encyclical letter of Leo's, *Rerum novarum* (1891), in which the pope clearly indicated the basic shift in world economy and societal classes.

In the second third of the nineteenth century, the papal State was passing through a period of stagnation. Once that State was lost, the papacy no longer had the physical means of participating in capitalism's high success. In any case, the ethical principles governing the papacy's economic policy had not evolved sufficiently to allow it to participate even if it had retained the papal State through the nineteenth and into the twentieth century. But it did lose its territory, and from 1870 onward the papacy was to coast along on the periphery of European capitalism but never be a working part of it, until once again at the end of World War II and under the impetus of its money-managers it attempted to regain a position of power. Dictator Mussolini and Pope Pius XI arrived at the "Decent Compromise" of 1929. The era of the managers began. The disasters and calamities of the sixties and seventies followed.

PART FIVE
RESTRUCTURING

CONCLUSIONS AS
GUIDELINES

With this history in mind, and in view of the twentieth-century scandals, there do seem to be good reasons why in the early eighties some began talking about the need to restructure Vatican financial agencies, and still others went as far as proposing total divestiture of all Vatican funds, maintaining that the Church should not have as one of its major instruments a portfolio and a banking status that would do credit to a multinational conglomerate equaling or even excelling Exxon, Mobil, and ITT.

Total divestiture is not a practicable matter today given the shifting sands of modern civilization and the caliber of Catholic prelacy. Total divestiture would only work under a great leader capable of lifting the weak and the corrupt, as well as the good and the saintly, onto paths of shining light that would dazzle all humanity by its purity as it met the profound expectations of the world. Christ has not blessed his beloved Church with such prelates.

The only alternative is a restructuring of the Church's system of financial administration to meet its present transitory exigencies.

Several significant conclusions follow immediately from the historical overview of papal financial history; and these are reinforced by an examination of the most recent forms into which the various financial agencies of the Church have been cast.

Fullness of Power

The basic idea giving shape and character to past and present financial structures of Vatican and Church is one born explicitly from that centuries-old effort, the Great Experiment. This, in essence, was an attempt to achieve sole, full, and continuous exercise of what was technically known as the fullness of power. *Plenitudo potestatis*. Fullest power. This fullness of power meant the pope was given absolute and undisputed moral authority, religious jurisdiction, and spiritual preeminence. It also implied the pope should have the undisputed right to judge the morality and religious value of any human action in any sphere of human activity, and possess coercive power to enforce that right. Authority, jurisdiction, preeminence, and judicial right imply here an obligation on the part of all concerned to listen and to follow the decisions made by the pope.

It is irrelevant that time and bitter experience have shown the present configuration of nations in the world community in no way permits any Catholic pontiff to exercise such a fullness of power. And this not because the nations reject the idea of either moral authority or, for that matter, the proposal of a predominant temporal power endowed with supreme authority, jurisdiction, judicial right, and coercive ability: The nations simply cannot agree who should be so endowed.

Moral authority today, according to international practice, belongs to whoever garners the most votes. The underlying morality is certainly not Christian. But it does claim to be a morality, an ethic of the nations. Physical power and coercive power are never granted freely to anyone by the nations. "Nobody gives you power," Soviet Foreign Minister Andrei Gromyko once said. "Power is something you take." Coercion at present is distributed rather equally among the two superpowers and their allies. Hence the stalemate of the United Nations.

What is relevant to our context is the coercive mechanism adopted by the Church and papacy in past history in order to enforce the acceptance of papal fullness of power.

Doubtless, part of that mechanism was composed of spiritual and ecclesiastical measures: doctrines about holiness and sinfulness, excommunication, censure, interdict, penances, and the like. But another and much used part of the coercive mechanism derived from temporal power: physical force, social ostracism, political domination, and financial weight. The sword or baptism: At times, whole populations were given this stark choice.

Sometimes, the papacy itself was strong enough to wield this physical mechanism of coercion. Most often, it depended on a secular right arm to do the job. The moral coercion of the papacy and Church on the secular power to do its bidding was so strong, so direct, so explicit, that ultimate responsibility for that coercive exercise by the secular arm must rest on that Church and papacy.

In this way, there arose the idea of the temporal sovereignty of the pope and, with it, the consequence that the papacy should necessarily enjoy economic independence and preponderance. Financial resources are at the very heart of that independence and preponderance.

It can be—perhaps should be—conceded that once upon a time there were solid reasons in the logic of history for adopting the proposal of papal temporal power. History would judge popes and papacy deficient if they had not stepped in and filled the dangerous void left by the fall of the Roman Empire. Billions of human beings were the beneficiaries of the ensuing Great Experiment, and western civilization was made uniquely possible by it.

But it is not overstepping the lessons of history to assert that the proposal of papal temporal power in its classical sense is, by now, a tainted one. So, also, must the economic independence and preponderance issuing in vast financial resources be judged and considered a tainted idea, for that was historically part and parcel of the now discredited papal temporal power.

Utopias

The other extreme is also unacceptable. To demand absolute poverty of the Church is misguided because it is totally impracticable for the Catholic Church as a whole or the papacy in particular. For the Church as an organization to undertake the practice of what has been called "evangelical poverty" or "Christlike poverty" or any such ideal would mean the end of the hierarchical Church. The latent but vicious heresy beneath the outcries of many who have preached such doctrine is double: They implicitly deny the need for an organized Church in their proposals; and they fall into the very ancient error of Manichaeism, the doctrine that saw material things—money, comfort, and plenty—as inherently evil.

One of the greatest men to write about this problem of the Church and its wealth was Dante. In *De Monarchia*, Dante proclaimed that political power was not derived from the pope or any other single man. It belonged, he said, to the people. And, through the people, it came to the ruler. God himself made the people the channel of political power which, in any case, was God's gift to the people.

As a Florentine, Dante naturally feared that the Rome-based papacy and the Church would usurp the power of the people. Resolutely opposed to the temporal power of the papacy, he could not separate religion from the reality of daily living, individual and societal. He did not want popes governing the daily life of Florentine citizens or indeed the citizens of any place.

Dante's visionary dream of universal peace and harmony is a dream all Christian believers share. His vision shimmers as their unconsciously entertained but truly desired goal. For many people in our day, just as for many in his far-off fourteenth century, Dante's idea exercises a strangely wistful attraction as the ultimate stage in the onward progress of the world community of men and women. The golden age of a universal republic. All the nations like so many closely knit families enjoying harmony and unthreatened peace. Politically, the reign of an all-ruling, all-just, utterly non-partisan management tied to no one country, colored by no one nationalism. Morally and religiously, a universal acceptance of a loving father, head of the Church, elected by the free votes of all. Dante's vision was of such a utopia.

For, in the final analysis, it was the people of the earth that mattered in the poet's mind. The earthly life and destiny of that people was in itself a revelation of divinity for Dante; and its rights were as sacred as those of Christ's Church. He has painted in words a ravishing picture of that humanity as a golden bird floating ecstatically in the air above the flowered meadows of paradise. Never before and certainly never afterward was humanity's fate so apotheosized.

In comparison with the lambent gentleness and godly peace of that vision, the pithy dreams of the early American settlers—the Beulah Land, the Beacon on a High Hill—seem but harsh symphonies celebrating fanatic sectarianism. And the attempted lyricism of Marxists who hail the glories awaiting humanity in "the stateless paradise of the workers" sounds like a song in honor of a dry skeleton. The fanatic bibliolatry of the Puritan and the specialized hate of the Marxist—both are sadly lacking in the all-precious element that Dante enshrined at the center of his vision.

The Florentine knew what Pope John XXIII in the twentieth century knew: Human beings can never be made peaceful and virtuous, individually or collectively, by the use of power, but only through the experience of love. The heretics and rebels twisted with pain in the dungeons of the fourteenth-century Inquisition held onto that love as their only hope. The old Catholics on their way to be hanged, drawn, and quartered at Tyburn by that most bloody of English sovereigns, Elizabeth I, as well as the hundreds of others tortured on the rack of Protestant England's Star Chamber or peering through the flames and smoke of their faggot-pyres throughout England and Germany could recognize Dante's ideal of civic love and political comity as their own. In the end, Dante—with his flaming hope that love was stronger than hate and could make all things new—was the father of them all.

In critiquing the various theories about the temporal stance and condition of the papacy, it is a rule that the ideal presented must be attainable without the destruction of Catholicism in its essence. Therefore, those who propose extreme and complete poverty for the Catholic Church are issuing a bland invitation to commit suicide.

One is forced to conclude that the attainable ideal in this whole matter was not presented either by the traditional Roman formula— the pope as temporal ruler endowed with the fullness of power— or by the proposal of absolute poverty and renunciation of any economic independence. Dante's vision remains just that—a vision of utopia.

The Compromise

The ideal that fashioned the compromise of 1929 and gave birth to the State of Vatican City as we know it today would seem at first to be quite attainable and a practical solution that could endure for a long time, satisfying the basic exigencies of the papacy. The pope now has his own independent territory, and its integrity as well as his access to the outer world are guaranteed by national treaty and international concordats.

Even during the 1940s when two major armies and half a dozen armed groups were fighting for supremacy in and around the State of Vatican City, its neutrality and integrity remained intact. What violations there were served only to emphasize the inviolability of the pope's tiny State. Only the Allies dropped bombs on Rome— and they apologized later. Their actions, for which they have never been called to account, constituted a gross betrayal of their pledge to Pope Pius XII and merely served the needs of an arrogant victor bent on the viciousness of psychological warfare. President Roosevelt and Prime Minister Churchill both "cleared" that betrayal, and they were the guilty ones.

In sum, no one can accuse the ruler of the minuscule Vatican State of being a territory-grabber or the autocratic ruler of a population chafing for democratic liberties. As with many other historical compromises which originally were accepted as temporary solutions, this compromise has produced what many see as a permanent condition. For very few people today can even imagine the circumstances under which the pope would be obliged, or would voluntarily decide, to renounce the territorial independence of the State of Vatican City.

There is, however, one set of conditions under which the State might be voluntarily liquidated; but, at present, such conditions belong to a far distant future. A consideration of those conditions concerns the deepest ecclesiastical question that the Catholic Church has yet to confront realistically: the unity of all those baptized within the spiritual and institutional embrace of Catholicism.

The Church claims to be the one and only Catholic Church, to have no sister church and no branches but heretical and schismatic portions (Anglicans, Greek and Russian Orthodox) and splintering offshoots (mainline and fundamentalist Protestant churches). Probably, the blame for those fractures is to be equally distributed between Catholic and (now) non-Catholic Christians of some hundreds of years ago.

The element that most repels the most desirable breakaway portions (Greek and Russian Orthodox) is what these "Eastern Christians" call "the imperialism of the Roman bishop." To the Orthodox mind, one prime factor in that "imperialism" is the temporal sovereignty of the pope (as much as his claims to ecclesiastical primacy and doctrinal infallibility). And this, although there is hardly an aware churchman in the Greek and Russian Orthodox churches who does not now wish that both Greek Patriarch Demetrios and Russian Patriarch Pimen enjoyed the territorial integrity of that same "Roman bishop," the pope. Yet they object to the pope's "imperialism" and "temporal stance" as unworthy of an apostle of Christ. In the course of interchurch relationships, and seeking of some formula to unite the whole of Eastern Orthodoxy once more with the ancient mother church of the Bishop of Rome, it is possible that the first casualty would be the Vatican State.

The present pope and, it is hoped, his Curia no longer look—if they ever did seriously—at the splinter Protestant churches as dearly beloved and desirable, if erring, children. But the Catholic Church is actively seeking unity with Orthodoxy. If it ever came to the point that prejudices could be abandoned on both sides, Catholic and Orthodox, then the idea of the pope's temporal stance and appearance would necessarily change in order to accommodate the final steps to that all-desirable unity.

But no competent observer of Eastern Orthodoxy, Greek or Russian, predicts at the present moment any serious move toward unity. Russian Orthodoxy is immersed in the vital ideology and sociopolitical system of the Soviet Union. Only if that system disappeared could Russian Orthodoxy be free even to contemplate an approach to unity. The end of the Soviet system will surely coincide with a totally new era in human history; for, if Soviet Marxism and its Gulag empire disappear, surely the democratic West will also disappear.

Greek Orthodoxy, centered around the Patriarch of Constantinople, is today utterly opposed to unity with the Catholic Church. Anti-Roman sentiment among Greek and Russian Orthodox Christians is as basic a prejudice as hatred of the Turks. Orthodox never forget that for hundreds of years popes and their churchmen preferred to see Ottoman Sultans, not Byzantine Greeks, in power at Constantinople. The Orthodox always responded by declaring their preference to see the "Turkish fez rather than the Roman tiara in the Basilica of Hagia Sophia [Constantinople]." Long before any genuine move toward unity between the Catholic Church and Orthodoxy takes place, the socioeconomic face of the world both churches inhabit will have changed.

The Catholic Vision

The realization in objective reality of the Catholic vision about the temporal condition of the Church would rest on two accomplished facts: the universal recognition of the Catholic Church as the sole repository of a salvation all men and women desired to obtain, and the Church's total divestiture of every trace of temporal power, financial sinews, and sociopolitical claims. Both of these would go together.

Universal recognition would mean that the material needs of papacy and Church would willingly be borne by all members of human society. It would mean, in other words, that papacy and Church could forego any effort in the temporal sphere to secure their material needs. Total divestiture would mean that Church and papacy were no longer primarily preoccupied with physical survival, that this was assured by another source, and that the full splendor of their spirit and the full riches of their supernatural treasure could be poured out to all human society.

Clearly, both universal recognition and total divestiture belong to a millennium that has been promised by God in the Book of Revelation; and, like the wondrous Child the prophet Isaiah predicted would be born of the Virgin, the best—the only—sign that a millennial ideal has been realized is the appearance of the ideal itself in reality.

Total divestiture, therefore, by papacy and Church of all wealth, of all claim to wealth, of all endeavor to develop wealth, must be placed on that millennial plane.

The lessons of history would seem to confirm that conclusion. On the one hand, none of the 267 popes has ever proposed divestiture. When divestiture, total or partial, has happened, it has come about always in the form of "the Vandal Solution"—a phrase historians attribute to that extraordinary personage, Frederick Barbarossa, German emperor from 1152 to 1190.

When the Germanic tribe called the Vandals streamed down south over the already Christianized Roman Empire in the fifth century, they destroyed literally everything they could not carry away on their horses and their four-wheeled wagons. To be "vandalized" originally meant to lose everything by destructive violence and systematic robbery. The citizens of the Empire abhorred them so much that they rarely named them but spoke merely of "the abominable race."

Applied to the Church, the "Vandal Solution" means that a superior physical force literally would strip it of all worldly possessions. This occurred more than once in papal history. In 1527, the papacy was reduced to nothing in material wealth and territorial possessions in Rome, elsewhere in Italy, and abroad. Within fifty years, all had started anew, and the losses of that year were made up. Napoleon Bonaparte went even further: He not only stripped the papacy of wealth and temporal power, he took the pope into exile. Within twenty-five years, the papacy was restored in its temporal power. Napoleon's empire was over.

In the twentieth century, the "Vandal Solution" has been applied to the Church by the Soviet Union in several countries: the Soviet Union itself; the Baltic states of Lithuania, Estonia, and Latvia; and the central and eastern European states of Poland, Czechoslovakia, Rumania, Hungary, Bulgaria, as well as the eastern portion of

Germany. The Church is literally "vandalized" and, furthermore, enslaved. Yet nowhere in these lands have the religion and faith of the Church died. On the contrary, the evidence is that not only has the Church maintained a toehold on physical existence; it has flourished in a way rarely to be found in Western countries. Even in Albania, rightly reputed to have the worst form of religious oppression, religious faith and the practice of religion continue; and, by strictly underground means, a rather exact picture of the internal Albanian religious situation is regularly available.

The lesson of history is that no "Vandal Solution" can do away with the temporal stance of the Church. Such solutions have only meant a temporary loss of regular revenues and an interruption in communication with the rest of the Church. Effective divestiture never resulted, for the simple reason that the same socioeconomic pressures remained at work. The Church never found itself and the world around it in any other condition, nor did it ever find the minds of its members changed concerning the use of wealth and the function of wealth in human society. That change is implicit in Dante's vision.

The Here-and-Now

The existence, the format, and the necessity of the Vatican State today emanate from the same source as the existence and necessity of the State's complicated and powerful financial agencies, namely: the world economic system and the sociopolitical systems that this economic system imposes. If that system were to change radically along with the sociopolitical system it spawns, doubtless the Vatican State would cease to exist as it is today. In the meanwhile, the present arrangement seems perfectly tailored to the system on all important levels.

The host country, Italy, has been associated with the Vatican for as long as the Vatican has existed. There is still a very strong Italianate tradition in the Vatican, and a strong feeling of pride among Italians about the presence in Italy of the papacy, even if they do not by and large obey the moral and ecclesiastical laws of the Church. Italy, too, originally granted and, with few changes, still allows the enormous margin of tax exemption the Church enjoys there even for ecclesiastical properties and ventures outside Vatican territory and its extraterritorial possessions. Even a Communist or Communist-dominated government in Italy would tread very cautiously in Vatican-related affairs. The pope could call on untold divisions among the Italians.

Would it make any difference to the spiritual mission and ecclesiastical authority of the pope if the Vatican State as such did not exist? If, to be sure, he were granted possession and ownership, title and deed in perpetuity, to all present Vatican land and property in Italy? If, however, he and all his entourage were Italian subjects, subject to Italian laws, served by Italian laws, while enjoying the present generous tax exemptions and the special status and protection guaranteed them by the Italian Constitution? Would that change of status remove from the figure of the pope the trait so many enemies and critics of the papacy and the Church find objectionable?

For most of the papacy's genuine enemies and for its most ardent critics, the only change in papal status that would dissipate the enmity and quell the criticism would be a reduction of the pope's status to that of a local bishop with no extra privileges, certainly no special tax exemptions, no formal relations with government, and, above all, with no jurisdiction or control over other bishops.

This negatively critical attitude leads us to the essence of papal statehood and sovereignty. The temporal power of the modern papacy has little if anything to do with what such power once could guarantee. For the Vatican State is as defenseless against physical force as any other ministate. Nor is there any way in which the papacy can threaten—as it did once—to commit aggression on other people's territory, even to acquire that territory. Those days are past. Sovereignty and papal temporal power mean something else today, and they accrue to the papacy because, as Gromyko asserted, the papacy was and is strong enough to take that power. This is probably what galls its enemies and spurs its critics.

But the brute facts are plain. The pope is head of an international community or family, the Catholics. Some portions of the world Catholic population enjoy much wealth and the prestige and influence that flows from wealth. Other portions—Latin America, for instance—are not wealthy, but their sheer numbers and key locations make them very important in the calculations of statesmen, economists, and military planners. They may not all be loyal to Catholic law and the Catholic spirit all the time; but sufficiently large numbers of them are faithful at least to the institution of pope and Church that local governments are usually very glad to be able to talk to the pope about their troubles and aspirations concerning the Catholics in their population.

What more logical step, then, than to have the pope's representative—an apostolic nuncio or a papal legate or, at least, a papal nuncio—accredited to the home government, and to return the favor by sending an accredited representative to join the Vatican diplomatic corps? It is so logical, in fact, that 109 countries have done so and those who haven't—the USSR and Israel, for instance—all maintain an unofficial representative permanently in Rome just for this purpose.

For, Catholicism apart, there are in our troubled world few locations where diplomats on opposite sides of the fence can find as conveniently neutral a ground as within the Vatican diplomatic corps. Besides, without exaggerating the point, one must admit that the information pouring into the Vatican is of an unusually wide span and of a very reliable kind.

The fundamental fact is that whoever heads the Catholic Church as pope wields genuine power. No government granted it to the papacy. It took that power upon itself. The pope, ex officio, is one of the world's most powerful men. The peculiar power entrusted to him cannot be measured by the usual yardstick. There is no other religious or political figure on our earth who could, as Pope John Paul II did, make a state visit to England and another one to the Argentine at the very time both were engaged in acts of war against each other.

There is no political leader, no statesman, no philosopher who could, for instance, enter a Communist military dictatorship such as Poland and literally speak to the Communist military dictator across a carpet in full television and radio proximity to Poles and millions around the world. Pope John Paul II did. Nor could anyone else have gone to Nicaragua and lectured the Sandinistas in public on their deviations.

The same general conclusion applies to the question many have raised about the Vatican's financial agencies. Given this power status of the papacy and the Vatican, a bank of its own is as logical and needed an installation as its diplomatic corps. Its tax-exempt status becomes part and parcel of that special status the pope enjoys. In fact, all the accoutrements of the present State of Vatican City seem to be perfectly fitting: The compromise of 1929 seems a permanent one.

When we turn to the present structure of the Vatican's financial agencies as they developed after 1929, we cannot really fault the general line of policy, which was directed at securing for Vatican representatives a place within the emergent managerial system that is gradually replacing the old ethos of capitalism. In one true sense, the developing situation seemed to be tailor-made for the papacy's position and its resources. In effect, those financial resources do not belong to any one man or group of men. Nor do they belong to the men and women of the Catholic Church alone. In Catholic truth, they belong primarily to Christ as head of the Church, and then not to Peter or any of Peter's successors. These have the resources at their disposal merely to manage, distribute, and conserve for the good of Christ's Church. All in all, they are merely managers of those resources. And that, within our new system of geo-economy, is title enough and title proper to active participation in the economic sphere.

No doubt, also, the policy adopted after 1929 succeeded this far. In liquid assets, in real estate, in gold deposits, in collateral, and in all the valuable and so-called intangibles—prestige, credit, quality of performance, durability, organization—the name of the Vatican stands high. Mao Zedong was so wrong in saying that power came out of a gun nozzle. And Bernardino Nogara was so right in pointing to the running tickertape as "the place where power flows."

There may be only one fault in the policy calculation that has dictated Vatican success these latter decades, and only time will tell. The managerial system may prove to be not the initiating process of a new era in world economy and financial structure; it may be the last, desperate gamble of a civilization already on its knees beneath the blows of historical failure. For the managerial system as such envisages the full gamut of human rights that, before the system itself was born, were championed by that most fragile of human inventions, democracy. And, in principle, the system is designed to give rein to liberty and competitiveness, two of democracy's gifts.

But the situation the managerial system creates may well turn out to be the cradle for another new regime in human affairs wherein the notion of human rights has no place, and where all the mighty efforts to salvage something of the past spirit will prove to have been just a sleepwalking to the end of the human night.

In that eventuality, doubtlessly the Catholic Church will have an alternative course to steer. There are already signs that, due to the peculiar situation of the Catholic Church in Poland, an utterly new concept of the Christian in human society may be developing under the tutelage of John Paul II's Vatican.

For the moment, however, our overview is limited to the here-and-now. The main criticism that can be leveled at the Vatican State today concerns its financial agencies. No one event and no one detail, but the weight of many events and a myriad of details, has convinced many people within the Vatican State, within the Church, and outside the Church, that the present structure of Vatican financial agencies—efficient as they manifestly are—must be judged not fitting.

The reason is clear. From being formally and according to charter an appendage of the Vatican State, the cluster of financial agencies seems to have become or at least to act like an independent entity enjoying an autonomy of decision and action which has enabled some of the financial functionaries to engage in activities that no recent pope countenanced. When these activities are judged even by the low standards of our modern international financial community they are unacceptable in any court of law. Besides, there is some evidence that at least isolated actions of more than one pope with a bearing on ethical and political problems were dictated primarily by the monetary advantages envisaged by the State's financial agencies. All in all, one can understand, if not sympathize with, the remark of one Italian treasury official commenting on the enigmatic convolutions of the 1982 Roberto Calvi case and the shadowy Vatican connections with it all: "It seems it is the tail that wags the dog."

Both the past history of the Vatican's financial agencies and the recent calamities suggest urgent need for a restructuring of those agencies in a way that is compatible with the religious character of the Catholic Church, the primatial claims of the papacy, and the economic needs of the administrative center for an ongoing institution such as the Catholic Church continues to be.

The Would-be Reforms of John Paul I

Albino Cardinal Luciani, the 65-year-old Patriarch of Venice, was elected Pope John Paul I at 6:20 P.M. on Saturday, August 26, 1978. He was found dead in bed thirty-five days later. Official medical bulletins ascribed his death to heart failure at approximately 10:30 or 11:00 P.M. on Thursday, September 28.

Of all the problems that confronted Pope Paul VI's successor at the outset of his pontificate, three were the most thorny. There was the popularity of the new liberation theology which was sweeping

through Latin America and providing a would-be Catholic justifi-
cation for armed and violent overthrow of existing governments.
Grave doubts were also entertained about the activities and loyalty
of the Church's most prestigious religious organization, the Jesuits—
many reports accused the Jesuits of fomenting Communism and a
Marxist interpretation of human existence. And at home, John Paul
I was faced with the complex and scandal-ridden financial agency
of the Vatican, the Institute for Religious Agencies, the IRA, headed
by Archbishop Marčinkus.

The untimely death of John Paul I[1] precluded any action on the
pope's part; his decisions concerning all three problems remain
shrouded in relative silence because, along with the stilling of the
pope's voice, two of the Vatican officials nearest John Paul I in his
short reign—Cardinals Jean Villot and Giovanni Benelli—have
since died.

Nevertheless, the broad outlines of John Paul's intentions were
made abundantly clear. The principal officers of the IRA who were
in charge during the entire period of Sindona's association with
Vatican finances—Archbishop Marčinkus being one of them—
were to be retired. But this was merely a beginning. What confronted
John Paul I was an agency of his own Vatican bureaucracy about
which very little was known.

There was no question of doing away with the IRA itself. What
John Paul wanted was control over its activities. But for control,
accurate information was needed. And even when such information
was available, there was a further difficulty: the relative immunity
and independence of the IRA, which does not fall within the normal
administrative structure of the Vatican. While, theoretically, the
pope is in control, no pope ever ascends the throne prepared even
to understand what is going on in the IRA, much less hand down
technical decisions.

John Paul I, therefore, proposed establishing a confidential committee of cardinals with their technical advisors. Their competency
was to include complete audit of all financial operations connected
with the IRA; an accurate assessment of the Holy See's worth at
this stage of its history; and a series of concrete recommendations
under three main headings: In what sectors of IRA activity was there
a possibility of scandal similar to the Sindona scandal arising? What
investments and investment operations of the IRA, if revealed to the
world at large, would result in a denigration of the Church? What
restructuring was necessary and advisable in order to bring the affairs

and operations of the IRA within normal supervision and regulation by the pope and his personal aides?

One part of the inquiry John Paul I wished carried out with alacrity concerned the confidential business associations of the IRA. In the first ten days of his pontificate he had been the recipient of many comments and reports that suggested those associations included relations with industrial, financial, and political figures whose aims were in direct contradiction to the ethos and beliefs of the Catholic Church. His informants spoke of associations with right-wing dictators, underworld figures, and one or more branches of the Lodge in Italy.

One important question over which John Paul spent much time concerned the very existence of the IRA. Did the Holy See really need a bank of its own? Was the very idea of a Vatican bank inimical to the spiritual and religious character of the Catholic Church? Finally, what net losses in funds and financial freedom would result if the banking function of the IRA were terminated and performed by a non-Vatican agency on behalf of the Vatican, and if, at the same time, the tax-exempt status of the Holy See was still respected by the Italian government?

It is not certain or even probable that John Paul I would have gone beyond a thorough investigation of the IRA and its ramifications. Apparently, his restructuring proposals were intended to obviate any reasonable possibility of a repetition of the Sindona affair. But we will never know accurately how far he had been able to penetrate the morass of complex and interwoven operations which enabled and still do enable the IRA and its associates to wield a considerable influence on the Italian economy and on political issues that affect the vital interests of other countries.

But he did insist on knowing what was afoot. Such knowledge could result in a dangerous breach in security for those who operate on the outer edges of civil law and quite outside the limits of Church canon law and the papal charter for the IRA. Death closed off those avenues from John Paul I.

HIGHEST IDEAL

There are a number of conditions which those who value the Catholic Church would like to see surrounding the acquisition, the management, and the distribution of its monies and—as a general term—its assets. We are not speaking here about the inner structuring of Vatican financial agencies, but rather of conditions resulting from an ideal structure. Some structural elements must enter into a list of such ideal conditions, of course, but here structure is a secondary consideration.

Apart from those who would prefer to see both Catholic Church and Vatican disappear from all existence, everybody agrees that such a huge institution must be adequately and correctly financed. Assuming, therefore, a desire to see the papacy and the Vatican maintained according to the Church's own doctrinal teaching, and also enabled to carry out its proper mission among men and women, what should be the necessary and sufficient general conditions in an ideal situation of its financial agency?

Full disclosure would seem to be the prime condition. The public, Catholic and non-Catholic, should have access to an accurate knowledge of all sources of Church funds, of all assets and possessions, all fiscal and monetary operations, all business associations and associates, all personnel whether directly employed, regularly consulted on a fee basis or not, or participatory even in a purely private capacity within the structure of Vatican agencies. No receipt, no disbursement, no acquisition, no salary paid, no expenses incurred, no element, in fact, should be hidden. The law of full disclosure must be applied to all salaried employees in the financial agency.

It could be argued on the basis of contemporary practice—say, when the person involved is the Queen of England, a head of government, a special government agency such as its intelligence services—that confidentiality should be allowed the pope in the matter of his Privy Purse. The sum involved would be disclosed under certain circumstances and to certain responsible people. But the actual disbursements or sources of the Privy Purse would remain undisclosed.

The argument would not hold, however, in the pope's case. His position cannot be compared to that of a constitutional monarch, a prime minister, or a confidential government service. He is first and foremost the vicar of Christ and head of an institution which must be above the suspicion or even the possibility of reasonable suspicion that he disposes of Church monies with as much immunity as those supposedly parallel secular counterparts.

The same restrictions would analogously apply to the question of confidentiality. Today, the operations of banks, financial institutions, large corporations, and governments are protected from public viewing by an accepted code of confidentiality. Without a doubt this confidentiality is partly dictated by the competitive conditions of business; but, equally certainly, it has been and is used to conceal transactions which may be legal but would be condemned by the public as unethical. The distinction is capital. There should be no room for that distinction in Vatican financial operations, which must always be construed as the actions of the pope's executive right hand. The use of confidentiality must therefore be limited.

The basic reason for full disclosure arises—almost imperatively today—from the present unalterable trend in the redistribution of wealth due to the decline of capitalism and the slow installation of the managerial system which has no religious component in its driving motor. There is in progress throughout the world a leveling of incomes as fewer and fewer people achieve personal fortunes, great or small, but in their majority have access to an across-the-board and equalized standard of living. It was never before considered to be a sign of religious authenticity or moral excellence to be without wealth, to be bereft of finery in clothes, in dwelling, in possessions. But that was a different era. As the present trend goes, the identification of any public body with unknown but presumably very ample supplies of money will diminish that public body's appeal as a source of religious authenticity and moral suasion.

The Catholic Church claims to be a public sign of spiritual

salvation and a repository of God's presence and God's law. The
pope is supposed to be God's vicar. There must be no possible way
those sacred functions—as sign of God's salvation, as vicar of God—
can be belied. People, ordinary people, must be able to verify for
themselves that the Church and the pope are above reproach in this
matter.

Only full disclosure will ensure this. There is no need to emphasize that full disclosure would go a long way toward precluding
fraud, embezzlement, nepotism, self-aggrandizement, unworthy
undertakings, and unseemly associations—all of these being elements that have constantly plagued Church and Vatican finances
from early on in its history right down to the last quarter of the
twentieth century.

Absence of clerical control would be the second prime condition
of an ideal structure.

There is here a fundamental question: Who owns the assets of
the Holy See? They were *considered* to belong to St. Peter, were
called *res pauperum* (the possessions of the poor), but in fact the
pope and the Curia dispose of those assets as if they were the owners.

Given the claims of the Catholic Church and its professed mission
to represent Christ without the encumbrances of worldly lust and
ambition, the formal and legal ownership of the Holy See's assets
should be affirmed as belonging exclusively to the real head of the
Church, Christ. Such an affirmation will have no value in the eyes
of the world unless the assets are placed in trust for Christ, who
would be represented by a neutral body of lay people drawn from
outside institutions with as impeccable credentials as are possible;
their function would be to own the assets in the name of Christ.
Each member would be guaranteed by the outside institution to
which he belongs; none would receive salary, emolument, or honorarium. The group would be subject to no clerical authorities or
any outside body. All of the assets of the Holy See would belong
to this corporate body, not to the pope ex officio as a "corporation
sole" and not to any group of clerics, clerical employees, or em-
ployers of clerics.

This corporate body, the ownership group, would have no say in
the management of assets or the distribution of funds. Besides ownership of assets, a derivative of its main function would be to consent
or object to the acquisition or the alienation of assets. Of itself, it
could propose neither acquisition nor alienation. There would be
no clerical control direct or indirect in the running of that ownership

body. Regardless of the number of its board members, the voice of this corporate body would be worth one vote in decisions of the plenary financial agency.

The third prime condition concerns the management of assets and the distribution of funds. The principle here would be to make sure that there is no clerical participation in the management of the Holy See's assets.

In the first place, such activity is in no way priestly. This does not mean it is evil or sinful; it means simply that clerics—men ordained to say mass, to give absolution, to help the sick and dying, to preach the good news of salvation, are not professionally adept at stockbroking, banking, insurance, money market haggling, stock market buying and selling. For these activities one does not need to be an ordained priest. It is a very significant part of the recent scandals that ordained clerics were immersed in such activities.

Needed is a management group of lay people skilled in this work, and with no say whatever as to the distribution of funds amassed by their efforts. The combined voices of the members in this management group would amount to one vote in the taking of decisions by the financial agency as a whole.

Distribution of funds would be the function of a distinct group of people composed of lay people and clergy. The clerical element would be of the second highest level (cardinalitial), and its number would always be one less than the number of lay people. On this combined group would depend the distribution of funds to cover legitimate expenses; that is to say, all authorization for the general Vatican budget, for the budgets of different Vatican departments, and for the pope's Privy Purse would be prepared, but not granted, by this group. They would have nothing to say in the management of assets, nor in the acquisition or alienation of assets.

Sufficient available funds would seem to be the fourth prime condition in an ideal situation. We are not talking here of the sufficiency required to meet the ordinary and extraordinary expenses of the Vatican, the pope, and the Church. It goes without saying that funds must be regularly available for the physical maintenance of the Vatican and all its associated buildings; for its regular payroll of Vatican employees; for its educational, cultural, and charitable institutions whether they be seminaries, colleges, universities, postgraduate research centers, libraries, clinics, leprosaria, orphanages, refuges, or hospices; for its missionary efforts; for its diplomatic corps; for its participation in international organizations. Extraordinary expenses would include general councils, papal trips, special funds (for relief, for disaster areas, and so on), and new projects.

All this funding should be taken for granted. The sufficiency implied here is rather that condition which ensures that the pope will not be financially at the mercy of the bishops of his Church, the cardinals of his papal Curia—or the Curia itself—or of any secular body of men. For, according to the second prime condition, the financial structure should be so fashioned that neither the pope nor any body of Curial clerics owns or disposes at will of Vatican assets. The danger then would be that the pope would be controllable by those who control the assets.

Time and again in the history of the Church, we can find popes who, because of financial dependency on bishops or Curia or secular authorities, were not free to discharge their papal duties as was fitting. There have in recent history been situations wherein bishops (especially those of northern Europe and the North American hemisphere) wished to declare themselves superior to the pope in doctrinal decision and in disciplinary regulation. This places the primacy of the pope in danger within the Church. Nobody asserts the bishops are independent of or superior to the pope in authority, but a growing number of bishops behave as if both propositions were true and accepted. If the full truth is to be known in this matter, it must be said that the relationship of pope and bishops in the Catholic Church still awaits further clarification. The funding of pope and Vatican must therefore be sufficient in that it places the pope beyond coercion by bishops through a dependency on them for funding.

In the decision-making process of the Vatican financial agency, the management and distribution groups would each have one vote.

On another front, there is a certain amount of evidence to suggest that the present financial agencies of the Church can act independently of the pope, have no felt need or constitutional obligation even to consult with him. In one sense, it would be very difficult: The day-to-day operations of the Vatican bank, for instance, could not be easily understood by anyone who had no formal training in the field. Trust has replaced disclosure to a large extent; and that trust has been, at least sometimes, violated.

The point is important, because the free disposition of assets by the technocrats of the Vatican bank can possibly produce hindrances to the execution of the pope's policies in certain areas of Catholic interest. Papal opposition to certain activities of the Vatican bank officials has in the past met with a suitable rejoinder: the refusal to make funds available for papal projects. That is why the functions of management and distribution must be kept separate. It is also why three other conditions should obtain in the ideal structure we are outlining.

Auditors-General

The assets of the Holy See are so substantial that built into the general finance agency of the Vatican there should ideally be an auditing unit that enjoys certain privileges. These auditors-general, all laymen, salaried to the Vatican, should have carte blanche to go anywhere in the service of Vatican financial operations, open any safe and any files and any desk, monitor all correspondence, telephone calls, and cablegrams, at any time and for any length of time that is required.

They would be appointed by the plenary finance agency and be accountable only to it. Neither management nor distribution group should possess any control over them. They could be countermanded only by the plenary finance agency, just as their authorization would come only from that agency. In decision-making sessions of the finance agency the auditors-general would cast one vote.

The auditors-general, as a group, would be a key element in controlling the whole agency. What was lacking during the Sindona–Calvi episodes was precisely such an independent, all-powerful body with one sole purpose: to know what was going on throughout the Vatican financial system.

Bishop and Cardinal

Two final groups would round out the balance of forces in the ideal Vatican financial agency.

Ultimately, the day-to-day running of the Church's millions is the task of the Church's bishops. Their voices will tell accurately what the condition of the Church is, and what the people in the Church need. In Catholic doctrine, they are the successors to the Twelve Apostles and, as such, possess a jurisdictional and teaching power in the Church which the Curial cardinals cannot have. Within the central bureaucracy of the Church, the voice and mind of the bishops are needed to balance the effect of the professional bureaucrats who are not pastors of souls.

Already the bishops of the Church are organized on a national and regional level. The elected bishop-delegates sent by the regional bishops' conferences would have one vote at plenary session decision making.

The cardinals who live and work in Rome, heading one or more of the Vatican ministries and offices, represent the permanent on-going center of the organized Church. Their function as electors of the pope and their bird's-eye view of the universal Church give them a perspective that is unique. Traditionally since the eleventh century, they have assumed a vast importance in general policy-making, introducing a republican counterforce that balances the monarchism of the pope.

Those cardinals who are bishops in various dioceses throughout the world would be on a par with any other non-cardinal bishop in the decision-making process of the finance agency.

It is the Curial cardinals who control the interlocking directorate overseeing the day-to-day working of the Vatican bureaucracy. In all budget and financing discussions, their voices must be heard. As with the other groups, those voices would constitute one vote.

Plenary Council of the Financial Agency

The supreme governing body of the Vatican financial agency would ideally be composed of one member from each of the preceding groups—ownership, management, distribution, auditors-general, cardinals, and bishops. A total of six votes. The pope, an ex officio member, would have the seventh vote.

Decisions would be taken according to a two-thirds plus one majority, and voting would be public. The pope would have a right of veto over any decision taken, unless an appeal was made to a consistory of all the cardinals; the consistory could upset the papal veto, again by a two-thirds plus one majority. Consistorial voting could not be done by proxy; and no age limit would prevent a cardinal from participating.

The organizers of the plenary council sessions would be the auditors-general, meeting on a regular monthly basis or whenever a simple majority of the council's members called for a session.

The power of the plenary council would have to be absolute in all major decisions affecting the fiscal and monetary status and activities of the Vatican. On it would rest the final responsibility for the type of investment allowed and for the distribution of funds.

By its structure it would not be a fiefdom of the pope or the Roman Curia or the bishops of the Church or of any single group of laymen.

One of its biggest responsibilities would be to decide on the morality of certain investments. Some issues would be clear (the council could not permit one of its agencies to invest in a company that manufactured and marketed contraceptives, for the Church forbids contraception as a crime against nature), others would not. At present Vatican representatives sit on the boards of various metallurgy and mining companies. In the annual budget which the boards must approve, there is provision made for the creation of "workers' recreational facilities," particularly for mining locations that are far from any town or city. Inevitably, these facilities include a brothel. May the Vatican representative on the board give his approval to this item? Will a simple protest or abstention from voting do? Should the Vatican be associated with a company that provides the wherewithal for violation of one of its cardinal rules? The Church calls it fornication and forbids it under pain of mortal sin. Aiding and abetting the commission of mortal sin is a mortal sin in itself.

There are a thousand and one other such cases, some of them far more subtle and complicated—cases involving currency laws and violations, competitive bidding, capitalist competition in real estate, building construction, armaments manufacture, the legitimate businesses of organized crime fueled with funds derived from the narcotics trade, from male, female, and child prostitution, loansharking, and contraband activities. May the Vatican conduct legitimate business deals with such businessmen as their associates and partners?

A different set of problems arises from an age-old and traditional practice of the Roman Curia and of every diocesan curia and parish authority throughout the length and breadth of the Catholic Church: the charging of fixed fees for the performance of spiritual acts and the obtaining of ecclesiastical favors.

Fees are charged for baptisms, marriages, marriage annulments, masses said for one's personal intentions, funeral obsequies, dispensations from a gamut of laws. Not so long ago, in certain areas, people were not allowed into church on Sundays and Holy Days unless they paid a minimum fixed sum at the door. The process was refined in places like Ireland. One sum (half a crown, equal to 5 cents in a 1939 dollar) would allow you enter and hear mass from the upper half of the central nave; one shilling permitted you to stay in the lower part. For anything less, you crowded into the side aisles or the back of the church. Such practices have all but died out. But the principle of charging for spiritual and ecclesiastical benefits still reigns.

Ideally, there should be no such charges. Ideally, too, local parishes as well as diocesan chanceries and the Roman Curia itself should receive monetary support from the people who use church facilities. But no practicable solution has yet been found. The problem is only a small facet of the larger universal problem about the economic viability of the Church.

For there are only three ways that economic viability can be assured: Either the State government guarantees it, or the members of the Church guarantee it, or Church authorities themselves, by their own business efforts, provide the monies that are needed to meet expenditures. History has shown that it is fatal when the State is guarantor; either the state enslaves the Church or the Church enslaves the state. Neither result is desirable.

A religious sect as moderate in size as the Mormons (approximately 3 million) or the Protestant Episcopal Church (approximately 4 million) might well be able to subsist on an income guaranteed by their members. (Actually, both Mormons and Episcopalians depend heavily on invested monies and endowments.) But what about the Catholic Church with over 761 million members, over half of whom live in Latin America and whose poverty and misery are exceeded only by that of India's forlorn millions?

Hitherto, when Church authorities themselves entered the business of providing for the economic viability of the Church, the organizational and visible bureaucratic side of the Church did indeed attain viability. In fact, at one stage, the Church bureaucracy bid fair to dominate not only the economic but the sociopolitical order as well. Even when this power-madness was amputated and, by 1929, the Church organization accepted the "Decent Compromise," within fifty years abuses crept into the organization which were rare even in their secular counterparts.

Those who have reflected long and deeply on the miserable results of this most recent period in the Church's financial history, seem to agree that the Church should undertake such a vast and all-embracing financial policy and aim only if the purpose was to aid mightily in effectively solving a socioeconomic problem as great and as festering as the one that has latched onto the emaciated frame of Latin America.

In the ideal order where this present consideration is located, much could have been done. By the middle of the sixties, when it was quite clear Vatican financial policy was paying handsomely ample dividends, and when it was also clear that the clock stood at five minutes to a Latin American midnight, if Rome had made it its business to tackle the socioeconomic cancer of Latin America, the Church would not now be confronted with a problem that defies any thinkable solution—financial, military, economic.[1] Now the clock stands at five past the hour. It is too late.

All these considerations of the highest ideal in the matter of finance and economic well-being have been, at one time or another, in part or in whole, the aim of more than one enlightened pope and churchman, not to speak of the many initiatives that have come from the laity of the Church.

Yet, nothing was ever effectively done. In all such cases, of course, there were economic and political reasons for the failure of the best laid plans. But in nearly all such former initiatives one can find at least traces of two very common human traits: greed and self-interest. The existence of such a longtime prestigious institution as the papacy and the Catholic Church, together with the wealth and financial leverage such an institution acquires—these have always created firmly entrenched lobbies of particular causes, business dynasties, family fortunes, and vested interests. Cloaked by the name and mission of Vatican and Church, such power centers would go to any extreme—even assassination—in order to prevent Vatican financial sinews to serve uniquely the primary mission of the Catholic Church: to be a recognizable and effective sign of salvation in the everyday world of men and women.

This is why, once we have considered what the ideal order of things would be, we have to seize the concrete situation as it exists, and consider how it can be bettered. For there is no way, as things stand, that it can even approach the ideal. A fateful caution blocks that direct path.

THE CAUTION

If one casts an unjaundiced eye over the Catholic Church as a whole during these last twenty years of the twentieth century, the word which leaps to mind as best characterizing the condition of the Church is "transition."

There is such turmoil at every level of Church life, such contradictory impulses, such variation in quality of belief and moral practice, such deep divisions on fundamental issues, and such a lack of firm unified leadership from the leaders of the Church—the bishops, together with John Paul II—that one conclusion imposes itself: The Catholic Church is undergoing a monumental change. It is in transition from the condition it was in up to the beginning of the sixties. But no one can define exactly in what form it will emerge when the transition is over—nor even how long that transition will last.

Judged from a traditional standpoint, the essence of this apparent transition is what ecclesiastical writers and Bible commentators have always called the "Great Apostasy." A powerful, determined, vocal pope, John Paul II seems impotent to control the destruction of traditional Catholic doctrine or to restore traditional Catholic practice. He keeps on reiterating that his will and determination are to apply the directives of the Second Vatican Council. But so far, he has not been able to make even a small beginning in this direction. Things are out of his control; and to make new rules would only provoke fresh revolts.

Great masses of Catholics no longer observe Catholic marriage morality. Great numbers of priests and nuns are firmly committed to a Marxist interpretation of contemporary history. Great sections of Church administrators throughout the world act in ways that are incompatible with Catholicism as it has been handed down by generations; when John Paul II or his Vatican protest or question what the bishops and priests are doing, the counterforce acts with a deafening negativity. The pope's personal representatives in each country—his nuncios and delegates—are practically dishonored, their voices unheard, their function sometimes despised as a relic of medieval thinking.

The bastions of papal support, the "pope's men"—as Jesuits, Dominicans, Franciscans, and Carmelites were once called—have by and large become little republics on their own, professing an ecclesiastical socialism (sometimes, too, a political socialism), intent on developing a "people's Church" in contradistinction to the "hierarchic Church" of yesterday. And only small pockets of nuns persist in faithful adherence to traditional religious life.

Within his Vatican bureaucracy, John Paul II stands isolated. It is not so much that the pope is not Italian—that has some bearing on his isolation. Principally, however, it is that Karol Wojtyla never had and does not now possess a Curial mind. Everything that went into the making of this pope has made him radically different from the men in the middle echelons of the Vatican bureaucracy. He has no social roots in the "Black Nobility," no political roots in the charade that constitutes Italian politics, where for over forty years the burdens of government have been passed around among the same couple of hundred agile politicians. Absolute rule he experienced under Nazi and Communist at home in Poland. But Rome's peculiar admixture of irredentist republicanism and oligarchic autocracy—this is something he never quite mastered. Yet, to rule and govern effectively, a pope must be able to run on both sides of that street.

Given the transition of his Church from cohesion to decadence, and given his own relative isolation, the last thing now possible for John Paul II is a top-to-bottom reform of a Vatican agency as power-sensitive and as coveted as the financial agency of his Vatican.

This is the caution expressed by his position in papal history and by the unraveling of traditional hierarchic Catholicism: To touch in a profound and thorough sense what has been built up over the last forty years as financial sinews and fiscal method would be to court a reaction so violent that it could only end in disaster of one kind or another. And his pain-riddled pontificate has already come close to disaster more than once.

We must remember that such a financial position as the Vatican agencies enjoy today is not built overnight, and is achieved by means of a vast, complex system of associations and joint ventures which involve not only Vatican interests but those of private and corporate entities. One cannot, then, shift the position of Vatican interests overnight without threatening longtime associates with a destructive dislocation. The reactions to such a threat would be, at the very least, quite defensive. They might possibly be offensive.

That caution is reinforced by the very disturbed sociological and political conditions obtaining in John Paul's Rome and Italy—not to speak of regions such as Latin America, where the Church looms large in the life of the masses. Violence lies always beneath the thin surface of law and order. If complete reform of the Vatican financial agencies was clearly signaled and if it were to be accompanied by anything like full and accurate disclosure of Vatican assets and business interests, one could predict the eruptive effect of such information on a variety of people among whom volatility of perception and violence of method are never absent from life. There is such a naked want in Third World countries, there are so many autonomous pockets of discontented men and women who secure their funding by terroristic means such as kidnaping, robbery, ultimatums of violence, that such disclosure could well bring on a series of social, political, religious, and personal calamities that are best avoided.

Besides, any reasonable prediction about the general trend of international politics in Europe, East and West, strongly suggests that an era of stiffening on the right has already begun, despite the apparent success of socialist regimes at the polls in western European countries. For East and West are now locked into a path of economic convergence. On that path, the price for the West will be largely monetary. For the East it will mean a dilution of their centralized, closed economies. As convergence seeps beyond the economic area and affects the cultural and political milieus, on both sides there will be a defensive stiffening. In the West, this will mean a new heyday for right-wing politics. At such a time, the caution of present history will be relaxed, less forbidding; and, at such a time perhaps, full disclosure and thorough housecleaning will be in order.

Thus, from all sides, the caution of contemporary history dictates that reform and restructuring of the Vatican financial agencies be a long-range goal accomplished, if at all, in several relatively feasible stages. It is also why the elements we have discussed as the highest ideal in a restructuring of those agencies must remain on the idealistic plane, as merely an outline of what should figure as an ultimate goal.

Holding the ideal on high but not attempting to implement it immediately, let us ask: What in the present circumstances would be the first and most feasible step in the direction of that ideal, but still a step respectful of the historical caution, one that would surely be a step to gain control of the present situation? Any practical, applicable plan of restructuring at the present time should and could aim at that. Control, in this context where so many powerful and vested interests are at stake, implies two main elements: full knowledge of what is going on, of all operations, and of what monies are involved; a balancing of the forces already involved, one counteracting the other, one supplementing the other, so that whoever sits at the center of the structure gains at least de facto control over the intricate machinery.

This would be the result of a first major restructuring and new configuration of the Vatican financial agencies.

THE FIRST
CONFIGURATION

A ny configuration of what a plenary financial agency of the Vatican should look like structurally must be comprehensive of the whole Church—the Church Universal, according to the time-honored phrase. It must outline an operational plan that includes not merely the sources of revenue belonging to the Holy See; it must also include diocesan and regional finances as well as those of other important units of the working Church.[1] Prime among such units are the religious orders of men and women. For these, by their revenues, constitute a sizable bulk of assets; and, officially, they represent the Church wherever they are, whatever their work. But their inclusion within a plenary financial system, as well as the inclusion of dioceses, is going to present thorny, and as yet uncontemplated, legal problems centering around de jure ownership.

The purpose of any new configuration in the Vatican financial agencies is to facilitate primarily the pope and, next, his personal advisory council so that he and they are constantly in a position to make "educated," fast, and sound business decisions for implementation by subordinate parts of the whole financial agency. This general purpose would be confided to a new entity in Vatican State: the Pontifical Finance Authority. The PFA would absorb and replace all existing financial agencies: the Prefecture of Economic Affairs, the Institute for Religious Agencies (IRA), the Administration of Holy See Property, and the General Administration of Goods of the Holy See.

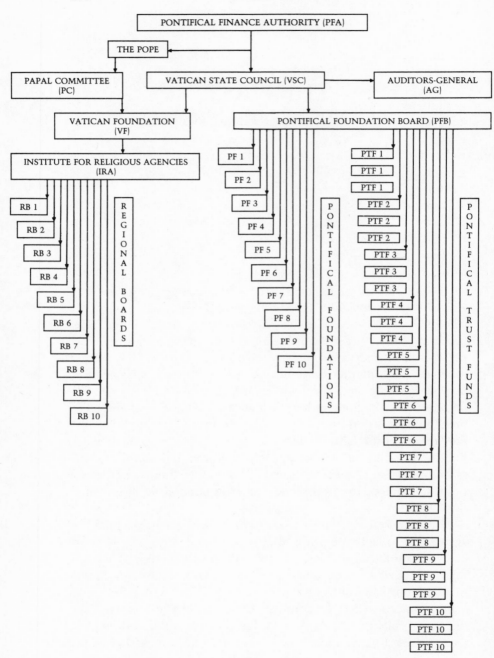

FIGURE 2

The Assets

Included under this term are all possessions in specie or in kind, of recent or former or future provenance, that belong to the Holy See, to any of its organs and agencies, to any of its ecclesiastical institutions in Rome or elsewhere. An ecclesiastical institution is understood here as any corporate body which depends on the approval of Church (canon) law for its right to represent the Church and its duties to work within the broad scope of the Church's divinely appointed mission, whatever be its civil status according to the territory where it is centered or domiciled.

Possessions is used in its widest sense. Land, landed property, property; valuable movables in precious metal, precious mineral, precious stone, *objêts d'art*, antiques; invested or in-trust funds dating from the past and the future, as well as all bequests and donations whose location and use are determined by the original donors; stock-market investment; private company participation; gold deposits; and, finally, any form on which collateral funding can be based, whether of a tangible or intangible kind.

There is one division of assets that must be mentioned here. Due to the long history of the Church and the Vatican, the *size* and the *quality* as well as the *kind* of certain assets make it impossible to arrange them on a systematic basis according to proper modern business and investment techniques. This may be due in large part to conditions attached to donated assets by the original donors. Thus the donor of certain revenues *in perpetuum* may have stipulated as a condition that those revenues be used in a certain way or for a delimited purpose. Other assets by their bulk or quality may escape management techniques. And, in general, all such assets have to be considered as nonmarketable. Such assets constitute actually a sizable source of funds, and must be managed separately from assets that are marketable in the modern sense of the term.

Ownership

The pope, as successor to St. Peter, as head of the Church, has among his primary duties to oversee the management and use of all possessions of the Holy See. He is the general overseer of, and the person ultimately responsible for, all those possessions that should be called "the patrimony of St. Peter."

He does not, however, own these possessions either as a public or private person. Nor should his status vis-à-vis those possessions in whole or in part be any longer denominated in legal documents and arguments as "corporation sole."

The "patrimony of St. Peter" belongs, in the proper sense of the term, to the State of Vatican City. Whatever goods, therefore, are reckoned to be or are co-opted to "the patrimony of St. Peter" belong to that State. The officials of that State—mainly three (the pope, the governor, and vice-governor), together with their uppermost State Council, are to be held as the overall administrators and managers of the "patrimony."

Their management and administration of the material goods involved must be performed according to a business philosophy that combines specifically outlined objectives in the economic order with the ethical and moral stance and teaching of the Catholic Church.

The prime change to be effected here concerns legal ownership, and the proposal touches on two areas where new and perhaps quite innovative formulas must be developed. There is, first, the area of diocesan law, the body of customs, habits, by-laws, and formal laws that amount to a constitution for each diocese in the Church. Whatever existing formulation there is in this area, be it by actual ecclesiastical law, by papal rescript, or by simple tradition, it must be reexamined so that title and ownership to the possessions of a diocese no longer belong in ecclesiastical law to the diocese. The same prescription should be applied to ecclesiastical bodies such as religious orders and congregations, institutes, universities, and foundations.

Whatever be the use and usufruct allowed locally, ownership should be effectively, that is to say constitutionally, ascribed and conceded to "the patrimony of St. Peter."

The most complicated legal question which arises at this point concerns the status of landed property. Belonging to the Vatican State, any property anywhere is the property of a sovereign state. That is, by definition, diplomatic territory, similar to the compound of an embassy in a foreign country. There are legal precedents to be consulted in this matter. For instance, the sovereign state of Kuwait acquired the Santa Fe Industries a few years ago. Did the plant and offices of Santa Fe Industries become Kuwaiti territory and enjoy all the immunities of diplomatic territory?

The first new unit to be created, therefore, is a Vatican State Council. For this, presided over by the pope, will be the supreme

authority for the management and distribution of whatever is included in "the patrimony of St. Peter."

The composition of the State Council should be one-third clerics,
two-thirds laymen. The clerical membership should not necessarily
depend on cardinalitial status, because those appointed or elected
to the Council should be educated in the managerial and financial
sense. Membership is not of itself an honorary title but a working
obligation. The offices of governor, vice-governor, treasurer, and
secretary in the State Council would be rotated among the members.
After the initial assembling of the State Council for the first time,
new members would be chosen by a simple majority vote, and
existing members could be dismissed by the same vote. Over both
votes, the pope could exercise a veto unless a two-thirds plus one
majority had so voted.

The lay portion of the Council should be composed of men whose
integrity and honesty cannot be called into question, and of proven
professional abilities with standing and personal prestige in the world
of finance.

The main functions of the Council would be to take major overall
management decisions; to entrust these for implementation to its
subsidiary and subservient bodies within the one Pontifical Financial
Authority; to determine the business philosophy of the PFA; to
supervise the general auditing of the PFA. Under no circumstances
could the Council of itself alienate or dispose of any portion of the
patrimony. That could only be a decision of a plenary meeting of
the PFA involving cardinals and bishops and heads of major religious
orders.

Attached to the State Council would be a committee of auditors
selected from outside firms. The mandate of these auditors-general
covers year-round examinations, entry to every agency in the PFA,
and discretionary powers to halt any operation in progress. Appeal
against the auditors-general could only be made to the State Council
or, as a final resort, to a plenary session of the PFA.

The State Council, at its own discretion, would create as many
committees as are needed for particular sectors of intra-Vatican
life—the care of St. Peter's Basilica, the curatorship of museums,
the archeology of St. Peter's, and so forth.

The management and distribution of assets and funds would be
allocated to a structured arrangement of corporate bodies, each one
an agency in its own right with a specific and confined series of
functions, and whose performance and achievements are funneled

up the organizational ladder to the highest authority. These corporate bodies must now be described.

The Papal Committee

The Papal Committee is envisaged as a selection of high-ranking clerics, in their majority cardinals, including the Cardinal Secretary of State together with the cardinals who head the Congregation for the Doctrine of the Faith, the Congregation for the Evangelization of Peoples, and the Congregation for the Oriental Rite. Each new pope is allowed to restaff this committee according to his own choices and wishes. No member of any other part of the agency would belong ex officio to the Papal Committee. It would be the right arm of each particular pope. Its function is to screen all reports and documents coming from below and presented to it on a monthly or quarterly basis by the appointed managers of the Vatican Foundation.

The Vatican Foundation

This central body would be composed of a maximum of twelve lay professionals, each of whom has a wide and recognized managerial experience. Membership in the Foundation would be only by appointment by a joint choice of the Papal Committee and the State Council.

The proper function of the Vatican Foundation would be to fashion sound professional judgments concerning the managed assets which on a previous page we grouped under the heading of *nonmarketable* assets. It was pointed out then that an appreciable bulk of existing assets would not be easily subjected to the new business guidelines that would guide the management of future assets.

Those nonmarketable assets would normally be managed by regional boards. The Vatican Foundation would be the final arbiter and judge of the regional boards' management.

Given the extent of the Church, and given the bulk of certain inherent parts of the Church, the number of regional boards would be a minimum of ten. Each of the seven accepted ecclesiastical divisions of the Church (Africa, North America, Central America, South America, Asia, Europe, and Oceania) would be served by one regional board. On account of the peculiar, even if transitory, status of eastern European countries as satellites of the Soviet Union, the European division would have to be divided into Eastern and Western Europe, each served by a separate regional board. Two other regional boards would have to be created to manage the non-marketable assets of the city of Rome itself and of the Church's religious orders and congregations of men and women religious. Nothing impedes the creation of further regional boards, according to the needs of sound management.

The regional boards can be directly subordinated to the Vatican Foundation. It may, however, be considered wiser to subordinate them directly to the Institute for Religious Agencies. Obviously, any restructuring of Vatican financial agencies is aimed, among other things, at avoiding the calamities that occurred when the IRA was the principal and sole agency for monetary matters. Altering the status of the IRA would be one of the prime objectives of this entire restructuring process. Subordinating the regional boards to the IRA as its subsidiaries, and through the IRA to the Vatican Foundation as to the parent group in this line of financial management structure, would be a wise move psychologically as well as organizationally. In a change that to all appearances enlarges the scope and jurisdiction of the IRA, the agency would actually receive very clearly defined limits and a vastly reduced scope of action. Complete change of personnel would, of course, be necessary in the IRA as it is presently constituted.

There is no statal, ethical, or religious reason why the membership and the functions of the State Council, the Papal Committee, the Vatican Foundation, and the regional boards should not be publicly known and acknowledged. This would apply also to a refurbished IRA as an agency of the Pontifical Finance Authority if the regional boards became its subsidiaries and it were subordinate to the Vatican Foundation.

This would not be the case for the remaining corporate agency of the PFA: the Pontifical Foundation Board, the Pontifical Foundations, and the Pontifical Trust Funds. Business confidentiality and statal reasons would impose a great wall of discretionary silence not only about their functions, but even about their very existence.

Pontifical Foundation Board

This board ideally would be composed of one-third clerics versed in financial and managerial skill, and of two-thirds lay people already established in their own right as dedicated professionals whose performance and integrity are known and appreciated in the world of international finance. Membership on the board would be a full-time job with its own fixed emoluments. Because of the leverage and information board members would have at their disposal, entry into the board would have to be preceded by a process akin to that imposed on those who join an American government administration. All conflict of interest must be avoided.

Initial membership in the PFB would have to be by appointment. Subsequent membership would have to be acquired by an intricate process involving the State Council, the Papal Committee, and the Vatican Foundation. But in organizational status, the PFB once constituted would be on the same level as the Vatican State Council.

The scope of the PFB's work is defined in terms of two sets of corporate bodies.

Pontifical Foundations

Each one of those foundations would correspond to one of the ten divisions already listed for the regional boards. Each would be a financial management agency empowered to deal with all assets in provenance from its territorial division. The foundations would be essentially transitional stations, subordinate to the Pontifical Foundation Board. This board would receive whatever was developed by a foundation in the form of assets, corporate profits, donations, and bequests. The PFB would have to analyze the assets and decide which assets should be further managed by the regional boards, and which should be confided to another set of management agencies, the Pontifical Trust Funds.

Before going on to discuss the Pontifical Trust Funds, something must be said here about the legal structure of the Pontifical Foundations.

Pontifical Foundations: Legal Structure   The Liechtenstein Foundation is the most adaptable to the business philosophy of the pope and his State Council. It is a legal entity depending solely on private law; its purpose as the legal owner of the foundation capital is the allocation of that capital for an exactly determined goal. The founder transfers ownership of the capital to the foundation. No Liechtenstein tax is imposed on donations for the founder domiciled outside Liechtenstein.

The foundation can be incorporated over the signature of a fiduciary agent, thus placing the actual founder at one remove from the public. Ecclesiastical foundations such as are envisaged here do not need to be inscribed in the public registry. Thus, they are assured added anonymity. Liechtenstein makes the foundation board members answerable with all their own property to both the foundation and the founder.

The founder can, under law, be another legal entity domiciled anywhere. He also determines the members of the foundation, its purposes, the conditions under which he may revoke the foundation, the auditing arrangements, and who or what entities will be the beneficiaries of the foundation.

Pontifical Trust Funds

These would be ten trust accounts opened under instructions of the Pontifical Foundation Board in three or more highly reputable financial entities in each of the ten territorial divisions. All those financial entities would receive the same instructions in the same terms from the Pontifical Foundation Board as to the business investment philosophy of the Pontifical Finance Authority. One of the Pontifical Foundation Board's main tasks would be to formulate that philosophy according to the ideas of the pope and his State Council.

The assets managed by the trust funds would be the marketable assets that exist or are developed by or are donated to the Church. The fact that all these assets could be regarded at the outset as cash or the equivalent of cash would make possible the uniform judgment of the management capabilities and performance of each trust fund.

The management performance of the Pontifical Trust Funds would have to be constantly monitored by the Pontifical Foundation Board. Its periodic judgment on each single trust fund would then be passed on to the Papal Committee and the pope for review in the light of overall papal objectives.

The Pontifical Foundation Board's major responsibility emerges clearly at this point. The board must maintain the liaison between the fund managers and their "client," pope and State Council, in order to ascertain and assure all concerned on a continual basis that the fundamental business philosophy of the "client" was being followed faithfully. In this, the Pontifical Foundation Board can be likened to the financial committee, say, of a General Motors type of firm, which is in charge of overseeing the management of various portions of the corporate pension fund entrusted to different financial entities. It is the undertaking of the Pontifical Foundation Board to draw up the guidelines within which the business investment philosophy of pope and State Council would be successfully and sustainedly applied.

Pontifical Trust Funds: Legal Structure   What is needed by way of legal structure in these Pontifical Trust Funds is a framework for the method of operation that can be tailored to suit exactly the aims and wishes of the pope and State Council. Under this heading the structure of the Liechtenstein Foundation is probably the most flexible to work with.

Liechtenstein is the only country in continental Europe that has evolved legislation specifically targeted on governing the trust. Its legal form, derived from Anglo-Saxon and American models, is recognized in both the U.S.A. and the U.K. with its associated Anglo-Saxon countries.

Basically, the trust is not a legal entity. It is a legal relationship in which the trustor or settlor—in this case, pope and State Council—entrusts to another, the trustee—in this context, each Pontifical Trust Fund—either goods or capital sum or a right called trust capital. The trustee undertakes to administer or utilize *in his own name* these goods or that capital sum or the trust capital in favor of beneficiaries designated in the deed of trust. For all third parties, the trustee appears as the owner of the trust capital.

Of the two kinds of trust fund, registered and unregistered, probably the unregistered is the most advisable for the Pontifical Trust Funds. It preserves the anonymity of the "client," and the trustee is responsible toward third parties. The trust is revokable only by the trustor.

The capital of the trust, in any case, is protected against seizure by the creditors of the trustee, for the trust capital is held by Liechtenstein law to be foreign patrimony and is immediately separated from the patrimony of the trustee. Nor have the creditors of the trustee any right over the trust capital. In case of litigation over a secret (i.e., unregistered) trust, the trustor must only prove the existence of the trust in order to achieve immunity from legal pursuit. The trustor (settlor) and the designated beneficiaries of the trust have the benefit of total protection. Finally, the tax imposed on the Liechtenstein Trust is a tax on capital levied at the rate of 0.1 percent of the trust's fortune. Payments made to beneficiaries domiciled outside Liechtenstein and taken from the capital and the income of the trust are tax-exempt in Liechtenstein. Distribution of trust capital, upon dissolution of the trust, is also tax-exempt.

The advantages to the Holy See from such a trust are distinct and obvious. All such trust capital is no longer the legal property of the trustor and therefore, where it originates, it is no longer subject to taxation on income and on donations wherever the trustor resides.

Business Philosophy

It would be, as remarked previously, the task of pope and State Council to lay out the essentials of the business philosophy that should govern the management and distribution of Vatican assets. Once that much was achieved on this superior level, it would be the Pontifical Foundation Board's further task to reduce that essential philosophy to precise guidelines for the Pontifical Trusts and Foundations. Those guidelines must be tailored to regional needs and standards. Whatever precisions the Pontifical Foundation Board formulates should also be assumed by the Vatican Foundation. Comparing the business conditions and conditions of assets in the regional boards under their supervision, the board members of the Vatican Foundation must produce their own guidelines adapted to the regional boards.

The overall objectives of the Pontifical Finance Authority should be six:

1. Adequate funds at the disposal of the PFA to finance all the organs particular to the Holy See and the pope's own projects throughout the world.
2. Funds to be managed in such a way that no pressure can be exercised on the pope or the Holy See for realistic economic or financial reasons.
3. Funds to be at the disposal of the PFA to finance fully the operation of dioceses and religious orders, in such a way that the stronger helps the weaker.
4. A position of prestige and influence in the sphere of international relations, insofar as that prestige and influence depend primarily on financial sinews.
5. The diminution and eventual dissolution of business associations already formed which necessarily imply political alliances.

6. The gradual shifting of money management from all clerical hands into the hands of competent and dedicated lay people who have been established as loyal to the Church and the Holy See.

Side by side with these main objectives, the PFA must issue its own general guidelines or general rules. The most relevant ones are as follows:

1. Preserve at least, if not increase, the existing value of investments.
2. No speculation; no venture-capital undertakings; avoidance of foreign-exchange speculations except under the most stringent rules. Sound revenue-bearing investments to be preferred, even though increments are slow and gradual.
3. Investments not to be concentrated narrowly, but over diversified fields; this may eliminate the chance of a great "killing," but it will also preclude sudden total loss.
4. In the final analysis, none of the subsidiary or principal organs of the PFA should underwrite an operation which, if the need arose, could not see the light of day and bear the scrutiny of ordinary men and women, without being condemned either as unworthy of the Holy See and/or as incompatible with the supernatural mission of the Church. An example would be real estate rentals and leases that due to market conditions allow "gouging." The rule cannot be simply "what the market can bear."
5. Whenever a course of action is ethically acceptable according to current business practices, but is not acceptable according to a moral opinion of churchmen, it is not to be pursued unless the moral opinion in question is one of two or more opinions sharing equal moral probability among theologians, *and* unless normally vital interests of the PFA are at stake—always retaining the norm expressed under #4.
6. The concept of confidentiality is to be understood exclusively as a facility for conducting ethically legitimate and morally acceptable business operations in a climate undisturbed by the strokes of competition or the uninformed dis-

traction of public opinion, but not as a cloak for operations that violate the conditions set forth in #4.

7. In business investment, no functioning part of the PFA should aim at, or develop revenues from, certain types of enterprise one of whose direct results is a violation of the natural law, of Church law, or of God's law. The manufacture of contraceptives is an example. Inevitably, there will be borderline cases. For instance, a medical supply company which produces, among other wares, the instruments specifically designed for abortion; drug companies which are known also to supply the underground drug market; companies that violate the explicit rulings of popes concerning the working conditions of workers; hospital facilities already burdened with legally sound leases to abortion clinics.

8. Even in what is established as an ethically acceptable and morally good business enterprise, participation should be avoided if it entails association with: business partners who are known to be (or to have been) or are reasonably suspected of being (or of having been) engaged in other business ventures that directly violate moral principles or the just demands of national loyalty; one political party so that the independence of thought and freedom of speech of the Church suffer thereby; partners whose primary source of capital is tainted; or members of any organization, clerical or lay, which aims at the destruction of the Church.

9. Investment in resource companies (coal, oil, metals, etc.) is to be preferred over investment in service companies. Investments in the latter should be either restrained or confined to software companies, avoiding as far as possible luxury goods (food, clothes, cosmetics, fashion).

10. Ordinary business competition can be ethically and morally acceptable. But the PFA's funds and assets cannot be involved in situations where competitiveness necessarily means direct falsehood in advertising, gross unemployment, adverse conditions in the economy of an entire section of the population, or violation of just laws concerning employment and the environment.

11. In the conduct of business, where the profit motive must be supreme, there will be enterprises—especially in banking, insurance, and reinsurance—where the immediate

goals to be achieved are politico-economic. The PFA may join such ventures provided that, even though it is thus involved in at least the political results, the vital religious interests of the Church are thereby bettered and cannot be otherwise bettered. But the PFA's position and motives must be made quite clear to all participants.

Plenary Session

Within the proposed Pontifical Finance Authority, ultimate responsibility and jurisdiction lie with the State Council. It is the highest agency in the bureaucracy. However, for certain sets of circumstances listed in the PFA's charter as extraordinary, there would be an instrument that could be used: the plenary session of the PFA.

A plenary session would not be conceived as a permanent body or a legal entity. It would be a legal instrument of convocation, to be used only on pre-specified conditions in pre-specified circumstances.

Convoked into a plenary session would be the following: the State Council, the Papal Committee, the Vatican Foundation, the Pontifical Foundation Board, the heads of the Catholic Bishops' Regional Conferences, the General Secretary of Superiors of Religious Orders, and the President and Treasurer of the Auditors-General. Convocation could be called in one of several ways. The pope may always summon a convocation, at his own discretion. Otherwise, convocation could occur if a simple majority vote of both State Council and Papal Committee, or a majority vote of State Council and the Pontifical Foundation Board together, or of the State Council and the Vatican Foundation, is in favor of it.

The extraordinary circumstances justifying but not obligating a convocation of the plenary session are to be determined by the Pontifical Finance Authority from the beginning. But certain of such circumstances are obvious:

—The death or incurable madness of a pope;
—The loss of a large part of PFA revenues or source of revenues;
—Gross crime committed within an agency or agencies of the PFA;
—Proposal of liquidation of any of the major agencies of the PFA;

—Appeal against the audit decisions of the Auditors-General, if those decisions involved the status of an agency, or if a majority of the Papal Committee support the appeal;

—Preparation for a General Council of the Church;

—A proposal to devote gross sums of money to purposes that involve the Church directly or indirectly in a relationship of conflict or close association with a secular government or organization.

Voting in plenary sessions is by secret ballot. To obtain victory at such a voting, there must be a two-thirds plus one majority in favor of the proposition about which the voting took place. Once the last vote is counted and announced, the proposition thus approved is considered to have become legally enforceable. The decision thus reached can only be overturned in another and distinct plenary session.

The First Configuration as a Beginning

It would be a mistake to understand the above proposed First Configuration as merely a means of avoiding events such as the calamities of the seventies. Such calamities would, or at least could, be avoided if direct control over all Church finances is exercised wisely and efficiently within a framework that allows the relevant authorities to make intelligent decisions at short notice. The PFA would seem to be one such framework. But that avoidance of calamities and the accompanying control over the financial life of the Church must be seen within the larger context of the Vatican Curia as the pope's own bureaucracy and the ongoing development of the Church as an institution.

Within that institution, the major issue at stake is and always has been the issue of authority and jurisdiction. The history of the papacy—even from the time of the apostles Peter and Paul, could be written in terms of that one issue. The main lesson of that history is that gradually over the centuries the original prominence and leadership that Peter obviously had conferred upon him by Christ and that he exercised, according to the Gospel accounts and the Acts of the Apostles, was explicated into a primacy of jurisdiction and a primacy of teaching authority. Both primacies were tempered always by what we have called the perpetual Roman balance between ecclesiastical monarchy and ecclesiastical republicanism.

At times, it was the inherent republicanism of the cardinals that balanced the papal monarchy. At other times, it was the republicanism—equally inherent—of the bishops which established an equilibrium with papal absolutism. The association of absolutism and republicanism was never an easy one. Sometimes it produced heresies. Sometimes it provoked violent and long-lasting schisms. For the fact is that the nature of the relationship between pope and bishops, and between hierarchy and laity, has not been probed and illuminated in the light of the latest experiences of the Church. The First Vatican Council (1864–70) did define as dogmas of faith the papal primacy of jurisdiction as well as the papal primacy of teaching. This second primacy is usually called infallibility. But that Council left its work unfinished and broke off hurriedly because the Franco-Prussian War of 1870 was about to explode. The Second Vatican Council (1962–65) did nothing whatever in this problematic area. All that remains dogmatically assured are the twin primacies of the pope, and the divine origin of the hierarchy—the bishops of the Church.

But the lack of final definition concerning that twin relationship—pope with bishops, hierarchy with laity—continued to be probed in the actual experience of the Church since 1965 and the end of the Second Vatican Council. Part of that churchly experience has been the varying fortunes of the Vatican's financial agencies, in which failures and deficiencies as well as successes now seem to call for a restructuring process in the light of bitter failures and signal successes.

But the financial agencies represent only one part of the Church's visible organization. In the other parts, the lived experience of the Church also suggests that sooner or later a similar restructuring process will have to be initiated. That restructuring will touch more fundamental elements of the Church than its mere economic power. It concerns precisely the twin primacies of jurisdiction and teaching.

One major factor that is fast imposing a restructuring of those two functions is the size and complexity of the Church in this very complex age. The growing difficulty in exercising the twin primacies was underscored at the time of the Second Vatican Council. Here were gathered three thousand bishops of the Church. Their mere number exceeded any human scale on which genuinely human dialogue is possible.

That number of bishops has already increased, and will go on increasing as the world's population creeps past the five billion mark and goes ever upward. Despite all the electronic means made available by modern technology, despite ease of travel to and from Rome, under what circumstances can, say, five or seven thousand bishops meet and hold a meaningful council?

Undoubtedly, there will soon be new initiatives concerning the exercise of those twin primacies. The only discernible trait to be seen at this distance in the now shadowy future of the governing structure of the Church is a diminution of the important role the cardinals of the Vatican have played since late medieval times. In any worthwhile projection for the restructuring of the financial agencies, clearly the preponderant role cardinals have played up to this time must obviously be diminished; and, correspondingly, the roles of bishops and laity will become more prominent.

In all likelihood, the same unbalancing of traditional roles will manifest itself when the time comes to restructure the two vital power exercises in the Church: authority and teaching.

Out of the Second Vatican Council there came the synod: a meeting of elected bishops-delegate every three years with the pope. Already between the synod of bishops and the Roman Curia of cardinals, the struggle for supremacy has been joined. It points to what the future holds. Already the synod has made plans each time it meets; hitherto, the execution of those plans has been in the hands of the Curia; but this will not continue. Already there are signs among the bishops of an insistent desire to have a say in the implementation of these plans.

THE TOWER OF THE WINDS

Thus the eternal churning of the Spirit goes on and will go on continuously within this visible institution which claims to be uniquely permanent in human history and uniquely privileged in the entire cosmos. After the attempted restructuring by Pope Paul VI —which really made way only for the calamities—and after the aborted reforms of Pope John Paul I, there comes now the obstinate will of Pope John Paul II, who is as resolute about a restructuring of Vatican finance agencies as he is determined in his enmity toward Soviet Marxism and its Communist dictatorship.

The first moves on his part are and must be suave, cautious, discreet, confidential. For no lethal threat must be offered to entrenched interests; and no sudden outpouring of shocking sludge must muddy the already troubled waters of Catholicism. Nor must there be any sudden break: All must appear organic—especially fundamental change. Threat could be met with more than threat. Scandal scatters loyalties. Sudden change instills panic. On John Paul II's side, there is Rome's immemorial advantage: time. Rome has always had an abundance of time when all else around it runs out of that priceless commodity, or is given the crusts of a few decades or the loaf of a century or the banquet of a millennium. In the present slow interval of planning and initiative, John Paul's papal Rome and his papacy must hold firm. What he starts now, the next pope will follow up on. And the pope after that pope will do likewise. The line will thus go on. It always has.

For anyone who can read 1700 years of history intelligently and apply its lessons objectively to the present, there is nothing, actually, in the long, labored past of papacy and Vatican, and really nothing in the present state of upheaval and ebullient trials-and-errors of the Church's members that suggests papal Rome and the papacy itself will ever lose their central and primary importance for Catholicism as for the great world around Catholicism.

Some, however, are fascinated by the glaring fact that the world of Catholicism seems wholly caught up in a febrile process of dissolution. Everything in the Church seems to be subject to change, to revolution, to decay, while papal Rome remains the same. So it is quite tempting for many an onlooker to think in contrary terms, and take all the present Catholic turmoil and its calamities as signs of the demise of the papacy and the Vatican and, ultimately, of the Catholic Church.

This appears especially true to observers who pass from the outer surrounding world of Catholicism into Rome and through the Vatican, on a visit. It is hardly possible for them to believe that this papal Rome, this papacy, this Vatican will long remain the rocklike center it has been for so many centuries.

Remembering the boiling cauldron of contention and diversity Catholicism today presents, what they need only see in Rome to confirm their negative judgment is a ceremonious assemblage of celibate clerics wearing ankle-length dresses, and odd hats, organized in a beehive bureaucracy, presided over by a constantly self-renewing gerontocracy preoccupied with its ranks and its dignities and its secretive, inner-wall life that seems full of so many figureless forms, insubstantial joys, lassitudes, voids. A beloved John XXIII or a charismatic John Paul II seem but pleasant interludes in an otherwise lugubrious situation.

Papal Rome seems to be an undue relic of a past age surviving in the middle of a too ancient city that displays sometimes an all-too-human beauty, sometimes a hoary and immobilized antiquity teeming with a mixture of sleep, of noise, of ruins, of pleasure, of sin, and dead memories of days of glory that cannot possibly return again. Long ago mighty Caesars rode in triumph; powerful families lit up life with panoply, strife, and wealth; and kings, princes, and emperors came in line to kiss the hand and instep of the Man in White because they believed he was clothed in Christ's persona.

But no more, the observers feel. No more.

Once they have visited the Belvedere Galleries,[1] they may be permitted to visit the rarely seen Tower of the Winds,[2] an astronomical observatory built by Pope Gregory XIII (1572–85) in the

middle of the Galleries. No other place in papal Rome conveys so
vividly a sense of what is *passé*, of what is given over to wan dissolution and uselessness.

A steep stairway, difficult to negotiate, leads to the airy, empty
Room of the Meridian at the very top of the tower. Frescoes on its
walls depict the Six Winds as godlike figures, and Roman life during
the four seasons. A zodiacal diagram on the floor coordinates with
the sun's rays that enter through a slit in one of the frescoed walls.
Hanging on the ceiling is an anemometer, its indoor pointer moved
by an outside weathervane to indicate which of the Eight Winds is
blowing—*Favonius, Africus, Auster, Auster Africus, Aquilo, Ful-
turnus, Subsolanus,* or *Eurus.*

The place is full of ghosts. Queen Christina of Sweden slept here
as guest of Pope Alexander VII. Poets John Milton and John Keats
sat here for long hours. The Gregorian calendar we all use today
was worked out in this room by Jesuit Father Christopher Clavius.
Pius IX, Leo XIII, Pius X, Benedict XV, Pius XI, Pius XII, John
XXIII, Paul VI all came up here once. Jewish refugees from the
Nazi terror huddled here for weeks during World War II. Now it
is always empty.

The visitor may come away saddened in some deep sense by the
forlorn impression made by that creaking stairway, the emptiness
of the room, the out of date drawings, the tiny sunrays peering
through the slit, the volatility of the ceiling pointer, the impossibly
peaceful scenes of seasonal life, the gently keening whistle of the
winds, the mausoleum effect of the surrounding galleries.

When visitors step away from the Belvedere Galleries and the
cultural wealth of the Vatican into the city of Rome itself, they
find—each one according to personal bias—that the withering hand
of time and decay is everywhere. Some will lament the ravages of
acid rain that now beset the sculptures on Trojan's Column, the
Arch of Titus, the Temple of Romulus and Remus, the Arch of
Constantine, turning the calcium carbonate of lovely marble into
the calcium sulfate of ugly plaster. Others will sorrow over the entire
region between Rome and Florence, which holds probably the dens-
est concentration of irreplaceable frescoes, mosaics, paintings,
sculptures, churches, and palaces in the world. The spirits of Giotto,
Cimabue, Simone Martini, Pietro Lorenzetti, Bernini, Michelangelo, Raphael hover everywhere. But that region sits in the earth-
quake belt of Umbria. Slowly quake after quake is shattering it all.
All of it seems so passing, so doomed. What pollution does not

waste and human neglect does not let die, violent nature will undo.

The city of Rome around the Vatican conveys the same impression in another way. For all its excitement and lively glitter seem to come from the crowds of passing visitors. Sip your espresso in the Piazza Navona with the cool evening breeze, the *ponentino*, freshening your face. Suffer indoors or out from the humid *sirocco*. Get caught in the showers brought by the sudden, gusty *grecale*, the northeast wind. Or wake up in the morning to find *aquilone*, the invigorating Alpine "eagle" wind cleansing all, with brilliant sunshine and the clearest, cleanest air filling a windswept luminous sky. No matter. You know from Rome's history that while all these Roman winds have been blowing since before Rome was Rome, all else that Rome became has passed away or is passing away slowly, sometimes gracefully, but inevitably. Many visitors include in this stricture the Vatican and the papacy.

They are viewed, in short, as human things in a latter stage of decay, as more or less condemned to topple slowly but surely to the earth with much the same surreptitiousness as the Leaning Tower of Pisa tilting inexorably by an annual average of four one-hundredths of an inch toward the horizontal. Any institution, writes a foreign visitor to Rome during the 1980s, which preserves the so-called foot of Mary Magdalene in a silver reliquary to be venerated at the Roman Church of Saints Celsus and Julian, and which exposes in the collegiate Church of Calcuta north of Rome a silver casket studded with rubies and emeralds and purportedly containing the foreskin of Jesus—surely that institution might strike some persons as culturally distant from us and our time as an African nail fetish is from a modern manicurist's salon. The oddities of old age and decrepitude! Lord Byron, an earlier visitor, summed it up laconically: "All is autumnal in this Rome."

But autumn is Rome's season of beginnings. It always has been—even for the ancient Romans with their belief that the goddess Lavinia showered her first gifts upon men in September. In the Roman spirit, spring makes false promises, the summer stifles and withers, the winter freezes the heart. But autumn with its languor and its mellow softness, its harvest gold and calm magnificence, autumn is the season of good counsel and the sign of Rome's perpetuity. Nobody should therefore be misled by autumnal Rome.

For Rome and its papacy will continue. Rome rests on law, and its hold on the human environment is finally through law. As popes die, the cardinals will gather in conclave and elect new popes, until such time as a change of electors is indicated by the living events crowding the Church's life. Bishops will come and go. Saints will be canonized, sinners shriven. Dissidents, recalcitrants, heretics, schismatics, rebels of all kinds will come and go. The Vandals may come and go in several modern guises. The pope may lose control of large contingents of bishops and people. The Great Apostasy may become a fact of history. That terrible figure of hideous strength mysteriously described as the Man, the Antichrist, may sit on the highest throne. All that is possible within the arc of Rome's span.

But all that time nothing will be dormant or dying or dead in Rome. Rome will keep on insisting that its laity, men and women, are essentially witnesses to the faith of Catholicism; that its priests are first and foremost offerers of a sacrifice; that its bishops are the only official pastors of divine revelation's grace; and that the Bishop of Rome is the unique vicar and present representative of Jesus Christ, true God, true man.

And the life of the Church will go on swirling around Peter's rock, even though its legal occupant may huddle on a promontory of the Gulag Archipelago, or hold a papal consistory in a Tasmanian forest clearing. Because that is what Christ called the first Bishop of Rome. Cephas. Peter. Rock. Every one of those successor-bishops will go on offering palpable security to men and women abandoned in the darkness of the human night; a personal assurance for each man and woman that the mystery of ultimate salvation was long ago accomplished on a skull-shaped execution-hill outside old Jerusalem; that they have each already been pardoned simply because they were loved; and that they can now afford to die in peace, even if not with dignity. "I have the ecstasy and the terror of being chosen," exclaimed that mad, dark French poet, Paul Verlaine.

Slowly the bureaucratic structure of Rome's Vatican will change because the world will have changed, and popes will succeed popes with these changes. Much of the beauteous and the noble in art may have perished from Rome by the time the first genuine restructuring of papal finance agencies by John Paul II has given away to a second, and the second to a third, and the third to a fourth, until those circumstances of time and space arrive when the Church in the world will have grown "in wisdom, age, and grace before God and men," as the founder of the Church is described by the Gospels in his human growing. Then the other-worldly radiance of the Spirit of Christ will visibly clothe the face of the Church—this visible institution—for all and sundry to see. The real poverty of Christ and the powerful love of Christ will be the Church's sole power—not financial sinews, not diplomatic prestige, not managerial excellence.

Men will understand then that all along this Holy Spirit did inhabit that visible institution. In its worst years. In all its mad years. Even in our time when the smoke of Satan entered the Church, as Paul VI once remarked somberly, and swirled around the Altar and the Tabernacle. The Spirit still abided within. Only now, that Church will be as palpable a sign of salvation as Constantine's vision of the cross was in the glittering evening sky above the Milvian Bridge.

Rome's time will be God's time, as it always has been. And in God's good time, papal Rome and its Catholic Church will be ready for the Final Day. The gentle *ponentino* and its sturdy cousin, the *ponente*, will no longer refresh a Roman evening. The brutal *sirocco* will cease to sweep from the Sahara over the Mediterranean with its red, choking sand-grains. The cold *aquilone* will fail to swoop down from beyond the frigid Alps. For then will be the Final Day when all the winds of the Almighty fill the cosmos and this earth; when all creation becomes one vast Tower of Winds fissured and fractured in a millisecond by the breath of divine love come at last to regulate and audit all accounts according to the heart of the Maker.

NOTES

Part One: THE MANAGERS

THE VACUUM OF POWER

1. Mussolini was the first person to use the expression. *"Il nostro fascismo è totalitario"* occurs in one of his early speeches.
2. For a while, the "gold bloc" countries (led by France) maintained gold convertibility, but they found their exports were at a competitive disadvantage in world markets.
3. Referred to, as always in the case of papal encyclicals, by its first few words, *Non Abbiamo Bisogno*. The text was smuggled out of the Vatican and published first in France, from where it made its way back into Mussolini's Italy.
4. The Lodge merely went more underground for the time being.
5. The initial sums paid by the Financial Convention did not equal what had been promised to Pius IX by the Law of Guarantees proposed and passed by the Italian parliament but rejected by Pius IX.
6. Mussolini appointed a troublesome Fascist Party member, Cesare De Vecchi, as his first ambassador to the Vatican, thus removing him from public life.

REENTRY INTO POWER

1. Founded in 1878 by Pope Leo XIII.
2. Founded in 1877 by Pope Leo XIII.
3. *Amministrazione per le opere di religione.*
4. *Istituto per le opere di religione.* Abbreviated IRA in this book.

ECONOMIC MIRACLE

1. The Democristians had as one of their nicknames *i preti* ("the priests"). Choleric Cardinal Tisserant used to refer to them as the *democretini* (roughly translated as "popular cretins").

2. Chief among these are: Bastogi, Credito Fondiario, SGES, La Sind di Milano, Efibanci-L'Ente Finanziario Interbancario.

3. Net profit in 1967 was $5.5 million.

4. Capital: $72 million.

5. Annual profit: $420 million.

6. Capital: $280 million. By this time it had captured almost 70 percent of passenger shipping in Italy and operated over 90 ships (including those in the Adriatica, Lloyd-Triestino, and Tirrenia lines).

7. Twenty percent of all bank deposits in Italy are held by them and the Vatican-owned, Rome-based Banco di Santo Spirito. The capital of the latter was $12.8 million with total deposits of $729 million in 1967.

8. Capital: $40 million.

9. Capital: $64 million.

10. Capital: $48 million.

11. Banca Provinciale Lombarda, Credito Romagnolo, Banco di San Geminiano e San Prospero, Banco San Paolo, Piccolo Credito Bergamasco, and Banco Ambrosiano.

12. Literally thousands of small banks exist in Italy and Sicily which were wholly owned by the Vatican agencies.

13. Assicurazioni Generali di Trieste e Venezia and Riunione Adriatica di Sicurtà.

14. The Vatican-owned Istituto Farmacologico Serono of Rome—with a capital of $1.4 million, a 250-person payroll, and an annual profit exceeding $150,000—produced and marketed for many years a popular contraceptive with the brand name Luteola. Nogara himself bought the IFS before World War II. Also Vatican-owned was the pasta company, Molini e Pastificio Pantanella S.p.A., with $15 million in assets. In the fifties, both companies had nephews of Pope Pius XII as board directors.

15. In Spain, Mexico, Brazil, Argentina, Luxembourg, and India. The British textile group, Courtaulds, was a shareholder of SNIA-Viscosa.

16. Nogara's takeovers of old, ailing companies often took a long

time to mature into profitable ventures. Manifattura Ceramica Pozzi, one of Italy's oldest companies, wholly owned by the Vatican (now specializing in bathroom fixtures, plastics, and chemicals), started to turn a profit by the end of the sixties. It had a capital then of $37 million but was barely profitable. With its foreign subsidiaries in Brazil and France and its expanding export trade, the Vatican eventually made a profit from it.

17. Capital: $20 million. Assets valued at $304 million.

18. Including Italcable.

19. Including RAI (Radio Televisione Italiana).

20. The 1983 reports on Montedison claim for it to be a pathfinder among European chemical companies. Montedison of the 1980s is concentrating on plastics and pharmaceutical products. Mario Schimberni, its present chairman, has started a financial restructuring of the Montedison group. The Vatican got out of Montedison some years ago.

21. Società Santa Barbara, Società Mineraria del Trasimeno, with combined capital of nearly $10 million.

22. The combined capitalization of some of the companies engaged in the above amounted to nearly $100 million.

23. Supplied steel furnishings for the *Raffaello* and the *Michelangelo*, two of the grandest passenger ships in the Italian Line that belonged to Finmare, a holding company of Finmeccanica, an IIR company in which the Vatican had controlling interest.

24. The Gran San Bernardo Tunnel was its work.

25. SGI acquired 70 percent of common stock in Watergate Improvements, Inc., Washington, D.C.

26. Immobiliare Canada built the Montreal Stock Exchange Tower.

27. In a fiduciary contract, an Italian bank would sign a secret agreement with a Swiss bank. The Italian bank would then transfer a client's money in the bank's name—not the client's— to that Swiss bank. The Swiss bank would be instructed to pay that money to the client in Switzerland or wherever the Swiss bank serviced its clients.

28. *Uditore* can be roughly translated as "clerk"; *consigliere* means "counselor."

29. A bishop without a diocese.

30. Egidio Vagnozzi of Rome, Joseph Beran of Prague, Cesare Zerba of Italy.

31. For some sparse details about this mysterious personage, see Luigi DiFonzo's *St. Peter's Banker*, published by Franklin Watts, New York, 1983.

PARTNERSHIPS AND DISASTERS

1. The best account to date in book form of Sindona's rise and fall is Luigi DiFonzo's *St. Peter's Banker*, published by Franklin Watts, New York, 1983.
2. The only published account of this event is *The Vatican Connection* by Richard Hammer (Holt Rinehart & Winston, New York, 1982). But the proof for the main event—the request by some employees of the Vatican financial agency—is guaranteed by the testimony of court-ordered wire-taps carried out, in the main, by Joseph J. Coffey, Jr., now Detective Sergeant and Commanding Officer of the Organized Crime Homicide Task Force, New York City. According to the book, the two Vatican people involved were Eugène Cardinal Tisserant and Archbishop Paul Marčinkus. There is no doubt in Sergeant Coffey's mind that both clerics were involved.
3. On August 2, 1979, while out on bail in New York, he disappeared, supposedly kidnaped, reappearing again on October 16. DiFonzo's reconstruction of what happened in those 74 days appears accurate.
4. Giuseppe di Cristina, officer of Ente Minerario Siciliano; Boris Giuliano, police superintendent of Palermo; Giorgio Ambrosoli, liquidator of Sindona's empire; Palermo judge Terranova, chief of the State Anti-Mafia Commission.
5. Graziano Verzotto, president of Ente Minerario Siciliano.
6. The commission consisted of Joseph Brennan, former chairman of New York Emigrant Savings; Carlo Cerutti, vice-chairman of Società Finanziaria Telefonica per Azioni; and Philippe de Wech, former chairman of Union Bank, Switzerland.
7. Terence Cooke of New York, and John Krol of Philadelphia.
8. Emmett Carter of Toronto.
9. Rosone narrowly escaped assassination earlier that year.
10. Abs had a phenomenal banking career in the Hitler era, being chairman of the executive board of Deutsche Bank, the largest bank in Hitler's Germany. His family expropriated part of the briquette works of the Petscheks, a Jewish family.

Part Two: THE FRAMEWORK OF POWER

CATHOLIC IDENTITY

1. The point is of capital importance today when clearly among certain groups of bishops—notably in France, Holland, and the U.S.—there are obvious attempts to establish "the French Catholic Church," "the Dutch Catholic Church," "the American Catholic Church." Several Communist countries—Poland, Czechoslovakia, China—have attempted to establish national Catholic Churches and break the connection between Catholic bishops in their home territories and the Roman Bishop.

2. As of 1981, there were 2,375 dioceses with a corresponding number of residential bishops, besides 1,980 other bishops employed at other jobs. There are other minor administrative categories: prelatures (80), apostolic administrations (8), apostolic prefectures (59), mission stations (3), and miscellaneous (47). The bishops of various regions are grouped into episcopal conferences (100). There are 10 international congresses of such episcopal conferences. The eastern section of the Catholic Church has 13 synods and episcopal conferences.

3. Some "Ordinaries" are archbishops, some patriarchs, some metropolitans. These are inner-clergy rankings.

4. The Vatican was originally a low hill on the right side of the Tiber, swampy around its base, solid land toward its flattish top. It is not one of the fabled Seven Hills of Rome, all of which are on the left side of the Tiber. In ancient times, priest-prophets functioned there (hence its name, from the Latin *vaticinare*, to prophesy). Later, emperors drained the lower section, and created terraced gardens and a stadium. The upper part was used as a cemetery. St. Peter was killed in the gardens below, and buried up on top. Christians built a chapel and then a basilica around his gravesite. Later still, St. Peter's Basilica, the Apostolic Palace (where the popes live today), and the other main buildings of the Vatican were located around that gravesite.

5. Originally the word Curia referred to the government bureaucracy of the Roman emperors. When that government was transferred to Constantinople, and the popes became the temporal as well as spiritual rulers of Rome, the papal bureaucracy inherited the name.

6. There are 11 congregations, 3 tribunals, 3 secretariats, and 19 commissions. See Figure 1 on page 84.

THE SHIFT IN HUMAN AFFAIRS
1. *New York Times*, July 15, 1983, editorial page.
2. In his *Unfinished Business*. Nash Publishing, Los Angeles, 1973, page 154.

THE PATHOS OF THE CATHOLIC CHURCH
1. *The Power of Silence*, 1895.

Part Three: THE GREAT EXPERIMENT

THE PROTO-PERIOD
1. A *soldus*, abbreviated from *solidus*, was reckoned as one seventy-second part of a solid (no other metallic compound mixed in it) pound of gold. In modern Italian, *soldi* is a current expression for the English "money." A florin was a ninety-sixth part of a pound of gold. A scudo was the equivalent of one U.S. dollar of the time. A ducat had the same value as a florin.

   Throughout this book, when sums of money are quoted in ancient coin values, no attempt is made to translate them into modern equivalents. This is the wise practice of historians who point out that factors of value in money have undergone such fluctuations that any attempt to translate ancient sums into, say, U.S. dollars of 1983 would be meaningless. The most that can be said is that a large sum of *soldi* was a very large sum by the standards of the time. This remark applies also wherever mention is made of scudi, florins, or ducats.
2. In its earliest form, this was called the *Camera Thesauraria Apostolica*.
3. Charlemagne bestowed on the papacy the cities of Capua, Aquino, Teano, Sora, and the towns of the Beneventan territory. Nicholas I (858–867) tried to make Bulgaria over into a province of the papal State, but this attempt failed. A successor, Sylvester II (999–1003), actually received Hungary as a province of the Roman Church in 1002; but this did not last beyond the end of the century.
4. Each ship was 170 feet long, had forecastle and castle on poop and stern, was propelled by 100 galley slaves manning 100 oars, and carried a complement of 50 marines.

THE FORMULA APPLIED

1. In 1882, the Vatican bought the company that supplied water to Rome, La Società dell'Acqua Pia Antica Marcia, which it sold only in 1962.
2. Literally "room" or "chamber."
3. One of the lowest denomination of coins.
4. The florin, so called because it carried the Florentine lily, was first issued in Florence in 1252. It weighed about 54 grains and was of pure gold. The Camera minted its own Cameral florins.
5. Tuscany: 10,000. Perugia: 40–50,000. The March of Ancona: 40,000. The Romagna: 50,000. Bologna varied between 90–180,000 florins.
6. Strong cotton fabrics with a pile face and twill weave.
7. *Vacancy Fruits*: When the holder of a benefice died and before his successor took office, the revenues were claimed by the Camera.

    Procurations: Travel expenses were paid to high-ranking Curial members by the nobles and churchmen in whose territory they traveled. One-half went to the Camera.

    Spoils: The personal property of deceased ecclesiastics went to the Camera.

    Quindennia: Sums equal to the benefice taxes the Camera would have received from benefices.

    Bad Fruits: Taxes levied on a benefice holder whose claim was exercised without canonical approval.

    There were several other minor levies for other papal services, and "compositions" (an indeterminate gratuity to be fixed when the Camera performed a service which carried its own price tag). St. Peter's Pence, once collected all over Europe, never brought in enormous sums, in spite of one pope's desire to have one penny "from each house out of which comes smoke." Even a penny from every party or 50 million houses would be a tidy sum, the pontiff realized.
8. *Armario* XXXVI, Vol. XXVII, fol. 793 verso.
9. Rarely has any body of men in the Catholic Church been liquidated with such wholesale cruelty and mercilessness. To be burned at the stake was the least painful alternative offered them.
10. Its disappearance as a social modality was slow. Germany was fundamentally a feudal state until 1806, Spain until the nineteenth century, the Low Countries until 1795. In the mean-

while, capitalism was governing the external trade and international relations of the political powers.

Part Four: CAPITALISM AND CATHOLICISM

CAPITALISM AND DEMOCRACY

1. *Octo Quaestiones*, ii, 7 (Goldast, *Monarchia*, ii, 341).
2. *De Concordantia Catholica*, ii, 14 (*Opera*, Basel, 1505), p. 730.
3. *Dialogus* (Goldast, ii, 603).
4. Reliable records would indicate a minimum of five simoniacal papal elections and a possible maximum of twelve.
5. All the italicized words are terms for specific papal taxes and fees in vogue at the time.
6. He paid Fra Angelico a paltry 15 ducats a month.
7. *The Idea of Nature*, Oxford Unversity Press, 1945.
8. *Werke*, 15 (2), 276.
9. In his May 1525 pamphlet: *Against the Thieving Bands of Peasants*. In *Werke* (18), 357.
10. *Institutiones*, IV, 20, 31.
11. Alison Philips, *Nineteenth Century*, December 1946, p. 908.
12. D. Wallace, *George Buchanan*, p. 11.
13. Literally, "Mountain of Mercy."

THE SLOW DECLINE

1. Innocent XIII (1721–24), Benedict XIII (1724–30), Clement XII (1730–40), Benedict XIV (1740–58), Clement XIII (1758–69), Clement XIV (1769–74), Pius VI (1775–99).
2. This appellation for the Catholic Church seems to have made its first appearance in the middle of the 16th century.
3. The Jesuit missionaries in China were persuaded that Christians could participate in ceremonies honoring Confucius and one's forefathers, without any taint of superstition. The Jesuits' enemies thought this was heresy and corruption of the Christian faith. Rome ruled against the Jesuits. Fierce persecution broke out in China against missionaries and converts. For the best modern account of this lamentable chapter of Roman Catholic history, see *Generation of Giants* by George H. Dunne, S.J. (University of Notre Dame Press, 1962).
4. Sicily and Naples at this time were rich and warlike kingdoms.

5. It included farms, buildings, forests, and estates.
6. In 1789, the bishops supported 562 grammar schools at which some 72,000 pupils were educated—over half free of charge. The school system cost a minimum of 30 million livres annually. They also supported 165 seminaries. With few exceptions, the bishops maintained charitable organizations in each parish—food kitchens, shelters, orphanages, old people's homes, and the like. There was no other charity-giving body in France at the time.
7. Duphot died apparently of a heart attack brought on by excessive drinking, eating, and carousing in Roman brothels.
8. The treasures lost to the French included the *Belvedere Apollo*, the *Laocoön Group*, the *Medici Venus*, the *Dying Gaul*, Raphael's *Transfiguration*, and Titian's *Sacra Conversazione*.
9. They included 333 emeralds, 692 rubies, 208 sapphires, and 386 diamonds; most were cut out of the papal tiaras.

THE GREAT INJUSTICE

1. A scudo is reckoned as one dollar; a baiocco (or bajocco) as one quarter of a U.S. penny.
2. A Roman lira of the time was equal in buying power to 50 U.S. cents.
3. See the text of this law in the Appendix, pages 248–49.
4. About $1.5 million in Italian lire at the time.
5. He was an executive of the Banco Ambrosiano of Milan, which almost a hundred years later attained international fame through the quite infamous "Calvi affair."
6. It was sold by the Vatican in 1962.
7. The Vatican still retains major equity in the Banco di Roma.
8. Some would see in this intermediate and quite secretive organization the forerunner of the P–2 organization that surfaced in the late seventies of this century in connection with the "Calvi affair." But this is incorrect.
9. Amministrazione delle Opere di Religione. Commonly (and literally) translated as "works," the word *opus* in this Vatican usage refers to any working unit, any ecclesiastical or lay agency, commercial or religious, which produces revenue for the disposal of the Holy See.
10. Literally, "the See being vacant."
11. 1963–78.

THE DECENT COMPROMISE
1. Individual rights.
2. Britain was the first nation to adopt the monometallism of gold. By the 1870s, France, Germany, and the U.S. had followed suit.

Part Five: RESTRUCTURING

CONCLUSIONS AS GUIDELINES
1. From the beginning, his death has been the subject of much rumor, the KGB being one of the prime suspects. After the attempted assassination of John Paul II in 1981, and a widespread theory that the assassin, Mehmet Ali Agça, was trained and employed by the KGB, attention was once more focused on the KGB as guilty of John Paul I's intended assassination.

HIGHEST IDEAL
1. The current proposal to establish a "People's Bank" or an "Agricultural Fund" in Communist Poland (largely with a Vatican participation topping at least $1 billion) does not fit into this category. Such a fund or bank may be precisely what will *not* help the situation in Poland, where the root-problem is not economic but political and ideological.

THE FIRST CONFIGURATION
1. Throughout this section, reference should be made to Figure 2 on page 216.

THE TOWER OF THE WINDS
1. These consist of the Gallery of Geographical Charts, the Hall of Parchments, the Secret Archives, the Room of Inventories and Indexes, Records of the Consistory, Picture Galleries, etc.
2. Finally put in disuse in 1906.

APPENDIX: GUARANTEE
LAWS OF MAY 13, 1871

The principal stipulations were:

1. The Pope's person is sacred and inviolable, and crimes against him will be punished in the same way as crimes against the Majesty of the King of Italy. The Italian Government will show to the Pope the same tokens of honor as to other sovereigns.
2. The Pope shall have the right to retain the usual number of Papal guards for the defense of his person and palaces. He shall have full liberty to exercise all the functions of his office, and to post notices concerning that office on all the church doors of Rome.
3. The Pope will be paid by the State the annual sum of 3,225,000 lire, free from communal or provincial taxes.
4. The Vatican, the Lateran, certain basilicas in Rome, and the Papal palace at Castel Gandolfo are to be at the Pope's disposal; these properties can be neither taxed nor alienated.
5. When the Papal See is vacant, the Cardinals may freely assemble; the Government will ensure that Conclaves and Councils are not in any way disturbed.
6. No Italian officials may enter the Papal palaces, unless the Pope has given permission; it shall be forbidden to make domiciliary visits, or to confiscate papers, books or registers in the Papal offices and congregations engaged in spiritual work.
7. The Church's officials shall be protected by the civil authorities.
8. The Ambassadors of foreign powers to the Pope shall possess the rights and immunities due in international law to diplomatic agents; the same for Papal envoys to foreign governments. The

Pope can without hindrance enter into communication with his episcopate abroad, and with the entire Catholic world.

9. The Pope may have his own post-office and telegraph facilities.
10. In Rome all seminaries, academies and colleges for the education of the clergy shall be subject solely to the Holy See.
11. The Government disclaims the right to appoint, or make suggestions as to the appointment to high ecclesiastical offices in Italy; and the Italian bishops shall not be required to take the oath of loyalty to the King of Italy.
12. *Exequatur, Placet regium,* and all other forms of governmental permission for the publication and execution of the decisions of the ecclesiastical authority shall be abolished.

INDEX